Unionization:
The Viewpoint of Librarians

Unionization:
The Viewpoint of Librarians

by
Theodore Lewis Guyton

American Library Association

Chicago 1975

Library of Congress Cataloging in Publication Data

Guyton, Theodore Lewis.
  Unionization: the viewpoint of librarians.

  Originally presented as the author's thesis,
University of California, Los Angeles.
  Bibliography: p.
  1. Librarians' unions—United States.   I. Title.
Z682.2.U5G88   1974   331.88'11'02   74–19164
ISBN 0–8389–0187–5

TO MY PARENTS

Contents

v

Tables

Acknowledgments

The author is grateful to many individuals who assisted in the research and writing of this study. I am particularly indebted to Professor Archie Kleingartner, my advisor during graduate studies at UCLA and Chairman of my Doctoral Committee. I am also indebted for the guidance provided by my Doctoral Committee members, Professors Robert Collison, John Hutchinson, Frederic Meyers, and Robert Vosper.

Numerous librarians and union and association leaders were of invaluable assistance during the research phase of this study. I am thankful to the many individuals who responded to inquiries, completed questionnaires, and consented to interviews. Special mention is due Carol Armstrong, Santa Monica Public Library; Frances Henselman, Long Beach Public Library; Thomas Lippert, Los Angeles Public Library; Anthony Mafrica, Los Angeles Public Library; Walley Pederson, Los Angeles County Employees Association; Harry Rowe, Jr., Orange County Public Library; and Marco Thorne, San Diego Public Library.

I am also thankful to Margaret Eaton, Brian FitzPatrick, Sheila Lane, and Barbara Williams for their technical assistance in this study.

While each of these individuals contributed to this study, they, of course, are not responsible for any shortcomings it may have.

Foreword

When Archie Kleingartner, professor of Industrial Relations in UCLA's Graduate School of Management, asked me and Professor Robert L. Collison of the School of Library Service to sit on Mr. Guyton's doctoral committee, we readily agreed. The topic intrigued us, the candidate was an engaging young man, and Professor Kleingartner—an expert on contemporary labor issues and particularly on collective bargaining among professional groups and white collar workers—had participated with campus librarians in various matters of mutual interest.

With equal readiness I agreed to write this introduction, because it was soon quite clear not only that Mr. Guyton had selected a timely topic, but also that his findings would be interesting and useful for librarians. Thus I encouraged the American Library Association to publish his study.

The management of large libraries, whether municipal or academic, is no longer a casual sideline for gifted professional librarians. It is an exacting, intricate, and responsible task, requiring its own special competencies and wholehearted commitment in addition to professional library insights. There are large numbers of libraries today that represent multimillion dollar public enterprises, involving complex staff groups numbering in the hundreds.

Administrative relationships have become complicated through the development of multi-institutional library systems, consortia, and networks. Rapid technological advances—in the applicability of computers, miniaturization, cable television, and other devices—require continuous organizational change, realignment of functions, and the development of new staff skills. Municipal libraries face new requirements in serving minority and underprivileged groups in the community. Additionally, the fiscal climate of multiple and shifting funding sources, persistent inflation, and limitations on tax income add appreciably to the complications of management.

As a result of these recent developments library administrators need access to a variety of new management skills such as operations research, systems analysis, program budgeting, computer simulation and modelling, decision theory, and the application of behavioral science theories to group management. The professional library schools are being pressed to modify their training programs in order to build in these skills. At the same time, library administrators are looking for young graduates of management schools who can be attracted into librarianship as planning officers, budgeting officers, and the like. The problem has become so important that the Association of Research Libraries, with funds granted by the Council on Library Resources, has established an Office of University Library Management Studies which is intended to foster research on the management problems of large research libraries, develop analytical tools for library managers, provide programs to train executives, and generally to improve managerial performance.

On top of these demanding requirements there is a whole group of new personnel issues to be dealt with these days. Increasingly sophisticated professional staffs expect and deserve more effective participation in decision making, collegial government on the academic pattern, peer evaluation procedures, and the like. At the same time, a better division of labor within the personnel structure is developing a para-professional staff group that is numerically larger than the professional group. These people are more likely to seek their best interests through union affiliation with like groups of employees in other jurisdictions. Yet increasingly, as Mr. Guyton points out, collective bargaining is being seriously considered also by professional groups, in both municipal and academic settings.

It has been suggested that among the several new management problems to be dealt with, collective bargaining may produce the most drastic changes in library management patterns. But library administrators are generally quite inexperienced in labor relations. Mr. Guyton is discussing public librarians, of course, but this is equally true of academic librarians. It is also true that union officials are often naive about the professional and academic marketplace. Thus it seems both timely and important that the profession begin to develop useful tools in the labor relations area. Mr. Guyton, I suggest, has provided one such tool by way of an historical review of unionization in public libraries and a case study in the application of industrial relations theories to the field of librarianship. His study should help us all in coming to grips with the fundamental issues we must face up to, instead of putting all of our attention emotionally on random "critical issues." One fundamental issue is whether unionism and participatory management or academic government are compatible.

I trust that what Mr. Guyton has to say will be illuminating for librarians in all types of libraries, as well as for teachers in library schools. I particularly hope that it will encourage further analytical and research studies in the new field of library industrial relations.

ROBERT VOSPER
University Librarian
University of California, Los Angeles

Chapter 1

Introduction

The recent wave of collective action among professional employees has touched what many consider the least likely profession to succumb: professional librarians. Like their professional counterparts, librarians have formed unions, bargained collectively, staged major demonstrations of protest, and closed down libraries through full-fledged strikes. The predominance of activity has occurred only in the past several years, although library unions have existed as far back as 1917.

Librarians are not as extensively unionized as teachers, nurses, and many other professionals, but the combined characteristics of the occupation make it a challenging area of study. First, the majority of librarians are women and many believe that female employees are a crucial obstacle to unionization. Second, librarians are a numerically small profession and are not as likely to be actively recruited for unionization as other professions because of the small potential return. Third, librarians possess minimum bargaining power since they are numerically small and do not perform an essential service. As one observer stated, "Even if librarians got up the courage to strike, who would really care?" Fourth, librarians are professionals. Although recently there has been a significant amount of union activity among all professionals, they still constitute one of the least unionized occupational categories in the country. Finally, the librarians analyzed in this study are local or county public employees. There has been increased union activity among these groups of employees, but not nearly to the extent as among federal government employees.

Objective

This book provides a theoretical interpretation of the pattern of library unionism from its inception to the present. The analyses focus on identifying factors that promote or hinder unionization among librarians and on developing theoretical statements concerning the emergence of library unions. As such, the focus is on the behavior of groups; not on the behavior of individuals. That is, the concern is with explaining why one library is unionized and another is not. The intent is not to examine why one librarian in a given environment joins a union while another in the same environment does not.

This study does not include an exhaustive list of factors that conceivably might explain library unionization. There are surely critical incidents that instigate union formation in particular situations. Such incidents, however, behave in a random fashion and are not always suitable for study. The concentration here is on isolating factors that have systematic and repetitive effects on library unionization, with the intent of providing a theoretical interpretation of the aggregate pattern of library unionism.

Definitions

There are three main types of librarians: public, college and university, and those maintained by industrial and special agencies. Unionization has been concentrated among the public librarians. As a result, they are the focus of this study. College and university librarians are less extensively unionized, although recently the amount of activity has increased. Special librarians have always been virtually nonunionized.

A professional librarian is normally defined as one who has completed a course of study in a graduate library school. This usually means at least five years of college: four to meet the requirements of a bachelor's degree and a fifth year or more of specialized study in library science, after which a master's degree is conferred. In actuality, however, many public librarians attain a professional position through experience and without a degree in library science. For purposes of this study, all librarians holding a professional position as classified by the employing public library are regarded as "professionals." In all cases, a professional position is defined to include the title Librarian I (a beginning professional position) and higher. All positions below Librarian I are considered "nonprofessional" library employees.

Also necessary to the discussion is a working definition of "unionization." The term must obviously include more than membership in a nationally affiliated labor union, but it should not be so broad as to include membership in a local staff association that does not act as spokesman for the staff. Likewise, the term naturally includes membership in an organization that actively negotiates for higher salaries, but it should not necessarily include an organization that sends a letter of protest over a minimal yearly salary increase. Rather than attempt to define unionization in terms of affiliation, extent of representation, or nature of activities, it seems more plausible to consider the intent of the organization's members. If a library staff determines either through a formal representation election or through an informal vote that they desire to form or join an organization to act as their representative, then they are expressing a desire for collective action and will be considered "unionized." The crucial point is that employees explicitly designate an organization to represent them in discussions or negotiations with library or other officials. The discussions or negotiations can involve exclusively economic matters, professional matters, or a combination of both.

Methodology

The dependent variable of this study is unionization, with the various factors analyzed being the independent or influencing variables.[1] The latter are conceptually distinct, and are analyzed as such in this study. At the same time, many of the independent factors are causally interrelated in practice; the interrelationships will be made clear in later chapters.

Numerous researchers have tested and attempted to demonstrate the relationship between unionization in selected occupations and various influencing variables.[2] Personal characteristics, such as sex, age, race, marital status, family background, educational attainment, political orientation, and economic position were investigated by Bain, Goldstein and Indik, Kleingartner, Lieberman and Moskow, Lipset, Lockwood, and Mills. Effects of employers' acceptance of unionism were studied by Bain, Blackburn and Prandy, and Goldstein. Worker attitude and acceptance of unionism were tested by Goldstein and Indik, Mills, and Shister. The effect of working in bureaucratic structures was analyzed by Blackburn and Prandy, Lockwood, and Kassalow. A closely related factor—employment concentration—was considered by Bain, Dvorak, Goldstein, Lieberman and Moskow, and Lipset. The employee's prospects of upward mobility and concerns over employment security were examined by Dvorak, Lockwood, Lipset, Mills, and Shister.

Structure of the work environment and employee attitude toward it were tested by Goldstein and Indik, Lipset, and Shister. The role of professional associations and professionals' acceptance of union membership in light of professional ethics were investigated by Dvorak, Kassalow, Kleingartner, and Lieberman and Moskow. The effects of contact with unionized employees, the availability of unions, union leadership, and

---

[1] The scope of the dependent variable is as defined in the objective of this study.

[2] Many of the studies mentioned here and their findings are cited in later chapters.

union recruitment were studied by Bain, Kassalow, Lipset, Lockwood, Mills, and Shister. Legal climate for unionization was considered by Bain, Kassalow, and Shister to be significant in influencing unionization.

These researchers, among others, provide a broad (although often contradictory) knowledge of variables that conceivably could influence the incidence and growth of unionization. A thorough review of these studies provided the working list of independent factors considered for analysis here.

The working list was constructed also in light of several theories of the labor movement. The theories do not cite specific factors that influence union membership, but provide theoretical frameworks of the emergence of unionization which are essential to the discovery of independent factors of unionization. Four theorists were examined in preparation for this study, and a short synopsis of their concepts is in order.

Robert Hoxie viewed the genesis of trade unions from the common needs and problems of the wageworker. Each wageworker develops an "interpretation of the social situation [which comprehensively includes the economic, moral, and judicial aspects of life] as viewed from the standpoint of his peculiar experiences and needs."[3] From this viewpoint, he develops a set of beliefs concerning what should and can be done to better the situation. "Workers similarly situated economically and socially, closely associated and not too divergent in temperament and training, will tend to develop a common interpretation of the social situation and a common solution of the problem of living."[4] The trade union emerges when workers' sentiments are crystallized. Thus, the union constitutes a group interpretation of the social situation and a remedial program of mutual assistance aimed at establishing and maintaining certain conditions of living. The union's social function in turn determines the specific form or structure which the union takes.

Sidney and Beatrice Webb saw the trade union as a "continuous association of wage-earners for the purpose of maintaining or improving the conditions of their working lives."[5] The essential cause of the growth of these associations lies in the divorce of the worker from the ownership of the means of production. This comes about through economic revolution. "The whole modern organisation of labour in its advanced form rests on a fundamental fact which has spontaneously and increasingly developed itself—namely, the definite separation between the functions

[3] Robert F. Hoxie, *Trade Unionism in the United States* (New York: Appleton, 1936), p. 57.

[4] Ibid., p. 58; for a more thorough discussion of Hoxie's theory, see pp. 31–102.

[5] Sidney and Beatrice Webb, *The History of Trade Unionism* (New York: Longmans, 1920), p. 1.

4

of the capitalist and the workman. . . ."[6] The trade union has only two expedients for the improvement of conditions of employment: the restriction of numbers in the trade and the establishment of uniform minimum standards required of each firm. The Webbs endorsed the latter, and envisioned the duty of the trade union as perpetually striving to raise the level of standards. This process may be achieved by collective bargaining or by legal enactment.[7] The function of the trade union is to provide for the democratic participation of workers in the conditions of sale of their services.

Frank Tannenbaum saw the origins of labor organizations arising from technological change. "The Industrial Revolution destroyed the solid moorings of an older way of life, and cast the helpless workers adrift in a strange and difficult world."[8] The core of his belief is that men seek the right to make decisions. Technological change threatened this right as business enterprises grew larger. Contact between the worker and his employer became less frequent, and "the opportunities for understanding and identity between the two decreased."[9] Unions arise as defensive organizations to protect the worker from the dehumanizing effects of the machine process. They also function to restore the worker's status to preindustrial conditions.

Through the unions, Tannenbaum states, workers attempt to limit the employer's decision-making function, and this strikes directly at the heart of the employer's security. Inevitably, a conflict develops between the employer, trying to protect himself, and the union, which exists to serve its membership at the immediate expense of the employer. Tannenbaum envisioned the unions' ultimate triumph over capitalistic opposition, and displacing it by industrial democracy, "an achievement which is implicit in the growth and development of the organized labor movement."[10] Tannenbaum insisted that the labor movement is not revolutionary; but that it is counterrevolutionary in purpose,[11] with the aim of returning society from the consequences of contracts—where the individual looses his decision-making rights—to an emphasis on status.

[6] Ibid., p. 5.

[7] John T. Dunlop, "The Development of Labor Organization: A Theoretical Framework," in *Readings in Labor Economics and Labor Relations*, eds. R. L. Rowan and H. R. Northrup (Homewood: Richard D. Irwin, Inc., 1968), p. 44; for a more thorough discussion of the Webb's theory, see Webb, *History of Trade Unionism*, pp. 1–63.

[8] Frank Tannenbaum, *A Philosophy of Labor* (New York: Knopf, 1952), p. 7.

[9] Ibid., p. 58.

[10] Dunlop, "Development of Labor Organization," p. 43.

[11] Tannenbaum, *Philosophy of Labor*, p. 11; for a more thorough discussion of Tannenbaum's theory, see pp. 3–13.

Selig Perlman gave primacy to the role of opportunity consciousness in the labor movement. He believed that in an economic community there is a separation between those who prefer a secure, though modest return; and those who are willing to take a bigger risk and the possibility of greater return. The former compose most of the manual workers, and the latter are the entrepreneurs. Which group an individual belongs to is a product of a survey of accessible economic opportunity and of a psychic self-appraisal. The manual worker perceives a world of limited opportunity while the businessman is more optimistic and perceives the world as being full of opportunities. If opportunity is believed to be limited, it becomes the duty of the group to prevent an individual from appropriating more than his rightful share, while at the same time protecting each individual against oppressive bargains. "The group then asserts its collective ownership over the whole amount of opportunity . . . and parcels it out fairly . . . among its recognized members, permitting them to avail themselves of such opportunities . . . only on the basis of a common rule."[12] The common rule serves to abolish or check competition for jobs and creates a solid bargaining front against employers. In contrast, if opportunity is believed to be plentiful, the enterprising individual would not submit to group control since he is confident of his ability to make good bargains for himself.

Perlman suggested that the safest way to assure group control over opportunity was for the union, without displacing the employer as the owner of his business and risk taker, to become the owner and administrator of the jobs. Where such an outright ownership of the jobs was impossible, the union should seek, by collective bargaining, to establish rights in the jobs by incorporating in the trade agreement regulations applying to overtime, to priority and seniority in employment, to apprenticeship, to the introduction of machinery, among others. As a technique, collective bargaining does not derive from a desire to displace or abolish the old ruling class, but from the wish to bring one's own class abreast of the superior class; to gain equal rights as a class and equal consideration for the members of that class with the members of the other class.[13]

The findings and insights provided by the studies on unionization and theories of the labor movement cited above laid the basis for developing the working list of variables to be considered for analysis in this study. The independent factors examined here were selected from the working list through the researcher's knowledge of library unionism and labor organization. The knowledge of library unionism stems from two years of gathering, studying, and synthesizing primary and secondary data on early

[12] Selig Perlman, *A Theory of the Labor Movement* (New York: Augustus M. Kelley, 1968), p. 242.

[13] Ibid., pp. 237–303; for a more thorough discussion of Perlman's theory.

and current library unions in the United States.[14] The selection of independent factors did not proceed in a manner where the researcher selected only those factors which he thought could be proved to be significantly related to unionization. Rather, he selected those factors which conceivably might have a systematic and repetitive effect on library unionization, in light of his knowledge of the field, with the intent of relying upon available data to prove or disprove the significance of each factor.

Data used to examine each factor are collected from a variety of sources. They include statistics published by the U.S. Office of Education, the U.S. Bureau of Labor Statistics, and the American Library Association (ALA); examination of documents; field interviews; and questionnaires. In all instances the source of the data is given in footnotes, with the exception of quotations, where the large number used and requests for anonymity prevent giving sources in every instance.

In some cases adequate data are not available for a thorough analysis. Part of the difficulty is due to the scarcity of research that has been conducted on librarians, particularly in the field of industrial relations and unionization. In cases where data are not complete, an explanation is noted.

In order to provide a quantitative measurement to the analysis, a questionnaire survey of public librarians was conducted. The survey is intended to represent librarians employed in various size libraries and in various socio-economic and political communities. In addition, the survey was to include both libraries with and without library unions. The sample was initially designed by making a list of public libraries in the southern California area (expenses necessitated limiting the survey to southern California). Libraries were then selected from the list so that the sample complied with the above guidelines. Questionnaires and self-addressed, stamped envelopes were distributed to all professional librarians employed at the sampled libraries. In total, 715 questionnaires were distributed; 490 were returned, giving a response rate of 69 percent. Thirty of the returned questionnaires were discarded for various reasons, resulting in a total sample of 460.[15]

---

[14] In addition to contacting known library unions, news items were placed in the major library profession periodicals requesting any helpful information on the topic. (*See*, for example, *ALA Bulletin* 63:692 [June 1969]. Requests were made in the name of the researcher's advisor, Dr. Archie Kleingartner.) The researcher is indebted to Ben Hirsch, union officer of the Chicago Public Library union during the early 1940s, for his assistance in obtaining information on early library unions.

[15] The unionized libraries included in the sample are Los Angeles Public Library, Los Angeles County Public Library, and Santa Monica Public Library. The nonunionized libraries are Long Beach Public Library, Orange County Public Library, and San Diego Public Library. The questionnaire response rate for each of the unionized and nonunionized libraries were, respectively, in percentages, 74, 53, 79; 85, 69, and 69.

Data from the survey, if strictly construed, are representative of only southern California librarians. But, as shown in later chapters, the survey results correspond in many respects with other national and regional surveys of librarians. The correspondence is most evident among such characteristics of the profession as median age, educational level, proportion of women, marital status, and social origin. In addition, several attitudinal responses measured by the survey—such as attitudes toward representative organizations and the compatability of union membership and professional standards—are similar to findings of other surveys. It can also be mentioned that the confinement of the survey to southern California should not yield a strictly positive nor negative union bias in the results, since the sample includes both cities with strong labor tradition and those with little union activity.

The questionnaire is shown in Appendix A. Part I elicits personal and background data. Part II measures degree of satisfaction with respect to three factors: material rewards, the library's organization and administration, and the intrinsic satisfaction provided by the job. The definitions of these factors and the items used to measure them are given in Appendix B. The items are selected from Baehr and Renck's employee inventory and Miller's scale of work alienation.[16] Each item has demonstrated high correlation with the factor which it represents.

Response categories for the items are (1) strongly agree, (2) agree, (3) disagree, (4) strongly disagree. Individual items are scored on a four-point scale, and a *scale score* for each factor is obtained from the mean of the scores of items measuring the factor. A scale score of 2.00 or lower represents a favorable attitude toward the factor; a scale score of 2.01 or higher, an unfavorable attitude. Thus, a scale score of 1 means the greatest amount of satisfaction in regard to the particular factor, and 4 means the least amount of satisfaction.

Part II also includes items designed to measure attitudes toward unionism in general. These items are adopted from Goldstein and Indik's study of engineers.[17] Response categories are the same as above, and responses are scored on a four-point scale. A mean score of 1 represents the strongest positive attitude and 4 the strongest negative attitude toward unionism. Part III includes a variety of miscellaneous items.

[16] Melany E. Baehr and Richard Renck, "The Definition and Measurement of Employee Morale," *Administrative Science Quarterly* 3:157–84 (Sept. 1958); George A. Miller, "Professionals in Bureaucracy: Alienation Among Industrial Scientists and Engineers," *American Sociological Review* 32:759 (Oct. 1967).

[17] Bernard Goldstein and Bernard P. Indik, "Unionism as a Social Choice: The Engineers' Case," *Monthly Labor Review* 86:365–69 (Apr. 1963).

Finally, respondents in the libraries with unions were asked to indicate whether they were a member of the union; respondents in the libraries without unions were asked whether they would be likely to join if a union were organized. Of the former, 61 percent were union members (which is proportionate to the percent of unionization in each of the libraries); 37 percent of the latter would be likely to join if a union existed. In the various analyses of this study, these two groups are often combined and referred to as "prounion" librarians. The remaining librarians of the sample, those who are not union members and those who would not choose to join, are referred to as "antiunion."

Tests of independence between any two factors are determined by chi-square analysis. In several instances, partial correlation is used to measure the association of two factors while adjusting for the effects of one or more additional factors. This is particularly useful in discovering those factors measured by the questionnaire that independently affect propensity to unionize. In addition, a correlation matrix was computed involving all the factors included in the questionnaire. This was used to provide a beginning statistic description of the strength of association between any two factors. All tests of independence are judged on a relatively strict level of probability (.01). Appendix C shows the statistical tests and formulas used in the study.

Value of This Work

The unionization of librarians has been a subject of little in-depth research. The majority of past and recent studies are primarily descriptive.[18] Several surveys initiated by ALA have sampled opinions of the profession toward collective bargaining and unionization.[19] The first reasonably analytic studies did not occur until 1970, when Vignone compared attitudes of Pennsylvania library directors, library board members, and librarians toward a constructed model framework of collective bargaining procedures; and Schlachter explored the type of associational representation desired

[18] The most comprehensive of these studies are: Bernard Berelson, "Library Unionization," *Library Quarterly* 9:477–510 (1939); John Clopine, *History of Library Unions in the United States* (Washington, D.C.: Catholic Univ. Pr., 1951); Erik J. Spicer, *Trade Unions in Libraries* (Ottawa: Canadian Library Assn., 1959); and Melvin S. Goldstein, *Collective Bargaining in the Field of Librarianship* (New York: Pratt Institute, 1968).

[19] The most recent surveys include: "Collective Bargaining: Some Questions Asked," *ALA Bulletin* 62:973–75 (Sept. 1968); "Collective Bargaining: Questions and Answers," *ALA Bulletin* 62:1385–90 (Dec. 1968); "Opinions on Collective Bargaining," *ALA Bulletin* 63:803–9 (June 1969).

by midwestern academic librarians and predictors of these librarians' interest in collective bargaining and union membership.[20]

Studies on professional employee unionization are numerous, but almost exclusively limited to the engineering and teaching professions. For at least two important reasons, this study serves to augment the findings of these works. First, it adds a new dimension to the research through the investigation of an unexplored profession. Second, many of the studies have used relatively unsophisticated research techniques. The most common fault is the failure to take into account the interrelations between variables examined as determinants of unionization. For instance, several studies demonstrate a relationship between age and salary, and propensity to unionize. But the strong association that generally exists between age and salary, or between these variables and other factors (such as attitude toward unionism) are not explored. Hence, the results do not provide a definitive explanation of unionization. As discussed in later chapters, a few of the more commonly cited determinants of unionization are age, sex, salary, social origin, and education. However, the results of this study show a high degree of interrelatedness among these variables, such that age is highly correlated with salary and education; and sex is highly correlated with salary, education, and social origin. The results also show that several of these variables are highly correlated with other factors, such that age and salary are both related to attitude toward the library's organization and administration, and whether the librarian is a member of ALA or a local library association.

The contribution this study might make, then, is to improve the exactness of accumulated research on professional unionization through a thorough analysis of unionization among professional librarians and an attempt at making theoretical statements concerning the origins of library unionism.

[20] Joseph A. Vignone, *Collective Bargaining Procedures for Public Library Employees* (Metuchen, N.J.: Scarecrow, 1971); Gail Ann Schlachter, "Professional Librarians' Attitude Toward Professional and Employee Associations as Revealed by Academic Librarians in Seven Midwestern States" (Ph.D. dissertation, Univ. of Minnesota, 1970).

Chapter 2

History of Public Library Unionism

The history of unions in public libraries in the United States is as long, or longer, than that of most other professional occupations. Bernard Berelson was the first to record the events of early library unions.[1] He provided an account of their activities from 1917 to 1939. During the 1950s, John Clopine and Erik Spicer added further details to Berelson's research, in addition to updating the history.[2] All three studies provide the most reliable data on early library unionism. This chapter synthesizes these studies and adds other pertinent information found in library periodicals and union publications, thus providing a brief but comprehensive history of library unions up to 1960.

The history of library unionization can be divided into three periods. The first dates from 1917 to 1920, when the original four unions were organized; the second is from 1934 to 1949, when fifteen unions were formed; and the third period begins in 1960, and continues through the present. Table 1 lists the unions formed in the United States during these periods.

The First Library Union Movement

The first unions of public librarians were formed in the years just before 1920 when "economic forces generated by the World War were stimulating organization of workers in all fields."[3] Unions were formed in four large eastern libraries: the New York Public Library in 1917, the Boston Public Library in 1918, the District of Columbia Public Library in 1918,

[1] Berelson, "Library Unionization," pp. 477–510.
[2] Clopine, *History of Library Unions*; Spicer, *Trade Unions in Libraries*.
[3] Berelson, "Library Unionization," p. 492.

TABLE 1
PUBLIC LIBRARY UNIONS IN THE UNITED STATES, 1917–70

Library	Union	Date Formed	Date Disbanded or Became Inactive
New York PL	Library Employees of Greater New York, Local 15590, AFL	1917	1929
Boston PL	Boston PL Employees Union, Local 16113, AFL	1918	1923
District of Columbia PL	Library Branch, National Federation of Federal Employees, AFL	1918	1924
Philadelphia PL	Philadelphia Free Library Union, AFL	1919	1921
Butte, Montana PL	Librarians' Union, No. 19178, AFL	1934	1941
New York PL	Library Workers Union, Independent	1934	1936
Boston PL	Boston Library Club, Independent	1936	1942
Cleveland PL	Library Local AFSCME, AFL (3 mos.); Local 48, SCMWA, CIO	1937	1948
Grand Rapids PL	Grand Rapids PL Union, Local 164, AFSCME, AFL	1937	1938
Milwaukee PL	Milwaukee PL Employees Union, Chapter 14, Local 2, AFSCME, AFL	1937	1940
Chicago PL	Chicago PL Employees Union, Local 88, SCMWA, CIO	1937	. . . .*
New York PL	New York PL Union, Local 251, SCMWA, CIO	1940	. . . .*
Detroit PL	Detroit PL Union, Local 304, SCMWA, CIO	1941	1942
Atlanta PL	Atlanta City Employees Union, Chapter 8, AFSCME, AFL	1942	1949

TABLE 1 (Continued)
PUBLIC LIBRARY UNIONS IN THE UNITED STATES, 1917–70

Library	Union	Date Formed	Date Disbanded or Became Inactive
Newark PL	Newark PL Union, Local 479, SCMWA, CIO	1943	1947
Boston PL	Boston PL Union, Local 731, AFSCME, AFL	1943	1949
Wayne County, Michigan PL	Library Employees, Local 771, AFSCME, AFL	1944	Not known
Minneapolis PL	Chapter 11, Minneapolis City and County Employees, Local 9, AFSCME, AFL. Later changed to Minneapolis Public Library Union, Local 211, AFSCME, AFL-CIO	1946	
Detroit PL	Local 1259, AFSCME, AFL	1949	
Philadelphia Free Library	Philadelphia District Council 33, AFSCME, AFL-CIO	1961	
Milwaukee PL	Milwaukee Public Library Employees Union, Local 426, District Council 48, AFSCME, AFL-CIO	1964	
Boston PL	Boston Public Library Union, AFSCME, AFL-CIO	1965	
Chicago PL	Chicago Public Library Employees' Union, Local 1215, District Council 19, AFSCME, AFL-CIO	1965†	
Cleveland PL	Cleveland Public Library Union, Local 1954, AFSCME, AFL-CIO	1965†	
Detroit PL	Detroit Public Library Union, Local 1259, AFSCME, AFL-CIO	1965†	
	Association of Professional Librarians, Independent	1966	

13

TABLE 1 (Continued)
Public Library Unions in the United States, 1917–70

Library	Union	Date Formed	Date Disbanded or Became Inactive
Brooklyn PL	Librarians' Guild, Local 1482, District Council 37, AFSCME, AFL-CIO	1966	
Buffalo and Erie, New York, PL	Librarians' Association, Independent	1968	
District of Columbia PL	American Federation of Government Employees, AFL-CIO, Local 1, AFSCME, AFL-CIO	—	
Contra Costa County, California, PL	Library Unit, Contra Costa County Employees Association, Local 1675, AFSCME, AFL-CIO	1968	
Enoch Pratt Free Library, Baltimore	Classified Municipal Employees Association	1968	
Los Angeles PL	Librarians' Guild, Local 1634, District Council 36, AFSCME, AFL-CIO	1968	
New York PL	Librarians' Guild, Local 1930, District Council 37, AFSCME, AFL-CIO	1968	
Queens Borough, New York, PL	Librarians' Guild, Local 1321, District Council 37, AFSCME, AFL-CIO	1968	
Santa Monica, California, PL	Librarians' Guild, Santa Monica Chapter, Local 1634, District Council 36, AFSCME, AFL-CIO	1968	
Youngstown and Mahoning County, Ohio, PL	Federation of Library Employees, Independent	1968	
Los Angeles PL	Library Employees Representation Unit, Los Angeles County Employees Association, Local 660, SEIU, AFL-CIO	1969	

14

TABLE 1 (Continued)
PUBLIC LIBRARY UNIONS IN THE UNITED STATES, 1917–70

Library	Union	Date Formed	Date Disbanded or Became Inactive
Oshkosh, Wisconsin, PL	Local 796-A, AFSCME, AFL-CIO	1969	
Berkeley, California, PL	Library Employees Union, Local 2077, AFSCME, AFL-CIO	1970	
Bloomfield, New Jersey, PL	Staff Association of Free Library of Bloomfield, Independent	1970	
Enfield, Connecticut, PL	Library Union Local 1029, AFSCME, AFL-CIO	1970	
Morris County, New Jersey, PL	Staff Association of the Morris County Free Library, Independent	1970	
Newark PL	Newark Public Library Employees' Union, Local 2298, AFSCME, AFL-CIO	1970	
Oakland, California, PL	Status not yet known— election contested	—	
San Francisco PL	Librarians' Guild, Local 400, SEIU, AFL-CIO	1970	

*Formed again as new union in third period of unionism.
†Unions were actually formed during the second period of library unionism (1940s), but were inactive until the mid-sixties.

and the Philadelphia Public Library in 1919. All four were affiliated with the American Federation of Labor (AFL): three directly by federal charter, and the Washington, D.C., union through the National Federation of Federal Employees (NFFE).

The least successful of the four was the Philadelphia union. In fact, authors disagree on whether such a union actually existed. Berelson wrote that the Philadelphia Free Library union was formed in June, 1919, but gives no other information. Clopine doubts that a union was formed, stating that there exists no documentation showing that an organizing movement ever reached fruition.

Each of the other unions enjoyed varying degrees of success. The District of Columbia union was the most successful. At one time, the union claimed a membership of about 75 percent of the clerical and professional staff. The percent of professional members is not known, but it was probably sizeable since the union was formed at their instigation. The Boston Public Library Employees Union, Local 16113, AFL, reported it had organized half the library employees but there is no account of the percentage of professional members. The New York union, Library Employees of Greater New York, Local 15590, was organized by workers in the lower grades of library service and apparently never developed a sizeable professional membership, if any at all. In fact, there is evidence of conflict between the professional staff and the lower grades. The union made published attacks on professional librarians, stating that "it [the union] is against the claim advanced by some people that librarians are 'professionals,' " and criticized the employment of library school graduates.[4]

The principal program of the Washington union was to work through NFFE to obtain improvements in salaries and to lobby for reclassification legislation. The federation included other librarians in federal employment, principally Library of Congress employees, and was instrumental in securing passage of the Reclassification Act in 1924. The Boston and New York unions were also formed for the purposes of obtaining better salaries and working conditions. Each claimed certain improvements in staff conditions as a result of their efforts, but whether the unions actually were successful is difficult to judge.

The New York union had the most liberal program of the four unions. In addition to better salaries and working conditions, the union advocated civil service coverage for library employees, equal rights for women in the library field, and labor representation on library administration boards. The union's only measurable success was passage of a resolution on these matters by AFL at its annual convention in 1919. At the ALA convention the same year, the New York union presented a resolution to the Executive Board asking that ALA go on record in favor of equal pay and equal opportunities for women in library work. The resolution was violently attacked as being unnecessary, and rejected by a vote of 121 to 1.[5]

Although the four unions had a minimal impact in respect to achievements, they caused a furor in library circles. Indignant articles appeared

[4] "Report of the Library Employees' Union No. 15590, Greater New York, 1917 to 1919," *Library Journal* 44:512–13 (1919).

[5] "Proceedings, ALA Conference, June 23–27, 1919," *ALA Bulletin* 13:359 (1919).

in the official journals of the profession. An editorial in *Public Libraries* said of the New York union, "No right-minded librarians can possibly favor this move for self-assertion as a creditable effort in library service."[6] The library journals did publish activity reports submitted by unions, but often failed to control their own biases. An editorial note accompanying an article reporting the achievements of the New York union warned that the salary increases referred to in the article may not be necessarily credited to union action.[7]

Just as the four unions began during a period of high union activity, they dissolved during the 1920s when labor union membership in the country was declining sharply. The Boston union disbanded in 1923, due primarily to opposition by the library administration. Clopine quotes a former member as saying that unionists were fearful of losing their jobs and that the administration had been successful in luring away key men in the union by offering them administrative positions.[8] The New York union disbanded in 1929, also due to strong administrative opposition.

The Washington union disbanded around 1924 for quite different reasons. It was the only union to enjoy the support of the library administration. The chief librarian acknowledged the union as "trying to accomplish the very things for which the trustees and librarian have been striving by means of official representation. If possible, it [the union] has made the members of the staff more sympathetic then ever with the administration thru better appreciation of the difficulties which must be met."[9] The demise of the Washington union was due to apathy on the part of its members. Berelson quotes a former member as saying, "For a number of years after the reclassification act went into effect in 1924, various members of the library staff kept individual memberships . . . out of gratitude and loyalty for what had been accomplished. Little by little, however, there seem [to be] no problems that concerned the library and the members dropped out one by one."[10]

The Second Period

The second period of library unionization began during the early 1930s. As with the first, it came at a time when union activity among all workers, including professionals, was high. To a large extent, the second period of

[6] "Editorial," *Public Libraries* 22:279 (1917).
[7] "Report of the Library Employees' Union No. 15590 Greater New York," p. 512.
[8] Clopine, *History of Library Unions*, p. 36.
[9] G. F. Bowerman, "Unionism and the Library Profession," *Library Journal* 44:365 (1919).
[10] Berelson, "Library Unionization," p. 495.

activity arose as a result of the depression, but it continued through the 1940s with library unions arising sporadically. Fifteen unions were formed during this period.

Library Unionism: 1917–60

The following conclusions can be drawn about the pattern of library unionism from 1917 to 1960. First, the percentage of union membership among librarians was very low. In 1939, Berelson estimated the total library union membership to be "something over seven hundred."[11] *Historical Statistics of the U.S.* reports 39,000 librarians of all types in 1940,[12] meaning that approximately 2 percent of the librarians in the country were union members at the time. The actual percent was slightly larger since Berelson's estimate did not include school and university librarians who were members of American Federation of Teachers locals and federally employed librarians who were members of departmental unions.

Second, library unions, with two exceptions, were organized in only large libraries in large cities. In addition, unions were confined to a limited geographical area, being concentrated in eastern and midwestern states. No unions were organized in the far West, and only one was organized in the South.

Third, the pursuit of higher salaries that was characteristic of most union programs implied that union activity was incited by poor economic conditions. The economic data available on librarians' salaries support this implication. The first library union movement (1917–20) coincided with the highly inflationary period of the late 1910s, when librarians' salaries moved slowly. Statements printed in library periodicals reflect the economic hardships. In 1918, an editorial in *Library Journal* stated:

> The question of salaries is of never-failing interest and importance in the educational world. From the newly-organized library unions to the special committee on teachers' salaries in the N.E.A., there is everywhere agitation and discussion of ways and means by which the librarian and the teacher alike can secure sufficient increases in wages to meet the rapidly rising cost of living.[13]

Another editorial the same year said, "It has not been possible anywhere adequately to increase the pay of librarians and library assistants to keep pace with the increased cost of living."[14]

[11] Ibid., p. 497.
[12] *Historical Statistics of the U.S.* (Washington, D.C.: Dept. of Commerce, 1960), p. 75.
[13] "Editorial," *Library Journal* 48:493 (1918).
[14] Ibid., p. 858.

Compared with the 1910s, the 1920s were relatively good years for librarians. According to one survey, salary increases for professionals in large public libraries ranged from 12 to 17 percent between 1923 and 1927.[15] The depression of the 1930s brought salary reductions and severe unemployment, and seemingly instigated the second library union movement (1934–49). Of 227 libraries surveyed in 1932, 73 percent reported salary cuts ranging from 1 percent to 34.5 percent. In the same libraries, only 78 professional positions were available to unemployed librarians during 1932, while in the same cities, it was estimated that 1,044 professionally trained librarians were unemployed, an approximate average of 14 librarians for each position.[16] Salaries during the 1940s were still at a low level, although generally not as low as during the preceding decade. Due to budget constraints, many librarians were unable to restore salaries to predepression levels plus cost-of-living adjustments.

During the 1950s, library salaries fared better. Between 1951 and 1955, beginning salaries for professionals averaged an increase of 6 percent per year; increases averaged 5 percent for the decade.[17] The relative prosperity of the 1950s created little interest in union activity.

Fourth, approximately one half of the unions which dissolved between 1917 and 1960, did so as a result of strong opposition by library administrators.

Finally, all library unions formed between 1917 and 1960, with two exceptions, were affiliated with national labor organizations. The implication is that librarians felt their needs could be served better through affiliation with the organized labor movement than through independent action.

In conclusion, library unionism from 1917 to 1960 represented a small number of librarians; was confined to large libraries in a limited geographical area; emerged in response to economic hardships in the profession; succeeded only in the absence of strong opposition by library administrators; and was aligned with the broader labor movement.

The Third Period

The present period of library unionism is the most significant in terms of total number of unions, total membership, total number of collectively negotiated agreements, and impact upon the profession. Between the middle 1960s and the present, several dormant unions were reactivated, and several new unions emerged. A greater number of library unions exist today

[15] "Trends in Library Salaries," *ALA Bulletin* 22:805 (1928).
[16] "Salaries and Unemployment," *ALA Bulletin* 27:94–95 (1933).
[17] "Trends in Library Manpower," *Wilson Library Bulletin* 43:272 (1968).

than existed in the first and second periods of union activity combined; they represent more librarians than in the earlier periods. In addition, the majority of today's unions have negotiated collective agreements with either library or city officials, whereas prior to 1960 collective agreements were a rarity. Finally, the impact of unionization upon the profession is reflected by the increase in number of articles published on the subject. Between 1921 and 1960, forty-four articles about library unionization were listed in the *Library Literature* index; whereas eighty-six were listed between 1961 and 1970, with seventy-nine since 1967.

Currently there are twenty-six public libraries where professionals or nonprofessionals are known to be unionized. The libraries, and the unions, are listed in table 1 on pages 12–15. This number was determined by reviewing references to library unions in the 1950–70 issues of the *Library Literature* index, and by examining other studies on library unionization. All but two of the twenty-six unions are affiliated with a national labor organization or operate under a collectively bargained agreement. The remaining two unaffiliated organizations discuss or negotiate issues involving salaries and working conditions, and can be appropriately considered unions. Organizations excluded from consideration here are those that either do not officially represent librarians as determined by an election showing the librarians' desire for representation, or that only represent blue-collar (maintenance, etc.) employees of the library. The two organizations most often excluded are the local staff association and the municipal employee association, whose roles in library unionization are discussed in a later chapter.

The following material does not exhaust the list of current library unions; in fact, the present extent of library unionization is undoubtedly understated. However, a sufficient number are examined to identify the general pattern of library unionization during the 1960s.

BROOKLYN. Employees of the Brooklyn Public Library, one of the three public library systems serving New York City, make up the third largest public library staff in the United States. Union organizing at Brooklyn began in early 1966 with a campaign by the New York American Federation of State, County, and Municipal Employees (AFSCME). By June, 1966, organizers presented a demand for recognition to the Brooklyn Board of Trustees. The trustees agreed to an election of library employees, under the supervision of the New York City Department of Labor, to determine whether a majority wished representation by a union. In the fall of 1966, an election was conducted among two separate groups of employees: the professional librarians and all residual classifications, comprised mainly of clerical and maintenance personnel. A majority of both groups voted in favor of union representation. The new union was designated Librarians' Guild, Local 1482, District Council 37, AFSCME, AFL–CIO.

In January, 1967, the union submitted its first set of preliminary demands to the library administration. The union's requests centered around obtaining a dues check-off system, establishing a grievance procedure, and substituting the union in the place of the long established Brooklyn Public Library Staff Association. The administration was reluctant to concede any points to the union, and talks between the two dragged on through June, 1967. Dissatisfaction with the negotiations reached a high point in June, and Local 1482 staged one of the first major demonstrations by a library union. Close to 300 members took part in a picket line protesting alleged stalling tactics by the administration.[18] Finally, in September, 1967, library trustees and union officials approved the terms of their first union contract.

The Brooklyn union, along with the other two New York unions (discussed next), must be recognized as three of the most successful library unions in the country. In 1969, the Brooklyn library had approximately 600 librarians of which approximately 80 percent were organized; and a similar number of clerical and blue-collar employees, of which some 80 percent were organized.[19]

NEW YORK. The success of AFSCME in organizing the Brooklyn library provided impetus for the organization of the New York and Queens Borough libraries. Employees of the New York Public Library formed Librarians' Guild, Local 1930, District Council 37, AFSCME, in April, 1968. It is the fourth union in the library's history.

Local 1930 was the most amicably formed and recognized of the three New York City unions. After two years of organizing effort, union officials submitted to the library trustees a demand for recognition. Rather than require a representation election, library officials agreed to recognize the union on the basis of membership cards signed by over 50 percent of the staff. The only issue raised by library officials was eligibility for union membership. They took the position that no staff members with supervisory responsibilities should be union members. Members of the union organizing committee, some of whom were supervisory personnel, felt this was unfair. Even here, library administrators agreed to submit the dispute to arbitration.

Since 1968, the union has negotiated a contract with the Library Board of Trustees, the terms of which are similar to the Brooklyn agreement. In

18 "News," *Library Journal* 92:2493 (July 1967).
19 Membership figures based on a letter from Stanley Propper, Director, Professional–Technical Division, AFSCME, dated Aug. 21, 1969.

1971, approximately 400 of the 600 professionals at New York were organized; and approximately 625 of the 1,000 nonprofessionals were organized.[20]

· QUEENS BOROUGH. The Queens Borough Public Library was the most difficult of the three New York City systems to' organize. In early 1967, union organizers requested a meeting with library trustees to discuss recognition. Immediately afterward, the trustees issued a statement to the library staff stating that they would not accept union representation. "The Board of Trustees feels that recognition of a union would not be in the best interests of the library, its staff, and the public." The reasons cited by the trustees were that "the Board cannot control rates of pay and thus cannot bargain on monetary matters, and as for other matters, would be negligent of the public trust placed in it if it should bargain away its responsibility to perform the management function."[21] The trustees stated as a further reason that they were exempt from the provisions of the New York law setting up the framework for collective bargaining by city employees.

Two of the trustees' reasons were valid. Salaries for the majority of library employees in New York City's three library systems are controlled by the city, not by the individual libraries. In addition, New York's Executive Order No. 49, which established collective bargaining rights for public employees, stated that nonprofit cultural institutions may elect to deal with a union, but were not required to do so.[22] Then, in April, 1967, the trustees reversed their statement on the advice of the New York Director of Labor Relations, who informed them that it was city policy to recognize union representation of its employees. On Friday, April 11, the trustees issued a new statement pointing out the unfavorable aspects of unionism, but stating that nevertheless a poll would be conducted to determine the will of the staff. They set the date for an election on the next Tuesday, apparently hoping to catch union organizers off-guard. Despite the immediacy of the election, the library staff voted by a substantial margin to be represented by a union.[23]

It was assumed by AFSCME officials that the election demonstrated that they represented the librarians. After the election, however, the trustees said in a memo to the library staff that the referendum results indicated only that the staff favored some kind of union representation, and the "results of the poll would be presented to a forthcoming board meeting for

[20] Figures based on letter from David Beasley, President, Local 1930, AFSCME, dated July, 1971.

[21] "News," *Library Journal* 92:722 (Feb. 1967).

[22] A subsequent amendment to the New York State Labor Relations Act extended its provisions to all nonprofit and quasi-public agencies.

[23] "News," *Library Journal* 92:1783 (May 1967).

possible action."[24] The federation proceeded to obtain designation cards from library employees, and by April, 1968, over 50 percent of the professional and 60 percent of the nonprofessional staffs had designated their desire to be represented by Librarians' Guild, Local 1321, District Council 37, AFSCME. The trustees finally recognized the existence of the union.

The union has since negotiated a contract with the trustees, but not until the librarians conducted a demonstration protesting delaying tactics by the administration. As of 1969, Local 1321 represented approximately 65 percent of the professional and nonprofessional staffs.[25]

LOS ANGELES AND SANTA MONICA, CALIFORNIA. With the organization of the Los Angeles Public Library, the three largest library systems in the country have library unions: New York, Los Angeles, and Brooklyn. The Los Angeles union, Librarians' Guild, Local 1634, Council 36, AFSCME, was chartered in April, 1968. It is the first union in the history of the library. Unlike the New York City unions, it represents only professional librarians. In 1971, a little over 55 percent of the professional staff were members.[26]

The union has not negotiated a contract with library or city officials largely because the city has not yet passed an ordinance providing for municipal bargaining. It has been active in presenting salary recommendations to city officials and urging reclassification of library positions. The thrust of the union's activities has centered around obtaining a voice in the administration of the library, reflected in the union's guidelines, which state:

> As professionals we feel that the formulation of [library] policy should be a cooperative process utilizing the intellectual resources of the entire professional staff. . . . As professional colleagues with the administration, we feel that our ideas are of value and that each of us from our vantage point in the library system has a contribution to make toward policy formulation.[27]

Because of the union's legal inability to negotiate a contract, it has shown more attention to strictly professional concerns, as opposed to wage and salary concerns, than most library unions in the country. The union's activities in this direction have not created a particularly harmonious relationship with the library administration, but the union has been instrumental in affecting several administrative decisions.

[24] Ibid.

[25] Letter from Stanley Propper.

[26] Conversation with Thomas Lippert, President, LAPL Chapter, Local 1634, AFSCME, Oct. 1971.

[27] Librarians' Guild Guide Lines, mimeographed, undated.

Professional librarians at the Santa Monica Public Library followed the Los Angeles example and organized a sister chapter in 1968. Of the nineteen professionals at Santa Monica in 1971, seventeen were members of the Librarians' Guild, Local 1634, Council 36, AFSCME. Because the city of Santa Monica has a municipal bargaining ordinance, the union has obtained exclusive bargaining rights and has negotiated a collective agreement with city officials.

LOS ANGELES COUNTY. In November, 1969, employees of the Los Angeles County Public Library voted by a substantial majority to be represented by the Los Angeles County Employees Association (LACEA). At the same time, professional librarians voted by a solid majority to be included in the same bargaining unit as subprofessionals. The union is officially designated as Librarians Employee Representation Unit, LACEA, Local 660, Service Employees International Union (SEIU), AFL–CIO, and is the exclusive representative of county library employees. The union represented slightly over 60 percent of the 170 professional, and 65 percent of the 165 subprofessional librarians in 1971.[28]

Many librarians, and other county employees, actually belonged to LACEA prior to 1969, but the association did not serve as a bargaining agent nor assume any traditional functions of a labor union. In 1968, Los Angeles County passed an employee relations ordinance. County employees were divided into units for the purpose of collective bargaining. Since the ordinance provided for exclusive representation of employees and an election procedure to determine representation, LACEA began an organizing drive to represent county employees under the law. The association appeared on representation ballots as an independent organization; and it was not until 1971 that LACEA affiliated with SEIU. Hence, it could be charged that county librarians were backed into union membership. Although an election was held to determine affiliation with SEIU, all county employees—blue-collar, white-collar, and professional—voted as a group. A ballot count of librarians alone is not available, but several librarians did relinquish membership because of the affiliation with a national union.[29]

The library unit negotiates directly with the county board of supervisors, and a separate agreement is negotiated covering only library employees. The union has recently signed its second agreement.

BERKELEY, CALIFORNIA. In the fall of 1970, librarians at the Berkeley Public Library voted to be represented by Library Employees Union, Local 2077, AFSCME. At the same time, professional librarians voted to be

[28] Conversation with Wally Pederson, Business Representative, Librarians Employee Representation Unit, LACEA, SEIU, Nov. 1971.
[29] Ibid.

24

included in the same unit as the nonprofessionals. In 1971, a little less than one-half of the libraries' 120 employees were union members.[30]

The librarians surprised the city of Berkeley by being the first group of city employees to conduct a strike. On August 1 and 2, 1971, seventy library employees walked off their jobs in protest over contract negotiations with city officials. The action closed all branch libraries and curtailed service in the main library. The central issue concerned disagreement over wage increases.

The union felt librarians' salaries were well below parity with other city employees and librarians in surrounding areas. City bargainers offered a 5 percent raise; the union demanded raises closer to 20 percent. After several months of negotiating, the city agreed to the union's terms, but with the stipulation that there would be cutbacks in library hours and personnel to counteract the wage increase. The librarians felt the city was not conducting the negotiations in a serious tone and called a strike. The city immediately called the union back into negotiations and an agreement was soon reached.

The Berkeley strike was actually promoted by the shortsightedness of city officials. Prior to the beginning of negotiations between the library union and the city, city officials and other unions had informally agreed that for a temporary period of time salary increases would not exceed 5 percent. The city had failed to inform the library union of this agreement. Once the union was informed, it quickly abided and an agreement was reached for a 5 percent raise without curtailment of hours or personnel.[31] Although the strike served notice to city officials that the library union meant business and effected an agreement between the two, it also made many librarians realize that they were actually in a labor union. Immediately after the strike, ten to fifteen librarians dropped their membership.

A second confrontation occurred between the union and the library administration when the latter decided to eliminate Sunday library service. Protesting the decision, the union urged all Berkeley residents to write letters of protest to the library, and obtained signatures on a petition to retain Sunday service. The result was that the administration decided to maintain Sunday hours and to instead close three hours earlier on Friday evenings.

BOSTON. Although there is an AFSCME union which Boston Public Library employees may join, the union includes no professionals. In 1965, the city adopted a permissive collective bargaining law. Immediately after-

---

[30] Conversation with Mrs. L. Scogren, President, Berkeley Public Library Employees Union, Local 2077, AFSCME, Nov. 1971.

[31] Ibid.

ward, a majority of the nonprofessional library staff signed for a union; few professionals signed. According to Massachusetts law, no collective bargaining unit may include professionals and nonprofessionals unless a majority of the professionals in the unit agree. So the city recognized the union as representatives of the library employees, with the exclusion of the professionals, and subsequently signed a collective bargaining agreement. Hence, the professional librarians were left with no representation.

This is an unusual circumstance for Boston librarians since they and the New York Public Library employees have had more unions in the history of library unionization than any other libraries in the country. The Boston professionals do have a staff association, but it is of "dubious worth, except for its facility in arranging teas for departing co-workers"[32]

BUFFALO AND ERIE COUNTY, NEW YORK. In July, 1968, the professionals of the Buffalo and Erie County Public Library formed the Librarians Association to represent them in collective negotiations with the library board. In the same month, the association petitioned the board for recognition as exclusive bargaining agent. The board consented, and the two immediately began negotiations over salary matters. Officials of the county of Erie filed a court suit to enjoin the library board from negotiating with the association, claiming that the board had no power to recognize the organization. County officials had previously recognized three bargaining agents for the county: the American Federation of Teachers for teachers; the Badge and Shield Club for the sheriff's department; and the Civil Service Employees Association for all other county employees. Although the library employees voted by a solid majority to form their own organization rather than be represented by the Civil Service Association, the county's court suit insisted that the librarians be represented by the latter.

The Supreme Court of Erie County ruled in favor of the library board. In what may prove to be an important precedent for other library employees, the court found that the library was not a branch of the county government, but was a distinct and separate corporation which received budgetary contributions from the county and was therefore a public employer within New York's labor relations laws. Furthermore, since the librarians are exclusively supervised and directed by the library board of trustees, they are public employees of the library. The court then enjoined the county of Erie from negotiating collectively with the Civil Service Association as the librarians' representative.[33]

The librarians' association and the library board have since negotiated

---

[32] Karl E. Nyren, "Librarians and Labor Unions," *Library Journal* 92:2119 (June 1967).

[33] Erie Co. v. Board of Trustees of Buffalo and Erie Co. Public Library, 308 N.Y.S. 2d 515, 62 MISC. 2d 396.

an agreement which deals mainly with salaries and fringe benefits. In 1971, the association had 120 members out of 180 employees.[34]

CHICAGO. The Chicago Public Library has had a union in continuous existence since 1937. Through the 1940s the union was quite active. During the 1950s and early 1960s, it was practically nonexistent, and carried only thirty to forty members, most of whom were nonprofessional personnel. In 1965, the union affiliated with AFSCME, and has once again assumed a relatively active role.

The present union, Chicago Public Library Employees' Union, Local 1215, District Council 19, AFSCME, has a membership of between 150 and 200, or less than 25 percent of the staff. Approximately 30 of these members are professional librarians; there are about 200 professionals employed at the library.[35]

The Chicago union has a dues check-off system, but otherwise operates under adverse conditions. Relations between the union, and the city librarian and the library board have been generally unhospitable. The board has refused to allow a representation election, and originally refused to even meet with union representatives. The union's power to demand recognition is limited since Illinois as yet has no legislation requiring public agencies to recognize or enter into agreements with their employees.

In retaliation against the board's hard position, the union called a strike for March 13, 1967. It was averted on the evening of March 12, when the mayor met with union and board officials. At that meeting, the library administration agreed that the union has a right to represent its members in the processing of grievances, and the right to submit suggestions for improvements in personnel practices.[36] Since that time, the union has annually submitted budget proposals and has actively processed grievances through the civil service grievance procedure. Other than this, the union has been waiting for the Illinois legislature to pass a pending bill granting the right for public employees to bargain collectively.

If the Chicago union is given legal permission to conduct a representation election and to negotiate, it will probably become an active representative of the library employees. Shortly after the cancellation of the strike threat, Chicago AFSCME officials claimed that a heavy majority of all library employees had signed cards indicating their desire to have the union represent them.[37]

---

[34] Letter from Jeffrey P. Mahaney, President, Librarians Association of Buffalo and Erie County Public Library, dated Sept. 1971.

[35] Figures based on conversation with Lyda Carter, President, Library Employees' Union, Local 1215, AFSCME, June, 1971.

[36] "News," *Library Journal* 92:1398 (Apr. 1967).

[37] Nyren, "Librarians and Labor Unions," p. 2119.

CLEVELAND. There has been a union in existence at the Cleveland Public Library since 1937. It was very active in the late 1930s and middle 1940s, but fell dormant during the 1950s. During the middle 1960s, the union once again assumed an active role. The union is now designated as the Cleveland Public Library Union, Local 1054, AFSCME. Although membership is open to both professional and nonprofessional librarians, the nonprofessionals have dominated. In 1969, the local's president estimated that approximately 50 percent of the nonprofessional and 10 percent of the professional staffs were members.[38]

There is also a staff association in the library which represents most of the professional librarians. The association and union are frequently in conflict, and despite repeated efforts to merge, no settlement has been reached. It is clear that the staff association deals more with social matters than the more wage-conscious union.[39]

The library administration has not granted exclusive representation rights to either organization, but has allowed both to attend all library board meetings, and consults each in the preparation of the library budget as it relates to salaries. No collective agreement has been reached between the administration and either organization, although Local 1954 does claim to have obtained certain benefits for the staff as a result of negotiations with the administration.

Once Ohio passes legislation enabling public employees to bargain collectively, Local 1054 can be expected to request a representation election. Since any librarian regardless of rank can join, the union has the potential to become an effective voice of the staff. But since the Cleveland professional staff has not supported the union in greater numbers even with the presence of a friendly library administration, it is probable that the main union activity will remain among the nonprofessional librarians.

DETROIT. The Detroit Public Library has had a union since 1949—Local 1259, AFSCME. It is not clear whether its membership initially included professional librarians, but events subsequent to its formation indicate that the majority of members were nonprofessionals. The union was not particularly active until 1965, when Michigan passed one of the most liberal collective bargaining statutes in the country. Shortly thereafter, the union was recognized as the exclusive agent for all clerical and production maintenance employees, and a contract was negotiated with the library commission.[40]

[38] Letter from Eleanor Grist, President, Local 1054, AFSCME, dated Feb. 12, 1969.

[39] Nyren, "Librarians and Labor Unions," pp. 2117–18.

[40] Melvin S. Goldstein, *Collective Bargaining in the Field of Librarianship* (New York: Pratt Institute, 1968), p. 38.

In 1966, several professional librarians formed the Association of Professional Librarians, and filed for recognition as the exclusive bargaining agent for the professional staff. A jurisdictional dispute arose when Local 1259 also filed to represent certain professional positions. The issue was resolved by the State Labor Mediation Board, which roughly divided the professional staff into supervisory and nonsupervisory units, and called for a separate representation election for each unit. The majority of employees within the supervisory unit chose to be represented by the association, while the nonsupervisory unit chose Local 1259. Since then, separate contracts have been negotiated between the two unions and the Detroit Library Commission.

MILWAUKEE. The Milwaukee Public Library Employees Union, Local 426, District Council 48, AFSCME, was formed in 1964. The union represents both professional and nonprofessional librarians. In 1967, a little over 25 percent of the staff was organized, with professionals represented in the leadership.[41] By 1966, the union had secured a check-off dues system, recognition by library and city officials, representation at library board meetings, and a collective agreement. These achievements are due largely to an amiable relationship between union and library officials and liberal legislation dealing with collective bargaining by public employees.[42]

The collective agreement under which Local 426 operates is part of a general agreement between District Council 48, which represents a variety of city employees and city officials. It pertains almost exclusively to salaries, fringe benefits, and establishment of a grievance procedure. There is no evidence that the library union has obtained results other than those gained by District Council 48, which lends suspicion to how active the library union is on its own. If the union assumed a more active role in representing the specific concerns of the library employees, a larger percent of the staff might join.

MINNEAPOLIS. The Minneapolis Public Library Union, Local 211, AFSCME, was chartered in 1946. It is autonomous from other city employees, and represents only professional librarians. The nonprofessional staff (clerical, bindery, and janitorial employees) are represented by a separate union. In 1968, the professional union represented approximately 80 percent of the eighty-five librarians.[43] Since 1968, the union's jurisdiction was expanded to include professionals of the Hennepin County Library, also located in Minneapolis, but this added only approximately twelve members at the most.

[41] Nyren, "Librarians and Labor Unions," p. 2120.
[42] Ibid.
[43] Goldstein, *Collective Bargaining*, p. 88.

The union enjoyed its greatest successes during the 1950s. In 1959, Spicer wrote that the union secured gains in wages beyond cost-of-living increases, the establishment of a five-day work week, and compensation for overtime at a rate of time and a half.[44] It also obtained union representation at library board meetings, a feat not achieved by too many unions during the 1940s and 1950s.

The current position of the union appears to be fairly weak, although this is based only upon speculation. Representatives of both Local 211 and the nonprofessional union still meet with the library board, and the library administration consults with the AFSCME business agent on proposals to be brought before the board. In addition, a union officer recently termed the relationship between the union and library administration as very cooperative. The closeness of the two is a theme that reoccurs in all writings about the Minneapolis union. Yet, to date the union has not negotiated a written agreement with the board despite the fact that in 1968, the union president stated this to be his main objective.[45] There has been nothing published during the 1960s on activities or achievements of the union.

It is curious that a union with such a reported high membership rate and long history is not among the leaders of library unions in negotiating an agreement. The reasons of course may be many, not the least of which may be the fact that the membership does not desire to have a labor contract. It is entirely possible that since the union was organized in 1946, and has had a close relationship with the administration since then, that many of the members are of the old guard and believe that a labor contract and other traditional union functions are unprofessional. It should be pointed out, however, that Minnesota does not have a particularly liberal public employee relations law.

Nevertheless, Goldstein seems to have a similar conception of the union. Interestingly, he points out that in 1955, there were 155 professional librarians in the library and in 1968, there were only 85. When the local was chartered in 1946, every one of the librarians belonged, and in 1968, only 80 percent were members. He quotes the union president as saying that "the average age grouping among the professionals is 'way up in the 40's' and a sizeable group of charter members may well be retiring in the next five years."[46] It appears that during the 1960s, charter members may have successfully held union activities to a conservative course. This in turn may be preventing younger staff members from joining and causing union

44 Erik J. Spicer, *Trade Unions in Libraries: The Experience in the U.S.* (Ann Arbor: Univ. of Michigan Pr., 1959).

45 Goldstein, *Collective Bargaining*, p. 89.

46 Ibid., p. 90.

strength to decline through attrition. A recent inquiry into the membership of Local 211 was returned with a confidential reply.

PHILADELPHIA. Some librarians of the Free Library of Philadelphia belong to the Philadelphia District Council 33, AFSCME, organized in 1961. There is no separate local for librarians. District Council 33 has a collective agreement with the city covering both professional and nonprofessional librarians, as well as other city employees. Few professionals belong to the union.[47]

In 1961, an ordinance was adopted by the city council providing for mandatory and voluntary union membership for certain city employees. Several nonprofessional library positions are covered under mandatory union membership, but the majority of positions are classified as voluntary; positions which may require supervisory responsibilities are precluded from union membership altogether. Although the ordinance was instrumental in stimulating unionization of some city employees, its provisions have effectively excluded many professional librarians from union membership.

SAN FRANCISCO. Professional librarians at the San Francisco Public Library are represented by the Librarians' Guild, Local 400, SEIU, AFL–CIO. Approximately 60 percent of the libraries' 140 professionals are members. Nonprofessional employees are represented by a separate Local 400 unit. The professionals formed an independent association in 1967, and remained unaffiliated until 1970, when they joined SEIU. The move to affiliate was instigated by a three-day strike of San Francisco city employees.

In early 1970, city officials froze a salary increment plan which had been in effect since 1943. With the high inflationary period of the time, city employees quickly felt the effect of the freeze. Local 400, which includes such city employees as social workers and nurses, threatened to strike if the pay plan was not restored; and on March 13, 1970, some 14,000 city employees went on strike. Close to 86 percent of the library staff joined the city employees, causing library administrators to close the main library for three days. The freeze was rescinded, and a 5 percent raise was granted to city employees. According to the Librarians' Guild president, the strike served to reinforce the opinion that librarians had little power to effect changes as long as they remained an independent organization.[48]

Since San Francisco has yet to pass an employee relations ordinance, the guild does not have exclusive representation of the staff, nor does it have

[47] Nyren, "Librarians and Labor Unions," p. 2117.
[48] Conversation with Mrs. T. Dillon, President, Librarians' Guild, Local 400, SEIU, Nov. 1971.

a collective bargaining agreement with the city. The liberal library administration, however, has given the guild informal recognition, and the two have reached a "memorandum of agreement" on several points.

YOUNGSTOWN AND MAHONING COUNTY, OHIO. In 1968, the employees of the Youngstown and Mahoning Public Library voted overwhelmingly to have its staff association, the Federation of Library Employees, represent them in collective bargaining with the library administration. In turn, the library administration agreed to recognize the federation as the bargaining agent of its employees, despite the fact that Ohio has no statute sanctioning the organization of public employees. Membership in the federation includes both professionals and nonprofessionals, and ranges from supervisory librarians to truck drivers and parking lot attendants. As of 1971, a little more than 60 percent of the forty-seven professional librarians, and over 70 percent of the nonprofessional employees were members.[49]

Early in 1968, the federation issued a statement to the effect that there was general agreement that it would deal only with salaries and working conditions, and not with library policies or administrative matters.[50] This position has changed somewhat because not only has the federation taken the library administration to binding arbitration over a dismissal case, but it has negotiated an agreement with the library director that goes beyond purely economic concerns.

Part of the federation's success is due to the liberal administration of the Youngstown and Mahoning County Library. According to federation president William Richards, the administration has given full recognition to the organization as the employees' sole bargaining agent. The administration's willingness to recognize the union, in turn, may be due to the fact that Youngstown is a heavily unionized area.

OTHERS. There are references to union activity in several other public libraries, but inquiries into the extent of unionization have yielded little information. Sometime during 1969, employees of the Oshkosh Public Library in Wisconsin joined Local 796–A, AFSCME. Membership is not open to professional librarians, but the library employs only five at the most. The union has negotiated a contract with city officials, the terms of which provided for a 20 percent and a 7 percent increase for hourly and salaried employees, respectively; establishment of a grievance procedure; and increased health and retirement benefits.[51]

---

[49] Letter from William G. Richards, President, Federation of Library Employees, dated Aug. 29, 1971.

[50] "News," *Library Journal* 93:1090 (Mar. 1968).

[51] "News," *Library Journal* 95:113 (Jan. 1970).

According to Goldstein, there is union activity at the Enoch Pratt Free Library, the main library of Baltimore, and the largest library in Maryland. Under Baltimore's employee relations ordinance, the Classified Municipal Employees Association was voted the exclusive bargaining representative for city employees. Since Enoch Pratt Library employees are not city employees, they did not participate in the election. Prior to the election, however, Goldstein reported that approximately 100 library employees, or slightly more than 15 percent, were members of the association. The number of professional librarians who were members was not known. Goldstein also mentions that the library's staff association meets with library administrators to discuss issues relating to salaries and employee welfare.[52]

Goldstein also cites union activity at the Public Library of the District of Columbia. Although there exists no separate unit of librarians, a few of the professional and nonprofessionals belong to either the American Federation of Government Employees, AFL–CIO, or Local 1, AFSCME.[53]

Professional and nonprofessional employees of the Newark Public Library organized in February, 1970, as the Newark Public Library Guild. In 1971, the guild affiliated with AFSCME, and is now designated Newark Public Library Employees' Union, Local 2298, AFSCME. Approximately 40 percent of the professionals and 50 percent of the nonprofessionals are organized. The union has signed a bargaining agreement with library officials.[54] The staff association of the Morris County Free Library in New Jersey is acting as a bargaining agent. According to an association member, fifteen of the eighteen professionals and fifty of the fifty-five nonprofessionals are members. The association has negotiated an agreement with the library commission.[55] The staff association of the Bloomfield Public Library in New Jersey is also acting as a bargaining agent, although no other details are available.[56]

A representation election was recently held among employees of the Oakland Public Library in California. All city employees were divided into units for purposes of conducting a representation election. Library employees were included among such city employees as legal secretaries, inspectors, zoning clerks, and a variety of clerical workers. Employees in this unit had a choice between the Oakland Municipal Civil Service Employees Association and Local 390, SEIU. Because of procedural irregu-

[52] Goldstein, *Collective Bargaining*, pp. 84–85.

[53] Ibid., p. 79.

[54] Returned inquiry from Charles Allan Baretski, President, NPL Employees' Union, Local 2298, AFSCME, dated Dec. 1971.

[55] Returned inquiry from L. Elliott, staff association, Morris County Free Library, dated Nov. 1971.

[56] "News," *Library Journal* 96:1662+ (May 1971).

33

larities in other units, the election was protested by both the Employees Association and SEIU. The Oakland Superior Court upheld the protests, set the election aside, and called upon city officials to establish more defined election procedures. Since the ballots were never counted, it is not known how many library employees voted for either organization. However, some employees did belong to the association prior to the election.

Employees of the Enfield Public Library in Connecticut voted to join Local 1029, AFSCME, in February, 1970. All of the fifteen nonprofessional librarians on the staff are members; the two professional staff members are not.[57] Local 1029 represents a variety of city employees, including highway, sanitation, and park employees. A contract has been negotiated with the town manager. Although the librarians may be few in number, they are making themselves heard. In September, 1970, the library staff filed a complaint before the State Commission on Human Rights and Opportunities, charging that they were discriminated against by town officials. While the labor contract was being negotiated, town officials agreed to raises of from 7 to 10 percent for all town employees except librarians, who were granted a 5 percent increase. The librarians charged that since they belonged to the same union as other town employees, they should be allowed the same benefits. A mediator agreed, found the town was discriminating, and ordered a 7 percent raise for all librarians.

Finally, librarians at the Contra Costa County Public Library in California are organized as the Library Unit, Contra Costa County Employees Association, Local 1675, AFSCME. In 1968, the unit made history by being the first library union to strike a major library system. The events leading to the strike involved salaries and recognition of the union. County officials refused to grant recognition and bargaining rights to the library unit. When the officials also refused to grant a 5 percent salary increase, the library unit staged mass meetings. The county finally relinquished, but the union desired to push the recognition issue. Approximately one-third of the library's employees walked off their jobs. The strike lasted eight days, but apparently accomplished very little since the union still does not have bargaining rights.

Organizing Efforts

Although the majority of library unions are affiliated with AFL–CIO, there is no documented evidence that the federation or any national union has pursued a major campaign to unionize librarians. Even among the

<hr>

[57] Returned inquiry from Mrs. Lucille Agro, Local 1029, AFSCME, dated Nov. 1971.

majority of current library unions, organization and labor affiliation have been instigated by librarians rather than by outside organizers. This is not to imply that the AFL–CIO or national unions have no interest in the profession. An official of AFSCME, AFL–CIO—the national union with which the majority of library unions are affiliated—refuted this assertion, but admitted that organizing efforts are not normally directed specifically toward librarians. Instead, he stated that librarians, as public employees, are included in general recruiting campaigns aimed at all city or county employees.[58]

There have existed few efforts among library unions to stimulate the growth of unionization. In 1938, several unions formed a committee within ALA (Library Unions Round Table) to coordinate the work of existing AFL–CIO library unions and to advise employees forming new unions. The committee's activities, however, centered around recommending resolutions to the association—which were never acted upon—and by the late 1940s, the committee was defunct. In 1968, library unions in the greater New York City area formed a joint council of school, college, and public library unions, but the activities of member unions have diverted the council from any significant organizing efforts. For the most part, there has been little liaison between library unions, and no intense effort among them to coordinate or expand the library union movement.

Structure of Collective Negotiations

The structure of collective negotiations between library unions and administrators depends largely upon labor-management relations statutes. Since these laws vary from state to state, and even between cities in a single state, the structure also varies. The structural aspects considered here are degree of recognition accorded the union; the types of employees included in the representation unit; parties to the negotiating process; and type of agreement reached as a result of the negotiating process. Table 2 summarizes the four structural aspects for each current library union.

Formal recognition has been granted to more than half of the unions. Such recognition is sanctioned by law, executive order, or some other administrative promulgation. All the remaining unions, with the exception of Chicago, have been informally recognized by the library administrators. The importance of formal recognition is that it generally connotes a relatively firm relationship, and usually requires library or municipal officials to bargain collectively or meet and confer with union representatives. Most

---

[58] Conversation with Douglas Barrett, Educational Representative, California Area, AFSCME, Apr. 30, 1972.

TABLE 2
STRUCTURAL ASPECTS OF CURRENT LIBRARY UNIONS

Union	Representation Unit			Type of Recognition		Collective Bargaining Agreement	Militant Action*	Officials Negotiated with:	
	Professional	Nonprofessional	All-City	Formal	Informal			Library	City
Berkeley	x	x		x		x†	x		x
Bloomfield	Information not available								
Boston		x		x		x		x	
Brooklyn	x	x		x		x	x	x	x
Buffalo and Erie	x			x		x		x	
Chicago	x	x			x				
Cleveland	x	x			x				
Contra Costa County	x	x			x		x		
Detroit:									
Local 1259	x			x		x		x	
Professional Association	x			x		x		x	
District of Columbia	x	x			x				
Enfield	x	x		x		x			
Enoch Pratt	x	x	x						
Los Angeles	x				x		x		x
Los Angeles County	x	x		x		x†			x

36

Milwaukee	x	x		x	x			x
Minneapolis	x			x			x	
Morris County	x	x		x	x			
New York	x	x		x	x	x		x
Newark	x	x		x	x			x
Oakland	x	x	x	x	In process of election	x		
Oshkosh		x		x	x			
Philadelphia	x	x	x	x		x		x
Queens Borough	x	x		x	x	x	x	x
San Francisco	x			x	x	x	x	
Santa Monica	x			x	x			x
Youngstown and Mahoning County	x	x		x	x	x		

*Participated in strike or major demonstration.
†Memorandum of understanding.

37

unions with formal recognition also have exclusive representation rights, meaning that no other organization can formally represent employees within the union's jurisdiction.

The unit of representation refers to the type of employees represented by one organization. The two main issues are whether professionals and nonprofessionals should be included in the same bargaining unit, and whether supervisory librarians should be represented at all. Most municipal and county laws provide that professional employees should be represented separately unless a majority vote for inclusion in the same unit with nonprofessionals. Where this has been the case, the majority of librarians have voted to be included with the subprofessional and nonprofessional employees. Since there is not always a strong community of professional interest between the groups, it could be argued that such a choice indicates more concern over salary and working conditions than professional matters, but material that follows shows the evidence does not support this. More than likely, such decisions reflect the realization that a library union can be more effective when a large number of the entire staff is organized.

Most librarians are represented in units which include only library employees; a small percentage is included along with other public employees. The difference is generally the result of each city's labor relations procedure, and the degree of organization in individual libraries. In Los Angeles County, for example, officials divided employees into representation units after the county's collective bargaining ordinance was enacted. All library employees were grouped together, with the provision that professionals could form a separate unit. In Oakland, California, on the other hand, library employees were grouped with such other city employees as zoning clerks, recreation leaders, inspectors, and legal secretaries. Because of the ruling of the Supreme Court of Erie County, New York, however, it appears that librarians can refuse to be represented along with other public employees. In all cases where a high degree of library unionization exists, separate units have been organized exclusively for library employees.

There is less consistency on whether supervisors can organize, and whether they should be included in units with other library employees. In most cases, the issue is resolved through arbitration or by an appointed labor relations board or commission. The Michigan Labor Mediation Board held, for instance, that supervisory librarians (chiefs of divisions and departments) of the Detroit Public Library may be represented by a bargaining agent, but directed that supervisory librarians and other professional librarians vote in separate units. The New York City Department of Labor ruled that supervisory and other professional librarians should be in the same unit, but excluded major administrative officers from representation. In other cases where supervisory librarians are precluded from organizing, the deciding criterion is normally title or position. Generally, supervisory librarians who direct subordinates in a nonroutine manner are not eligible for representation. This would include directors, department heads, division heads, and branch heads. Assistants to these positions are generally eligible.

For the most part, representatives of library employees negotiate directly with city or county officials. These officials are usually the personnel officer or other persons who simultaneously deal with other public employee unions. Library administrators are sometimes represented in the negotiations, but their inexperience in labor relations generally prevents them from assuming an active role. It is often the case that negotiations will proceed on two levels. Employee representatives will meet with city or county officials on matters dealing with wages, and meet with the library director or the library commission on matters involving working conditions and professional concerns.

Library unions with national affiliation are usually represented by experienced union bargainers. In a few cases where the union is unaffiliated, negotiations are conducted between elected representatives of the librarians and the library director or commission.

The majority of library unions studied here have reached some type of written agreement with city or library officials. Virtually every union which has been accorded formal recognition under existing ordinances has reached an agreement. The type of agreement varies, depending upon the particular labor relations ordinance. Some unions have formal bilateral collective agreements, and others have informal bilateral agreements or "memoranda of understanding." In New York City, for example, the city collective bargaining law permits the unions and city officials to reach a binding collective bargaining agreement. In San Francisco, legislation only allows the two parties to reach a written memorandum of understanding which is not binding upon either party. In some cases, such as in the Detroit library, where professional and nonprofessional employees are represented by different unions, separate agreements are negotiated with each union.

Scope of Negotiations

The scope of negotiations is also influenced by the laws of each state, county, or municipality. In most statutes the scope of negotiations is defined to cover wages or salaries, hours, and other terms or conditions of employment. Some statutes explicitly forbid negotiations on certain subjects. In Wisconsin, for example, matters covered by civil service regulations are excluded from bargaining. Connecticut protects the merit system by excluding merit examinations, lists, and appointments from negotiations. New York and Connecticut laws provide that an agreement calling either for an amendment of law or for additional funds does not become effective until approved by the appropriate legislative body. Similarly, Massachusetts provides that if a contract provision conflicts with an existing law or ordinance, the latter shall prevail.[59] Most union security provisions are prohibited from negotiations. The check-off of union dues is allowed in several states, but few statutes permit agency shops, maintenance of membership, or union shops.[60]

The basic issues library unions are negotiating do not differ markedly from those of unions in the private sector, although approaches to the issues often do differ. Of the unions studied here, seventeen have negotiated and reached collective agreements. Table 3 shows the types of issues most frequently covered in agreements for fourteen of these unions.

TABLE 3

TYPES OF ISSUES FREQUENTLY CONTAINED IN AGREEMENTS

Salary matters	14
Fringe benefits	13
Grievance procedure	10
Working conditions	8
Union security	8
Promotions and job classification	6
Professional matters	9

NOTE: These figures pertain to agreements for a total of fourteen of the unions studied here. Data were obtained from sections of union agreements and from news articles in *Library Journal*. The data pertain to contracts negotiated between 1968 and 1970.

As can be seen, all fourteen agreements contain provisions relating to improvements in salaries. In most cases, salary increases followed the standard for all city or county employees. Detroit's Association of Professional Librarians is the only contract not to mention specific salary increases, but instead states that the association and the library commission will cooperate to gain improvements in various areas, "especially wages." Several contracts additionally have provisions relating to overtime and

[59] Joel Seidman, "State Legislation on Collective Bargaining by Public Employees," *Labor Law Journal* 22:15–16 (Jan. 1971).
[60] Ibid., p. 16.

call-back payments. Overtime payments typically call for time and a half for time worked over eight hours per day. Most provisions relating to call-back-to-work payments specify that an employee receive a minimum of four hours credit, either in pay or compensatory time off. In all provisions relating to salary matters, unions have negotiated for minimum salary rates or percentage increases for all grades, leaving room in each job classification for merit increases. Thus the unions have not followed the standard union practice of establishing automatic salary increases with little leeway for merit considerations.

All but one of the contracts provide for improvements in fringe benefits. Areas most frequently mentioned are hospital, medical, and surgical care insurance plans; retirement and pension plans; holidays; vacations; and sick leave. As in the case of salaries, improvements granted were generally in line with those given to other public employees.

Provisions relating to working conditions usually call for an 8-hour/5-day standard work week. The New York contracts include a unique provision on operation of the library in extreme weather conditions. Under terms of the contracts, each agency is equipped with a hygrometer to record the temperature-humidity index. If the reading inside an individual agency reaches eighty and remains at that reading for one hour, the supervisor may excuse or reassign all except a minimum staff. If the hygrometer reading reaches eighty-two, or if the indoor temperature remains below sixty-four degrees two hours after the beginning of the work day, the supervisor is to call the library director to obtain a decision with regard to closing the agency.

Ten of the agreements outline steps of a grievance procedure. In the majority of cases, the procedure cumulates to outside arbitration. In other cases, the library commission or a special panel of union and administrative representatives is the final hearing board. All contracts define a grievance to include questions relating to interpretations, inequitable application, or alleged violation of the written agreements; and questions relating to rules or regulations governing personnel practices or conditions. However, not all grievances can be taken to arbitration. The Los Angeles County agreement, for example, specifies that only those grievances which directly concern or involve the interpretation or application of the terms and provisions of the agreement may be submitted to arbitration. In other instances, such as the Youngstown and New York City libraries, dismissal and disciplinary cases may be submitted to binding arbitration.

Eight agreements have provisions relating to union security. In six of these, the provision establishes a check-off of union dues system. The two Detroit contracts provide for an agency shop, and stipulate that employees may join the union or pay a service fee equal to union dues. Failure to do

41

either results in termination of employment. In addition, the New York City agreements provide that the contract will be reopened for the sole purpose of negotiating an agency shop provision "at such time as the City of New York implements the agency shop in a reasonable number of mayoral agencies encompassing a substantial number of employees." In general, however, the agreements tend to stress the voluntary nature of union membership. It is impossible to judge now whether this is a manifestation of professional unionism, or whether it is simply due to the fact that most statutes do not permit the union shop, maintenance of membership, and other traditional means of union security.

Negotiations involving promotions and job classifications represent an attempt by unions to share in the administrative processes of the library. Only four unions have thus far actually negotiated provisions relating to them. The greatest involvement has been secured by the Brooklyn union. That contract establishes procedures whereby the union may challenge administrative decisions relating to promotions. The Queens Borough and New York contracts allow employee representation on promotion boards. Detroit's Local 1259 contract provides that promotions are to be based upon the applicants' ability and seniority. However, a senior applicant who is denied a promotion can file a grievance. The Detroit Association of Professional Librarians contract grants that the ultimate decision for promotions and transfers resides solely with the administration, but it calls for an association-management committee to review and formulate procedures and guidelines for various personnel practices, including hiring and promotions. The only substantial provision relating to job classifications is contained in Detroit's Local 1259 contract. It states that new positions requiring new classifications and salaries are to be discussed with the union.

Finally, nine agreements contain provisions relating to professional matters. These provisions mark the major distinction between professional and blue-collar unions. They reflect issues which have arisen as a result of the professional nature of library work. Four contracts have provisions concerning sabbatical leave for professional and educational development. The provisions are not liberal since at the most they provide salary allowances at only one-half rate during leaves. Four agreements provide for tuition reimbursements for courses taken in the field of librarianship. The reimbursements, however, are subject to approval by the library director and to the availability of funds. One contract provides that employees shall participate in book selection policies. One provides that employee representatives and administrators shall discuss library priorities and that no new programs be introduced without discussions. The Berkeley union has reached agreement with administrators for the implementation of an affirmative action program to recruit more minority librarians. Several agreements call for periodic meetings between librarians and administrators to discuss policy and programs. Although each of these provisions is narrow in scope, each indicates that the unions have more than purely economic objectives.

The principle of seniority is given little weight in each of the agreements. In fact, in contrast to general union policy, most agreements specify that merit is to take precedence as the basis for rewards. Where contract provisions relate to promotions, they usually state that promotions are to be based on merit with length of service as only one of the factors to be reviewed. Some contracts specify that transfers to new work locations are mandatory for persons with the least seniority within a class of positions if no one else volunteers, and that layoffs and recalls are to be based upon seniority, but such provisions are a minority.

Among the unions which have written agreements, there is no tendency for those which include only professionals to emphasize professional matters more than unions which include both professionals and nonprofessions. The sample is not large enough, however, to suggest this as a firm conclusion. There is a tendency for those few unions which include only nonprofessionals to emphasize only economic issues.

Pattern of Library Unionism

The unions discussed here suggest the following pattern of library unionism:

First, during the past ten years library unionization has become an institution to be reckoned with in the library profession. According to an estimate computed for this study, 7 to 10 percent of the country's public librarians were unionized in 1968–69. Although the degree of unionization is relatively small, the library profession is currently more extensively unionized than at any other time in history. In addition, library unions have become more militant. Since 1968, at least six unions have sponsored strikes or major demonstrations that have curtailed library service. Prior to 1968, no documented evidence exists showing that strikes or demonstrations occurred.

Second, during the third period of unionism, a few unions have been formed in small libraries in relatively small cities. Prior to 1960, unions existed only in large libraries, with two exceptions. The predominance of activity since 1960, however, still has occurred in large libraries in well-populated cities. It could be argued that the methodology used to identify the current unions biases the pattern in favor of this direction. That is, library periodicals may be more prone to report union activity in large rather than small libraries. However, all the small libraries listed in table 1 were identified through this method. Instead of mentioning only large libraries, periodicals are more likely to report on only the most active unions, in which case the sample would not be biased.

Third, unions formed during the first and second periods of unionism were confined to eastern and midwestern states. This pattern still holds for the third period, with one important exception. Whereas no unions were formed in the West before 1960, seven currently exist in California. No unions have been formed in libraries of southern states during the third period.

Fourth, it is evident that the periods of union activity have conformed with periods of high union activity within the general labor movement. All the current library unions have been formed or reactivated since 1965, with the majority emerging only in the past three to four years. There was practically no library union activity during the 1950s and early 1960s. Data on total union membership in the United States show that membership declined between 1956 and the early sixties. During the mid-sixties, total membership began to recover, and it has risen each year since 1964.[61]

Fifth, library unions in the first and second periods appeared to emerge as a reaction to economic hardships within the profession, and the primary concern of most of these unions was to improve salaries and working conditions. Today's unions still strive toward improvements in economic conditions, but the concern is not as pervasive. This is evidenced by the fact that during the 1960s there has not been as much comment in library periodicals and by library unions over the necessity of improving librarians' salaries as existed in the earlier periods. Instead, there has been more comment concerning attempts to improve the administration and personnel policies of today's public libraries.

Sixth, early unions were hampered by library administrators who attempted to discourage activity. In fact, many unions dissolved as a result of administration opposition. Current unions do not necessarily enjoy administration support, but, in most cases, they are protected by legislation which did not exist prior to 1960. The result is that even the most reluctant library administrators are forced to accept unionization of their staffs through state or municipal statutes. Over two-thirds of the current unions were formed at a time when legislation existed to protect the right of public employees to organize; and all but four of the current unions exist in a state where local public employees are given the explicit right to organize.

Finally, the majority of unions formed during the third period have followed the pattern established by unions of the first and second periods

[61] *Directory of National and International Labor Unions, 1969* (Washington, D.C.: Bureau of Labor Statistics, 1970), Bulletin No. 1665, p. 66.

44

of affiliating with national labor organizations. Nineteen of the twenty-six unions studied in the third period are affiliated with AFSCME, AFL–CIO; only four are independent organizations. Significantly, however, unionized librarians are not represented by a national library union established exclusively for the profession, as is the case for many other professionals (such as nurses and teachers). Nor has there been noticeable liaison between library unions. In only a few instances have efforts been made to establish a regional or state federation of library locals for the purpose of coordinating and promoting union activity.

In summary, the library unions studied here suggest the following pattern of library unionism:

1. Although a small percentage of professional public librarians are unionized, the degree of unionization is greater now than at any other time in history.
2. Unionization is generally confined to large libraries in large cities (see table 1).
3. Unionization is concentrated in eastern and midwestern states, and California, with no unions currently existing in southern states.
4. The growth of library unionization closely follows the growth of total U.S. union membership.
5. Unions formed prior to 1960 appear to have emerged as a result of economic concerns; whereas current unions, while still showing an interest in economic matters, also display interest in matters relating to library administration and personnel policies.
6. The formation and success of current unions seem to have been aided by protective state and municipal legislation.
7. Most library unions have affiliated with the organized labor movement.

Chapter 3

Professional and Employee Associations

Eldred Smith observed that the lack of interest by librarians in unionization should not be surprising in view of the strong antipathy that most professionals have traditionally felt toward unions. All professions have recognized the importance of organization, but they have formed professional associations in place of unions.[1] Carr-Saunders observed that the formation of associations is generally regarded as one of the basic features of professionalization.[2]

Professional associations can perform many functions normally attributed to labor unions. Among the self-employed professions—law, medicine, dentistry—associations have effectively assumed roles of labor unions: they have established standards, limited membership, improved working conditions, and helped achieve a high level of material reward.

Among the salaried professions, the American Nurses' Association (ANA) offers the best example. This association, the dominant organization of the nursing profession, adopted an "Economic Security Program" in 1946. It states, in part, that

> the American Nurses' Association believes that the several state and district nurses' associations are qualified to act and should act as the exclusive agents of their respective memberships in the important fields of economic security and collective bargaining. The Association . . . urges all state and district nurses' associations to push such a program vigorously and expeditiously.[3]

[1] Eldred Smith, "Librarians and Unions: The Berkeley Experience," *Library Journal* 93:717 (1968).

[2] A. M. Carr-Saunders, *Professions: Their Organization and Place in Society* (Oxford: Clarendon Pr., 1928), pp. 7–9.

[3] Archie Kleingartner, "Nurses, Collective Bargaining and Labor Legislation," *Labor Law Journal* 18:237 (1967).

As a result, ANA has had no serious challenge from a labor union for representation of nurses.

On the other hand, the National Education Association (NEA), the dominant professional organization among classroom teachers, consistently maintained an emphasis on purely professional matters, with little attention given to economic concerns of its members. The American Federation of Teachers (AFT), the AFL–CIO affiliated union, had never been until recently a challenge to NEA. However, in 1961, AFT surprised NEA by winning exclusive representation rights for New York City's 40,000 teachers. The victory served as a boom to teacher unionism throughout the country, and had a profound impact on NEA. The next year, NEA responded at its national convention by passing two resolutions, both camouflaged sanctions for its affiliates to negotiate collective bargaining contracts with school boards and to engage in coercive action if necessary. Since 1962, many NEA affiliates have negotiated contracts and have endorsed classroom walkouts in support of teachers' demands.[4]

A similar change has occurred with the American Association of University Professors (AAUP). Garbarino observed,

> When the collective bargaining issue first arose [on college campuses in 1966], the AAUP saw itself as the national spokesman for the profession with local faculty senates handling operating problems. The inexorable momentum toward competition for bargaining rights generated by the public employee collective bargaining laws has forced the AAUP to enter the fray as an all purpose representative.[5]

At its annual meeting in 1972, AAUP endorsed the following position on collective bargaining: "The Association will pursue collective bargaining as a major additional way of realizing the Association's goals in higher education. . . ."[6]

Archie Kleingartner concluded after studying professional associations among nurses, teachers, and engineers, that these associations, and in all probability those associations of other salaried professionals, appear to have the capacity for discouraging large-scale unionization by adopting to changing needs and conditions of the professions.[7] In this chapter, the role of library associations in discouraging unionization is investigated and the activities of public employee associations are examined.

---

[4] Walter Fogel and Archie Kleingartner, eds., *Contemporary Labor Issues* (Belmont, Calif.: Wadsworth Publishing Co., 1966), pp. 253–54.

[5] Joseph W. Garbarino, "Precarious Professors: New Patterns of Representation," *Industrial Relations* 10:15 (Feb. 1971).

[6] AAUP Chapter Conference Letter, No. 4, p. 1 (May 23, 1972).

[7] Fogel and Kleingartner, *Contemporary Labor Issues*, p. 255.

American Library Association

The dominant association among librarians is the American Library Association, formed in 1876. Its activities have been described as follows:

> Notable among them are its efforts to improve library services in rural and urban areas through public, school and college libraries; its interest in the development of libraries all over the world; the raising of standards for [the] profession through better professional education [and] better salaries for librarians; encouraging improved book production; guiding the architectural revolution in American library building programme; and encouraging . . . free reading. It serves as an information bureau for public, school, college, hospital, prison, business and special libraries. It co-operates in cataloguing, compilation of bibliographies; supplies authentic information on subjects of library routine such as book buying, book binding, childrens' library problems [and] other technical matters concerning libraries; conducts general investigations in connection with the libraries, their personnel problems, etc. It participates in the interchange of librarians, books and other information material on [an] international basis. To make the activities lively, it holds annual conferences.[8]

The association has a complex organization structure to handle these activities. In 1970, there were 14 organizational divisions, each responsible for a specified area of concern; and 397 committees, groups, and sections to serve these divisions. In addition, there were 35 ALA committees responsible for other areas affecting library and association concerns.[9]

The association has a unique membership provision in that both individuals and organizations may join. Individual membership is open to any librarian, librarian administrator, or anyone interested in library service. Organizational membership is available to any organization with an interest in library service, such as local or state library associations. As of August, 1970, ALA membership included 26,259 individuals and 5,241 organizations.[10]

The principal concern here is an examination of ALA activities pertaining to the economic and professional position of librarians. It is dissatisfaction within this broad area that has instigated unionism among most professional employees, and the area in which associations must be effective

---

[8] T. C. Jain, "Role and Functions of Library Associations," *Herald of Library Science* 2:21–22 (1963).

[9] *ALA Organizational Information* (Chicago: American Library Assn., 1970–71), p. 2.

[10] Ibid., p. 1.

if unionization is to be discouraged.[11] Action in this area is within ALA's province. One of its stated purposes is "improvement of professional library standards through better professional education, working conditions, salaries, and certification."[12] The material following examines and evaluates ALA's action and programs in regard to each of these concerns.

American Library Association: Professional Education

First consideration will be given to the issue of education for librarians. At the beginning of this century, library schools were little more than trade schools run by larger libraries to train their own recruits. During the first two decades of the century, some professions were raising educational standards for admission. Law schools, for example, increased the course from two to three years; they then instituted two, three, or four prelaw years. In 1920, many teachers had as little as two years of college, whereas teaching in the public schools now requires a minimum four-year college course. During the 1920s, the library profession, too, began to question whether the qualifications of librarians had kept pace with the responsibilities of the profession.[13]

In 1923, Dr. Charles Williamson, an economist turned librarian, wrote the first reasonably comprehensive study of library education in this country. His study, *Training for Library Service*, has probably been more influential than any one person's point of view in determining the present status of library schools.[14] Williamson's high regard for the potential of the profession is reflected in his statement, "In any community in which the average person has enough education to get at the thought and information in the printed page, the librarian has an opportunity for service quite equal to that possessed by the minister, the doctor, the teacher, or the editor."[15]

The dominant theme in Williamson's report was that a distinction need be made between the professional and clerical work of libraries. "Until the distinction between clerical and professional workers is sharply made and adhered to, the demand for adequate salaries for the professional

---

[11] Herbert Northrup, "Collective Bargaining by Professional Societies," in *Insights into Labor Issues*, eds. Richard A. Lester and Joseph Shjster (New York: Macmillan, 1948), pp. 134–62.

[12] *ALA Organizational Information*, p. 1.

[13] Ralph H. Parker, "Ports of Entry to Librarianship," *Library Quarterly* 31:344 (1961).

[14] Edward A. Wight, "Standards and Stature in Librarianship," *ALA Bulletin* 55:871 (1961).

[15] Charles C. Williamson, *Training for Library Service*, a report prepared for the Carnegie Corporation of New York (Boston: Merrymount Pr., 1923), p. 113.

group will prove ineffective because they will be economically impossible."[16] His solution for achieving a distinction was the institution of higher standards in library schools. Williamson conceived of a national body that would accredit library schools and issue a uniform national certificate to the graduates of its accredited schools. It was his thought that after a uniform national but voluntary professional certificate, the next step would be uniform legal certification of librarians, at least in the public library field, and that this would come when the public recognized the educational and social importance of the work of the certified graduate librarian. This latter thought has never materialized on a national basis.[17]

Williamson's recommendations were quickly adopted by ALA. The year following his report, ALA created the Board of Education for Librarianship (now the Committee on Accreditation). In 1925, the board established minimum standards for library schools, and in 1926 twelve schools that met these requirements were accredited.[18] Thus, ALA's initial move into the area of professional education was based on a desire to improve the status of the profession through improving the quality of education.

During the late 1920s and early 1930s, most professions were faced with an oversupply of practitioners. Since the economy could not absorb the supply, accreditation committees in various professions became more concerned with controlling the number of recruits than with improving the quality of education. When unemployment within the library profession first began taking its toll, librarians, too, realized the need for restrictive policies. An article entitled "Limiting the Library School Output," printed in 1929, stated:

> . . . It is not too soon now to begin considering the future of professional training. There is the fallacious contention that an oversupply tends to raise the standards of the profession. . . . What the guilds did in the Middle Ages should be undertaken by every trade and profession today. . . . The library profession today stands in a strategic position to lead the way. . . . A Committee representing the library schools, or the Board of Education for Librarianship . . . should have absolute power to assign to each library school . . . the maximum number of students to be enrolled the following autumn.[19]

Beginning in 1930, when unemployment among librarians was sharply

[16] Ibid., p. 9.

[17] Wight, "Standards and Stature," p. 872.

[18] Parker, "Entry to Librarianship," p. 344.

[19] Louis Shores, "Limiting the Library School Outpost," *Library Journal* 54:64–65 (1929).

increasing, ALA began to consider the problem at length. The ALA Activities Committee stated in its report of December, 1930, that "a constant check should be made on supply and demand, for with the present low salaries an oversupply would, undoubtedly, react disastrously on the profession."[20] The Board of Education for Librarianship, after deliberations, stated its position as follows:

> Library schools should be encouraged to reduce the size of their classes through a more rigid scrutiny of applicants, both as to scholarship and personality. . . . The establishment of new agencies for educating librarians . . . demands continued careful consideration. . . . The library profession should take advantage of present conditions to strengthen its future personnel. Only young people of exceptional ability who show marked personal qualifications and promise for success as librarians should be encouraged to prepare for librarianship.[21]

In 1933, ALA instituted a new system of classification of library schools based upon entrance requirements. In Class I were schools that required four years of college for admission; in Class II, schools where the admission requirement was three years of college; and Class III, schools accepting students with less preparation.[22] During this period, few schools were granted accreditation. According to Parker, from 1932 to 1936, only two schools were founded and they were not accredited until after the depression. The Graduate Library School of the University of Chicago was the only school accredited during this period. And in the five years from 1937 to 1941, only two schools were established and six were accredited, most of them being founded before 1931.[23]

By adopting this policy of exclusion, ALA displayed more concern over raising the salary standards of professional librarians than the quality of education. Several library schools were understandably opposed to ALA's deliberate attempts to restrict the entry of new persons into the profession. In defending the association's stand, the chairman of the ALA Committee on Salaries stated:

> The legal, medical, and engineering professions make no pretense of limiting the numbers entering their ranks. The library profession is small and compact; the difficulty of controlling our personnel is less

[20] Charles H. Compton, "Our Obligation to Maintain Standards," *ALA Bulletin* 26:91 (1932).

[21] *ALA Bulletin* 27:811 (1933).

[22] Wilhelm Munthe, *American Librarianship from a European Angle* (Hamden, Conn.: Shoe String, 1964), p. 133.

[23] Parker, "Entry to Librarianship," p. 345.

difficult on that account. Why should we not take the lead in this respect? Certainly the difficulty of control should not be as great as the disastrous consequences of flooding the market.[24]

Parker wrote in 1961 that the same policy of exclusion prevails today, though largely unnoticed. "Those who now direct the libraries, the library schools, and the library associations entered the profession immersed in the philosophy of restricting production. Perhaps the failure to recruit sufficient librarians results in part from this unconscious set of attitudes."[25]

The last time ALA revised its standards for accreditation of library schools was in 1951, and the revision reflects the philosophy of the 1930s. In 1932, the director of the University of California School of Librarianship wrote:

> If the recommendations as future prerequisites for professional status are four years of college plus one of library school and that the title of librarian be then limited to those who complete such preparation, we shall have at once . . . a quite promising means of limiting library school students. If effective . . . this would eliminate undergraduate study for librarianship.[26]

The net effect of the 1951 revision was to remove accreditation of schools which gave only undergraduate instruction in library science. The idea that only a graduate program in library science could offer acceptable training had been generally accepted.[27]

What can be concluded about ALA's educational program with respect to its effect on improving the economic and professional standards of the profession? First, Parker's conclusion that the policy of exclusion still prevails seems accurate. In 1932, there were twenty-three library schools accredited by ALA standards; in 1963, thirty-five schools had been accredited by the 1951 standards; and by 1970, only forty-three U.S. schools were accredited by 1951 standards.[28]

The principles of supply and demand for labor normally dictate that when a profession is successful in restricting the supply of its practitioners such that it lags behind the demand, salaries within the profession will

[24] Compton, "Our Obligation," p. 92.

[25] Parker, "Entry to Librarianship," p. 346.

[26] Sydney B. Mitchell, "Ways and Means of Limiting Library School Output," *ALA Bulletin* 26:424 (1932).

[27] Parker, "Entry to Librarianship," p. 347.

[28] The number of accredited library schools was obtained from, respectively: "Accredited Library Schools," *ALA Bulletin* 26:H–341 (1932); "Accredited Library Schools," *ALA Bulletin* 57:963–64 (1963); *Bowker Annual of Library and Book Trade Information* (New York: Bowker, 1970), p. 150.

be aided. This has occurred among several professions, notably law and medicine; and among several blue-collar professions, such as electricians, plumbers, and carpenters. For several reasons it has not been the case in the library profession.

A primary factor involves entry into the profession. According to Parker, there is only one recognized port of entry into the library profession: the accredited graduate library school.[29] This conforms to the original basis upon which ALA entered into professional education. However, to control entry, a profession must also have a program of licensure. As discussed in the following section, the library profession has not obtained this, and it marks an important distinction between the library profession and other professions that have also controlled the training of its practitioners. The latter have successfully obtained legal licensing requirements to limit admission to those who have graduated from accredited schools. Medicine and law are obvious examples; cosmetology and architecture are others. The port of entry into the library profession, however, is not actually limited to graduates of accredited schools.

An analysis of library schools shows that in 1968, there were at least 384 library programs in the United States of which 39 were accredited by ALA.[30] In terms of enrollment, in the fall of 1967, 17,928 students were enrolled in graduate library schools; 7,131, or just under 40 percent, were enrolled in ALA unaccredited schools.[31] The demand for professional librarians has been able to easily absorb graduates from both accredited and nonaccredited schools.

A second factor more directly explaining why restricting the supply of professional librarians has not aided salaries involves the substitutability of professional and nonprofessional labor. To consider the extreme case, a shortage of medical professionals cannot be easily rectified by hiring nonprofessionals to perform the same tasks. On the other hand, this has not been the case in the library profession. The trend in the growth of nonprofessionals is pervading the field of librarianship. The ratio between the professional librarian and population served has fluctuated since 1939, but the population/nonprofessional ratio has declined significantly. From 1939 to 1962, the population served per nonprofessional employee decreased from 7,920 persons to 5,440.[32] The trend of hiring nonprofessionals has been particularly acute in the public libraries. From 1959 to 1966, the number of professional librarians employed at all types of libraries increased by 34 percent. In the public libraries, the employment of

[29] Parker, "Entry to Librarianship," p. 347.
[30] *Bowker Annual*, 1969, p. 164.
[31] Ibid., p. 168.
[32] "Trends in Library Manpower," *Wilson Library Bulletin* 43:271 (1968).

professionals during the same period rose by only 12.5 percent, indicating an emphasis on the use of nonprofessionals.[33]

A large part of the substitution can be explained by the knowledge base upon which the profession is built. Professions such as medicine are based upon an immense body of knowledge, and can generally be practiced only by those who have received the necessary formal training. To some extent the work can be performed by a nonprofessional, such as a laboratory technician, but the distinction between the professional and nonprofessional is clear. The knowledge base of the library profession is less exact, and the dividing line between professional and nonprofessional is obscure. One writer observed that the specific knowledge which a librarian must possess is not clear; another stated that it is difficult to define a problem for whose solution one would uniquely go to a librarian.[34]

By means of diluting the professional character of positions and training nonprofessionals who are capable of performing the work, employing librarians have been able to provide substitutes for the professional. If the statements of at least two authors on the subject are illustrative, substitution may be easily accomplished without even the dilution of positions. Goode states that while library school curricula teach communications theory, the sociology or psychology of mass communications, and the psychology of learning as it applies to reading, most day-to-day professional work utilizes rather concrete, rule-of-thumb, local regulations and rules, and a major cataloging system.[35] Leigh states that perhaps some two-thirds of library work is nonprofessional in character.[36]

In conclusion, if Parker's thesis is accepted that the professional education program of ALA still reflects the philosophy of exclusion adopted during the 1930s, ALA has little opportunity to significantly affect the economic and professional standards of librarians. As long as there remains no control over ports of entry into the profession, and the relative inexpert knowledge required by the profession makes it possible to substitute less highly paid nonprofessional workers for the professional librarian, ALA cannot influence salaries and status of the profession by restricting the supply of practitioners.

[33] Ibid.

[34] Neil C. Van Deusen, "Professional Education for Librarianship: Summary," in *Education for Librarianship*, ed. Bernard Berelson (Chicago: American Library Assn., 1949), p. 193; William J. Goode, "The Librarian: From Occupation to Profession?" *Library Quarterly* 31:312 (1961).

[35] Goode, "The Librarian," p. 312.

[36] Robert D. Leigh, *The Public Library in the United States* (New York: Columbia Univ. Pr., 1960), p. 186.

American Library Association: Professional Certification

The American Library Association is also committed to improving professional library standards through certification. Although it has consistently favored certification, the thrust of its activity has been to support state library associations' drives in promoting licensing legislation.[37] The association itself has been somewhat reluctant to enter the field of legislative action in behalf of licensing.[38]

Professional certification is a license to practice a certain skill or to hold a particular job. Receipt of the license is generally based upon completion of a course of professional training and examination before a board of inquiry composed of members drawn from the profession. Certification is effective only when it is sanctioned by law; otherwise, there would be no authority to punish persons who practice the professional skill without licensing.

There has been certification of public librarians under some state laws since about 1910. Table 4 lists states which currently have certification statutes. As can be seen, twenty-one states have made certification a mandatory legal requirement of municipal or county professional library personnel.[39] However, nine require certification only of head librarians. In fact, requirements for certification vary from state to state. All twenty-one states require graduation from an accredited library school as a condition for receiving a professional certificate, although only eleven states specifically stipulate that the school be accredited by ALA.[40] Variation also occurs in respect to the grades and types of certificates awarded, required length of experience, and whether or not an examination is administered. In most instances, a board—usually with an appointed membership including representatives of both the library profession and the general public—is given responsibility for administering the program.

In nine states, where certification is not demanded by law, voluntary certification has been effected through the efforts of state library associations. In these states, the association issues certificates to qualified per-

---

[37] See resolution passed by ALA Council in *ALA Bulletin* 26:211 (1932).

[38] Paul Howard, "Associations and United States Legislation," *Library Trends* 3:279 (1955).

[39] In actuality, twenty-two states provide for mandatory certification, but statutes in Arkansas and Tennessee are inactive.

[40] The eleven states which require ALA accredition are: Georgia, Maryland, New Mexico, North Carolina, Ohio, Oklahoma, Pennsylvania, South Carolina, Texas, Virginia, and Wisconsin. Even several of these states permit accredition by either ALA or another state board.

TABLE 4
CERTIFICATION OF PUBLIC LIBRARIANS

Mandatory Certification (required by law)

Arizona*	New York
California*	North Carolina
Georgia	Ohio*
Indiana	Oklahoma
Kentucky	Pennsylvania
Louisiana	South Carolina
Maryland*	Texas*
Michigan	Virginia
Montana*	Washington
New Jersey	Wisconsin
New Mexico	

Voluntary Certification (having no legal basis)

Kansas	Nevada
Massachusetts	New Hampshire
Missouri	South Dakota
Montana	Vermont
Nebraska	

SOURCE: *Certification of Public Librarians in the United States*, (Chicago: American Library Assn., 1965).
*Statutes apply to county librarians only.

sonnel. The certificates have no legal basis, and are not required as a condition of employment.[41]

State library associations deserve nearly all the credit for obtaining passage of certification statutes. The national association has limited its role to encouraging state associations to initiate campaigns, pressing for standardized state legislation, and publishing national surveys on certification plans. With legislation in less than 50 percent of the states, however, state associations have had limited success. The recent record has been poor. During the past decade, only one state, Pennsylvania, passed a certification statute for librarians, and that was in 1961.

Even if ALA succeeded in a nationwide campaign to bring about state certification, just how beneficial would it be for the profession? Theoretically, mandatory certification would serve to elevate librarianship in the eyes of the public to the unequivocal status of a profession; and this in turn would be followed by increased appropriations for librarians' sal-

[41] For a detailed summary of legal and voluntary certification plans in the states, see *Certification of Public Librarians in the United States* (Chicago: American Library Assn., 1965).

aries, which would effectively attract to the profession more and better recruits.[42] The record indicates, however, that the theory will not be turned into practice. Many of the twenty-one states with certification statutes seldom enforce them. The fundamental problem is that certification is impractical since job vacancies have generally outnumbered qualified candidates. At least six of the twenty-one states with certification laws stated, in effect, that there are limitations to the effectiveness of the laws due to the shortage of trained librarians.[43]

The prospects for certification in the future do not appear to be brighter as long as the trend toward substituting nonprofessionals for professionals continues. One writer observed that, among librarians, the general attitude toward certification has been one of apathy: "The great majority of library employees, those untrained or partially trained workers in libraries over the country could feel only apprehension over certification laws. The truth of the matter, which they well know, is that they themselves are the ones whom certification laws are designed eventually to eliminate.[44]

American Library Association: Professional Salaries

The association also has as its purpose the improvement of professional library standards through better salaries and working conditions. The program adopted by ALA to achieve this objective has entailed establishment of unenforceable standards of library employment, and encouragement for individual libraries to obtain sufficient financial appropriations to meet these standards.

The first official concern of ALA over salaries dates back to the inflationary period of the late 1910s. At its 1919 convention, the ALA Council passed the following resolution:

> *Whereas,* Investigations made by some of the most prominent members of the American Library Association have shown that salaries paid to library workers in the United States are inadequate to meet living expenses, and to compensate for the value of the services rendered; and
>
> *Whereas,* The only way to meet the natural demand under present conditions for higher salaries for library workers, is to secure increased appropriations; therefore be it

---

[42] Bernard Schein, "Certification of Public Librarians in the United States," *ALA Bulletin* 50:660 (1956).

[43] See *Certification of Public Librarians.*

[44] Harold Lancour, "The Librarian's Search for Status," *Library Quarterly* 31:375–76 (1961).

RESOLVED, That the American Library Association strongly urge all governing or legislative bodies, federal, state, county, city, town, or village to increase the appropriations for library salaries, in order to retain in the library service library workers who are forced by sheer necessity into other fields where the compensation constitutes a just return for scholarship and professional training; and further be it

RESOLVED, That the American Library Association take every available means to give this resolution the widest publicity, especially among those controlling appropriations for library salaries.[45]

The interest in the economic plight of librarians was translated in 1922 into the creation of the ALA Salaries Committee. The committee's initial program was to print salary statistics of public, and college and university librarians. The committee also recommended that ALA annually print facts regarding library salaries, that every state library association appoint a standing committee on salaries, that ALA Council consider establishing a standard for minimum beginning salaries, and that ALA be constantly making studies of various phases of the library salary problem and printing them. "The Salaries Committee's primary object should be to supply ammunition to the librarian in his fight for the development of a favorable community attitude toward better library salaries. The Committee . . . can best do this by making available such facts bearing on salaries as have been indicated [above]."[46]

Later the same year, in the official publication of ALA, *ALA Bulletin*, the first salary statistics for public librarians were printed. In later years, the statistics were expanded to include academic, high school, and special librarians, plus comparisons with salaries of other selected professions.

In 1924, ALA enlarged the scope of the Salaries Committee to include insurance and annuities; and in 1930, the committee published a survey of of pension and annuity plans for librarians in the United States, giving a state by state account of where librarians are covered.

In the same year, the committee recommended that a separate committee be established to devote itself exclusively to pensions and annuities, recognizing that the question of annuities for librarians was rapidly increasing in importance and interest. In 1931, the new Committee on Annuities and Pensions formulated a comprehensive retirement plan for librarians, to be underwritten by an insurance company, but operated under the auspices of ALA. Librarians, as most public and professional groups, were excluded from old age benefits of the federal social security plan. In

[45] "Proceedings, ALA Conference, June 23–27, 1919," p. 355–56.
[46] "Papers and Proceedings, Detroit Conference, 1922—Annual Reports, Salaries," *ALA Bulletin* 16:215–17 (1922).

order to provide protection for librarians, the association's retirement plan went into effect in 1934. The plan, underwritten by the Metropolitan Life Insurance Company and offering "incomparably" low rates,[47] was slow in growing. Most libraries installed the plan on a noncontributory basis, or employee-pay-all basis, and the difficult economic times of the 1930s prevented many librarians from joining. As a result, during most of the 1930s and 1940s, the Committee on Annuities and Pensions spent the majority of its efforts in promoting the plan. A modified version of the plan is still in effect today.

In 1933, when librarians began to feel the effects of unemployment, ALA expanded the Salaries Committee to include the study of employment and methods of relief for unemployed librarians. The chairman of the newly established Subcommittee on Unemployment stated that

> the experience during the last four years has demonstrated forcibly to us all that the library profession was not the master of the situation when confronted by conditions of unemployment. . . . Is it not possible for librarians to organize their forces so that they might be in a better position to control a similar situation in the future. . . . In order to prevent unemployment we must regulate the supply of professional workers so that it will never exceed disproportionately the potential demand.[48]

As discussed previously, the long-range plan of ALA was to regulate the supply of trained workers and limit entrance into the field through certification laws.

Up to this time, ALA's main activity in improving salaries and working conditions was largely restricted to publishing surveys and studies. Beginning in 1935, the association began taking more affirmative action. In that year, ALA became concerned with the lack of standardization of personnel policies in the country's libraries. The Salaries Committee was expanded to include the study of classification and pay plans. In 1937, it was again changed to the Board on Salaries, Staff, and Tenure, and had the responsibility for all personnel problems which might concern libraries, but it retained its basic concern over improving salaries.[49] In 1937, the board stressed what was needed for better library salaries: a cost of living survey, the need for encouraging certification, compilation of classification and

---

[47] "Committee Reports; Annuities and Pensions," *ALA Bulletin* 30:363 (1936).

[48] "Proceedings of the Fifty-sixth Conference, Unemployment," *ALA Bulletin* 28:718 (1934).

[49] "Committee Reports; Salaries, Staff, and Service," *ALA Bulletin* 31:601 (1937).

pay plans, and the fostering of local staff associations devoted to professional, social, and economic welfare.[50]

The main program of the 1935 Committee on Salaries, Employment, and Schemes of Library Service was to publish a manual to provide systematic and standardized employee classification pay plans for all public libraries. The majority of library compensation plans at the time were informally based on compensating an individual on the basis of his professional qualifications. The aim of the committee was to promote "class specification," or have compensation related to the requirements of the position as in the civil service principle. The manual was to include the identification of all professional and clerical library jobs, a description of the qualifications for each job, classification of the jobs into grades, and the assignment of minimum salaries. When the manual was published in 1939, the director of the Civil Service Assembly for the United States and Canada commended ALA for meeting ". . . one of its professional responsibilities." He went on to say:

> It is natural that every professional group should be interested in raising and maintaining personnel standards in its field. The soundest approach to this problem is through the development of a classification plan by which positions in the profession are classified on the basis of their duties and responsibilities. . . . By adopting this method for improving personnel standards, the library profession has effectively placed itself among the leading professions of the country.[51]

In 1940, ALA published another manual on organization and personnel procedure for public, college, and university libraries. It included suggested policy for organization of the library, classification of positions, salary schedules, promotions, tenure, working conditions, welfare and economic security (retirement, insurance, credit, and accident plans), and training.[52] This manual was revised in 1953, and again in 1968.

During this same period, ALA also began recommending minimum salaries for various library positions. The first recommendations were included in the 1939 manual on classification and pay plans. Then, in 1946, ALA launched its first and (up to the date of this study) last nationwide campaign for improving library salaries. The depression had forced most libraries to reduce salaries, and by the 1940s, many libraries had not re-

[50] Ibid., p. 602.

[51] *Classification and Pay Plans for Municipal Public Libraries* (Chicago: American Library Assn., 1938), p. v–vi.

[52] *Organization and Personnel Procedure of the . . . Library: A Suggested Plan* (Chicago: American Library Assn., 1940).

stored salaries to even predepression levels. This, coupled with the inflationary period of the forties, made salaries a critical issue in the profession.

The nationwide campaign included a two-phased program. The first phase was the establishment of minimum salary standards. In 1946, the ALA Council adopted a "Salary Policy Statement" which recommended beginning salaries for professional, subprofessional, and clerical positions.[53] This statement was revised in 1948 to reflect cost-of-living increases.[54]

The second phase of the national program was aimed at promoting and encouraging libraries to adopt the standards. First, ALA policy statements were given as much publicity as possible. They were released over the press wire services, published in full in the *ALA Bulletin* and other library journals, sent to all chief librarians in the country, and mailed to library trustees of each state. Second, symposiums and open discussions on library salaries were held at the association's annual convention in 1948. Third, individual librarians were urged to work through state and local groups for adoption of the standards. The *ALA Bulletin* stated, "No amount of study or publication at the national level alone will improve salaries or working conditions in a single library. Effective results can be obtained only through the positive action of individual librarians working together. . . ."[55] The association was careful to point out, however, that the work be accomplished "preferably through a staff association."

Unfortunately, it is difficult to measure the effectiveness of ALA's campaign since no comparable salary statistics were printed during the 1940s. Statistics for other decades show that beginning professional and subprofessional librarians received the largest percentage increase during the thirteen year period 1939–52, than in either the preceding or proceeding thirteen year periods.

In 1957, there was a major reorganization of ALA. The Board on Salaries, Staff and Tenure—which in 1944 was changed to the Board on Personnel Administration—became the present Section on Personnel Administration, under the Library Administration Division. The new section has essentially the same functions as the Board on Salaries, but there has been much less emphasis on improving library salaries. The last comprehensive salary survey conducted by ALA which sampled the profession as a whole was in 1955;[56] the last minimum library salary standards published by ALA were in 1951. A brief survey of salaries of ALA members

[53] "Board on Personnel Administration," *ALA Bulletin* 40:369 (1946).
[54] "Minimum Library Salary Standards for 1948," *ALA Bulletin* 42:104–6 (1948).
[55] Ibid., p. 158–59.
[56] Anita R. Schiller, "A Survey of Salary Surveys," *ALA Bulletin* 58:279 (1964).

was conducted in 1970, but this was in place of a national survey which never materialized since the ALA Executive Board believed funds were not available.[57] Why the association has stopped setting salary standards for the profession is unexplainable.

American Library Association: Conclusions

What conclusions can be drawn from this historical analysis of ALA activities? First, ALA generally has been attentive to the economic problems of the profession. Its concern over the low level of salaries during the 1920s and 1940s, and over the problems of unemployment during the 1930s, are cases in point. Second, in some instances, ALA has taken affirmative action to deal with economic problems. The nationwide campaign in 1948, the establishment of minimum salary standards from 1939 to 1951, the program to upgrade the quality of library education through accreditation, and the institution of the ALA pension plan have been predominant actions. Otherwise, ALA has dealt with economic problems by conducting full-scale studies and sponsoring symposiums, discussions, and resolutions in the particular area. Third, relative to the twenties and forties, the association has displayed diminished attention to economic problems during the past two decades. This is evidenced by the reduction in ALA-sponsored studies and activities.

It is not possible to measure whether activities of ALA have hindered the growth of unionism in the profession. It is possible, however, to pass judgment. From the period 1920–50, ALA probably showed sufficient concern for economic problems of the profession that librarians felt their interests were being served. To this extent, the majority of librarians had no need to turn to other organizations for protection. This is not to say that ALA necessarily hindered unionism; but at least the association did not encourage unionism through neglect of economic problems.

Activities of ALA during the past two decades reflect a different picture—a picture that may partially explain the increased interest in unionism. Not only has there been diminished attention to economic problems, but the organizational structure of ALA has grown so complex that librarians question whether the association is even capable of representing them. Articles in library periodicals during the past ten years show considerable comment over whether ALA has become too bureaucratic to effectively serve the interests of its members.[58] One report, written by a

---

[57] "ALA Salary Survey: Personal Members," *American Libraries* 2:409–17 (1971).

[58] *See* Ralph E. Ellsworth, "Critique of Library Associations in America," *Library Quarterly* 31:382–95 (1961); Robert Sheridan, "A Membership Dilemma," *American Libraries* 1:52–55 (1970); "Democratization of the Association," *American Libraries* 1:366–78 (1970).

special ALA panel in 1970, broadly categorized dissatisfaction with ALA, as the following material will illustrate.

First, there is concern that ALA's purpose is wrongly directed to libraries rather than to librarians. The association, the report states, does not support adequate salaries and working conditions, does not gather or publish salary data, fails to take a position on social issues, and concerns itself with trivia (awards, for example). Second, ALA organization is undemocratic. Younger members have no opportunity to participate in policy-making, structure does not involve the general membership in the decision-making process, and ALA is inflexible and unresponsive to individual needs. Third, ALA's procedures are slow and cumbersome. Months or years are required to achieve action on even relatively simple matters.[59]

ALA is aware of this criticism, and in June, 1969, established the Activities Committee on New Directions for ALA (ACONDA) to reinterpret and restate the philosophy of ALA and to reexamine its organizational structure. To date, however, ALA has made no substantial organizational changes. Whether it will remain the dominant spokesman for the profession remains to be seen. It appears that ALA's structure has become so cumbersome that it can no longer adequately represent all librarians in the country without a rigorous reorganization.

American Library Association and Collective Bargaining

The official stand a profession's dominant association takes on unionism and collective bargaining may affect the propensity of its members to join labor organizations. Until very recently, ALA has been uncommitted on these issues. A review of ALA history shows, however, that it never officially and actively opposed library unionism. The first time ALA considered library unionism was at a meeting of the Trustees Section in 1919, when speakers were invited to discuss the advantages and disadvantages of union membership among library employees.[60] The trustees of the association did not present their view at this meeting.

Then, in 1938, an ALA committee named the Library Unions Round Table (LURT) was formed by library union members to coordinate the work of existing AFL and CIO library unions, and to act as a clearinghouse of information and advisory agent for employees forming new unions. Membership in LURT was never numerically strong, and by the late 1940s, it became inactive. Its main activities centered around recommending resolutions, such as labor representation on library boards, which

[59] Ibid., p. 367.
[60] "Asbury Park Conference: Catalog Section—Trustees Section" *ALA Bulletin* 13:375–86 (1919).

never were acted upon by the ALA Council; maintaining booths at ALA conferences as a meeting place for those interested in library unions; and counteracting criticism made against library unionism.

One such criticism was made the same year as LURT was formed by the ALA president. In a convention address, Ferguson, who was speaking more for himself than for the association, charged, ". . . if ever unionism comes into the library, then we will lower our standards, our morale, our self-respect, and our appeal to those we serve."[61]

The first semiofficial comment on unionism by ALA came in 1939, when the Third Activities Committee included in its final report on reorganization and evaluation of association purposes the statement:

> . . . Unions may be not only a desirable but a necessary means for the extension and improvement of library science. . . . The ALA, therefore, must frankly recognize that library unions may be able to contribute to the promotion of library service and should be encouraged and aided in so far as their efforts tend toward this end.

The report was sent to the 1939 ALA Council, but reportedly was not discussed due to lack of time.[62]

The subject of unionism was not brought into the open again until 1968, when the ALA president, in his inaugural address, recognized that library unions ". . . have begun to move into a vacuum that we have, by inaction, helped to create."[63] McDonough went on to say, "I am not against unions per se; I don't feel that unions can, or will, exhibit the same concern for the profession that we [the association] do." The speech provided the impetus for ALA studies into the extent of collective bargaining among librarians, and a special program at the 1969 convention devoted to exploring the problem of professional associations versus unions.[64]

Finally, in January, 1970, ALA presented a statement of position on collective bargaining. The position paper read:

> The ALA recognizes its national, occupational, and professional responsibilities to educate and assist all concerned groups and individuals regarding responsible library unionization and collective bargaining. As a national organization of librarians, trustees, in-

---

[61] The text of Ferguson's speech is found in "The Library Crosses the Bridge," *ALA Bulletin* 32:421–26 (1938).

[62] "Activities Committee, Library Unions," *ALA Bulletin* 33:796 (1939).

[63] Roger H. McDonough, "An Inaugural Address," *ALA Bulletin* 62:873 (1968).

[64] "Collective Bargaining: Some Questions Asked," *ALA Bulletin* 62:973–76 (1968); "Collective Bargaining: Questions and Answers," *ALA Bulletin* 62:1385–90 (1968).

dustries which serve library needs, and other concerned members, the ALA will:

1. encourage the development and passage of laws which provide a sound framework for effective collective bargaining by libraries and library employees.
2. inform librarians, library administrators, trustees, and officials about collective bargaining trends, methods, and techniques . . .
3. assist librarians, library administrators, trustees, and officials in gathering data and information to enable them to develop better employment patterns and contracts.
4. encourage and conduct educational programs to train librarians, library administrators, and trustees in collective bargaining, and in working effectively within contractual employment patterns.[65]

Then, ALA precluded itself from becoming an agent for collective bargaining as a result of the following reasoning:

> The collective bargaining concept and collective bargaining laws generally preclude the membership of both managers and other personnel in the same union or bargaining group.
> Article III, Section I, of the ALA Constitution is as follows: "Members. Any person, library, or other organization interested in library service and librarianship may become a member upon payment of the dues provided for in the Bylaws . . ."
> The above constitutional provision precludes ALA's becoming a bargaining organization within its current membership and dues structure.[66]

Local Staff Associations

Local staff associations exist in the majority of public libraries. They occasionally assume functions not too dissimilar from labor unions, and as such can be instrumental in hindering the emergence of library unions. From evidence that is available, however, their role in this capacity has been minimal.

The growth of staff associations up to 1936, the date of the last study on their growth pattern, has generally followed the formation of library unions. Thus, from 1916 to 1919, five associations were formed; from

[65] Position Statement, "The American Library Association and Library Collective Bargaining," adopted by the Library Administration Division Board of Directors, Jan. 21, 1970.
[66] Ibid.

1920 to 1929, ten were formed; and between 1930 and 1936, fifteen were formed.[67] In another study made in 1949, Bryan found that "the majority of the associations are to be found in the largest libraries."[68] In terms of activities, however, the similarity with library unions ends.

In 1936, ALA initiated the above cited study to determine the activities of staff associations organized at that time. The following results were based upon thirty-six organizations surveyed. The lack of stress on economic matters is conspicuously apparent.

> . . . Nearly all have definite social programs, a few emphasize especially professional interests, several conduct book reviews for and by the staff and many watch staff welfare programs. One association sends a delegate to both the State and American Library Association conferences, *two others are mainly engaged in working for pensions and economic improvement* [emphasis added], one 'watches the city government to protect staff interests' and several mention benefits to raise money, staff hobby shows, and teas.[69]

Another study conducted in 1940 concluded: "If thirty-one staff associations are indicative of the total picture, vigorous action in economic matters is characteristic of only a small minority of those which exist in the public libraries of the country."[70]

Bryan's study in 1949 produced the most revealing results. She surveyed the activities assumed by 58 staff associations, and also asked a national sample of over 2,000 public librarians the type of activities they would desire their association to assume. The results are shown in table 5.

As table 5 shows, working toward improved economic welfare was not a common activity of the associations, yet their members believed this was the most desirable form of activity. Bryan does not offer an explanation for this inconsistency, although she did find that a majority of employees who were members of an association belonged to one which was sponsored by the library administration, while a majority of the same group expressed the opinion that, if given a choice, they would prefer to belong to an association that was independent of management. Nevertheless, her results cast doubt on the ability of staff associations to substitute as unions.

[67] Helen T. Ziegler, "The Staff Association Picture, 1936," *Library Journal* 61:944 (1936).

[68] Alice Bryan, *The Public Librarian* (New York: Columbia Univ. Pr., 1952), p. 264.

[69] Ziegler, "Staff Association Picture," p. 943.

[70] E. W. McDiarmid and John McDiarmid, *The Administration of the American Public Library* (Urbana, Ill.: Univ. of Illinois Pr., 1943), p. 191.

TABLE 5
SURVEY OF ACTIVITIES OF STAFF ASSOCIATIONS
(In Percentages)

Activities	Activities Carried On	Activities Desired
Organizing social activities for staff	38	79
Aiding professional development of staff	26	93
Working toward improved economic welfare of staff	29	95
Handling grievances for staff or individual staff members	17	64
Acting as liaison between chief administrator and staff	27	71
Making recommendations regarding administrative policies and problems of library	24	81
Cooperating with staff associations in other public libraries	24	83
Other activities	2	. . . .

SOURCE: Alice Bryan, *The Public Librarian* (New York: Columbia Univ. Pr., 1952), pp. 269–70.

The current picture of staff associations is given by a survey conducted in 1969. It estimated that although 69 percent of the country's libraries have staff associations, they are "not used extensively to influence change either in service or in improved working conditions and the following percentage breakdown of activities was reported:

Social activities	78
Staff welfare (e.g., maintenance of staff room, hospital visits)	43
Professional and educational programs	26
Fundraising and allocation (e.g., staff scholarships)	23
Liaison with administration, i.e., grievance channel	22
Community charitable activities	13
Very little	7
Other	8[71]

As indicated, only a small portion of the associations perform any form of protection function (liaison with administration).

It is concluded, then, that only a few cases have local staff associations been likely to hinder union formation by performing a substitute role. Nor does it appear likely that a significant number will do so in the future. One

[71] Mary Lee Bundy and Paul Wasserman, *The Public Library Administrator and His Situation* (Washington, D.C.: Office of Education, June, 1970), final report, p. 56.

public library administrator made the following comment when asked whether staff associations should be bargaining agencies:

> There is no reason that a library staff association cannot become a bargaining unit for library employees; the wishes of the members of the staff association and the members of the library will determine whether or not the staff associations will assume the role of a bargaining unit. . . . As a practical matter, very few library staff associations will be transformed into bargaining units, and it is more likely that a collateral organization will be established to represent the employees in its negotiations with the library administration.[72]

State Library Associations

In addition to local associations, public librarians may join one of forty-five state library associations. Activities of these organizations vary. For the most part, programs are limited to scholarly concerns, although some associations have been instrumental in obtaining passage of state certification laws, lobbying for higher library appropriations, and publishing statewide statistics.

Recently, at least five associations have considered acting as bargaining agents, but as of yet no affirmative action has been undertaken. There seems to be doubt among these associations as to whether librarians would support such a move. For instance, an official of the Massachusetts Library Association stated, ". . . librarians in the larger cities will affiliate with an existing national association such as the AFSCME because they have the wherewithal."[73] According to Vignone, a committee of the Michigan Library Association "concluded that there was an impressive number of librarians who might use collective bargaining, 'but the likelihood of their choosing MLA over more powerful and effective groups is not great.' "[74]

There are also other ALA affiliated associations representing specific fields of interest in the profession. Examples are the American Association of Law Libraries, Association of Research Libraries, Medical Library Association, and the Music Library Association. They normally pursue professional programs not shared by most public librarians.

Public Employee Associations

As public employees, librarians may also join public employee associations. These organizations are normally unaffiliated with national labor

[72] "Collective Bargaining: Questions and Answers," p. 1389.
[73] Goldstein, *Collective Bargaining*, pp. 23–24.
[74] Vignone, *Collective Bargaining Procedures*, p. 18.

unions, and traditionally have acted as fraternal and benevolent organizations. Most do not bargain collectively in behalf of their members, but instead lobby before legislative bodies on such matters as health, welfare, and retirement issues. Dues are typically nominal, and membership generally offers such benefits as charter flights and reduction in ticket prices for athletic and cultural events. Many public employees automatically join as a matter of employment.

The importance of these organizations in a study of unionization lies in the fact that many public employees are turning to these associations for representation in preference to unions. Some associations, as a result of pressures from their membership and from competing unions, are in turn making a transition to becoming "near unions." Hence, public employee associations could be a crucial factor in preventing the full-fledged unionization of public employees.

A recent Bureau of Labor Statistics survey of municipal public employee associations provides an indication of this trend. According to the survey, the number of municipal associations has increased in the past decade. Of the associations surveyed, more than one-third were formed during the 1960s; and over half were established between 1950 and 1968. Membership has also increased in the past decade. For associations reporting membership data for both 1962 and 1968, the total increase in membership was 28 percent. By comparison, the growth rate for the same period was lower for total union membership (15.1 percent) and substantially higher for government union membership (75.9 percent).[75]

The survey also shows that lobbying is no longer the dominant activity of many municipal associations. During 1968–69, over three-fifths of the associations surveyed, involving more than four-fifths of the total membership, were engaged in legislative activities and, at the same time, represented city employees in collective bargaining situations on wages and working conditions. The types of issues most frequently discussed were pay matters, working conditions, fringe benefits, and grievance procedures.[76] In addition, close to 60 percent of the associations surveyed reported having been granted formal recognition under existing law.[77]

The number of librarians belonging to public employee associations

---

[75] *Municipal Public Employee Associations* (Washington, D.C.: Bureau of Labor Statistics, 1971), Bulletin No. 1702, p. 8.

[76] Ibid., pp. 6, 20.

[77] Ibid., p. 10. The proportion of municipal associations having formal recognition is overstated since the Bureau of Labor Statistics sent questionnaires only to organizations designated by city managers as having a relationship with the city. Associations in municipalities in which no relationship exists, if included, would diminish the proportion.

cannot be accurately estimated. Some indication is provided by the Bureau of Labor Statistics survey. It gives the following percentage breakdown by function of employees most often represented by associations in 1968–69:

Police protection	83
Fire protection	76
Public works	60
Parks and recreation	40
Other occupational functions (including librarians)	40
Public utilities	32
Public health and hospitals	11
Noninstructional education	8
Public welfare	6[78]

As can be seen, the function which includes librarians is not among the most highly represented.

It is clear that public employee associations can hinder unionization. First, the Bureau of Labor Statistics survey shows that many associations currently offer the protection of traditional unions but at less expense to the employee. The survey states that of the employee associations reporting both legislative and representation activities, only 20 percent have annual dues of thirty dollars or more. Dues for the majority of these associations is closer to ten or fifteen dollars. In contrast, two-thirds of those national unions establishing dues minimums in their constitutions required payments of thirty-six or sixty dollars a year (three or five dollars a month), and local unions have the option to set the dues even higher.[79]

The survey of southern California librarians conducted for this study shows that dues structure is of some importance in discouraging union membership. Statements such as the following were often given as reasons for not joining library unions: "I am not a union member because the dues are too high for benefits received;" "I do not belong to the union because at the present I feel I cannot afford the membership costs." It should be remembered, however, that as associations increase their representation activities, operating costs will increase, causing dues to be higher. So this advantage over traditional unions may be only temporary. A case in point is the Los Angeles County Employees Association, which recently affiliated with the Service Employees International Union, AFL–CIO. As the association has expanded in scope, its dues have increased. As one nonunion librarian complained, "Seven years ago the Employee Association dues were twelve dollars a year; now it is a union and dues are sixty dollars a year."

[78] Ibid., p. 13.
[79] Ibid., p. 9.

Another reason associations can hinder unionization is that many are long established institutions which have gained the respect and confidence of public employees. The following statement made by a Long Beach librarian is reflective of the feeling that to join another organization would be a betrayal to an association which has thus far served so well: "In Long Beach, the City Employees Association is a de facto union. It is less expensive, locally controlled, and gets results. I have no desire to join any other labor union."

In addition, association membership can offer many of the benefits of unionization without the employee actually feeling he is a union member. The following statements were made by municipal employee association members: "Employee associations as distinguished from unions do an excellent job of collective bargaining for all except management"; "There is a municipal employees association to which I belong. It serves many of the same purposes that a union does."

The survey of southern California librarians shows that the majority of association members do not view their organization as a union. Employees of three libraries where close to 99 percent belong to employee associations were asked to respond to the following question: "Are you a member of a union organized within your library or a union of other city or municipal employees?" Slightly over 55 percent chose the response "none exists."

A major disadvantage of employee associations is that a variety of employees are often placed in the same bargaining unit. For example, in Oakland, California, library employees have been grouped with such other city employees as legal secretaries, zoning clerks, and a variety of clerical workers. Under such circumstances, particular concerns of library employees may be passed over during negotiations, especially when librarians represent a small proportion of the bargaining unit and when they have no professional counterparts in other city departments. The administrator of one library where it was decided to join other city employees for collective bargaining evaluated the situation as follows:

> I'm not sure whether or not this will be a pattern to continue indefinitely because few of the negotiators know library problems of staffing, educational requirements, certification, etc. We can only try to educate them as time goes along. Special considerations should be given to library employees for such items as evening and Saturday work schedules which were not considered in this year's contract with the city.[80]

---

[80] "Collective Bargaining: Questions and Answers," p. 1388.

Librarians have been critical of employee associations for similar reasons. One association member stated she would join a library union if one existed "because this is the only kind of bona fide organization that would be representative of and interested solely in working librarians' working conditions, pay rates, etc." Another stated, "I belong to one [association] because of life insurance and other benefits. Otherwise [I] would not belong, as the Municipal Employees Association does not do much for librarians."

Conclusion

Of the organizations examined here, the local staff association and the public employee association are in the most favorable position to hinder library unionization. The majority of the former, however, seem too reluctant to assume protective and representative functions. The ability of employee associations to represent unique concerns of librarians is questionable as long as librarians are grouped with other public employees; but in respect to representation over economic matters, they can be important in hindering the growth of unionization among public employees.

The American Library Association is the most dominant organization in the profession. Its relative inattention toward economic problems during the past ten to twenty years, coupled with the mounting criticism that it is no longer capable of representing librarians, suggest that as a professional association it has not been instrumental in discouraging unionization during the past decade. The association's recent endorsement of collective bargaining may, in fact, act to spur further union activity. Thus, ALA has placed itself in jeopardy. In effect, it has told librarians that if they desire collective bargaining, they should seek their own organization. This leaves librarians who wish representation the choice of modifying their local staff associations or joining public employee associations or unions. Whatever the case, ALA is encouraging other organizations to assume its role as spokesman for the interests of the nation's librarians.

Chapter 4

Occupational Characteristics

Some writers have speculated that librarians are not more extensively unionized due to several of their occupational characteristics. For instance, Phelps states,

> It is not difficult to explain the limited success of trade unions among library employees to date. Library personnel may be characterized fairly easily, and each of the characteristics, in turn, is associated with a group which has proved unresponsive to the organized labor movement. . . . An overwhelming proportion of them, almost 90 percent, are women. Almost without exception they are white-collar workers, with a large percentage of professionally trained personnel.[1]

Other experts have noted that such characteristics as social origin and age are important in propensity to unionize. Several occupational characteristics of librarians will be examined here to determine their potential effect on unionization.

Sex and Marital Status

Women make up a large proportion of the country's librarians. According to a 1962 study, approximately 87 percent of all librarians were women.[2] Data show that women constitute a lower relative percentage of

---

[1] Erik J. Spicer, *Trade Unions in Libraries* (Ann Arbor: Univ. of Michigan Pr., 1959), p. 4.

[2] Henry T. Drennan and Richard L. Darling, *Library Manpower: Occupational Characteristics of Public and School Librarians* (Washington, D.C.: Office of Education, 1966), p. 2.

union membership than men;[3] hence it is often advanced that they are more recalcitrant toward unionization.

Evidence demonstrates that this proposition is not necessarily true. Bain concluded that female employees have no inherent characteristics which make them more difficult to organize than men. He explains the lower proportion of union membership among women by the fact that they tend to be employed in industries which have a low degree of employment concentration; and that this, more than the proportion of women, is the cause of a lesser degree of unionization.[4] Similarly, a National Industrial Conference Board survey showed that sex had no bearing on whether a unit of employees voted for or against unionization. Sixty-three units of predominantly (80 percent) male employees were compared with thirty-one units of predominantly (80 percent) female employees. Unions won elections in thirty of the former, and seventeen of the latter units, indicating that the predominantly female units were not less likely to be unionized.[5]

Several studies provide evidence that among librarians sex is not a determining factor in propensity to unionize. The survey of southern California librarians conducted for this study shows that in both unionized and nonunionized libraries, women are about as likely to be members or to choose membership as men. Among females in the total sample, 49 percent were anti-union and 51 percent, pro-union; while among males, 40 percent were anti-union and 60 percent were pro-union. Vignone obtained similar results when studying attitudes of Pennsylvania librarians toward a model of collective bargaining procedures. Females were found to be as favorably disposed toward the model as males.[6] Bryan found in a 1949 national survey of professional librarians that 4 percent of the men, and 3 percent of the women had been members of a library union; and that an equal percent of both (9 percent) were currently members.[7]

Several librarians have suggested that women should be *more* prone to unionize due to the inequality of opportunity for women in the field. One surveyed librarian stated, "A collective unit of librarians would be at a greater advantage to aid us in an equalization of job levels between males and females in librarianship." Another commented, ". . . most librarians

---

[3] In the mid-fifties, only about 16 percent of the females in the labor force were union members, in contrast with 31 percent of the males. In 1968, women accounted for 19.5 percent of all union members. See *Directory of National and International Labor Unions* (Washington, D.C.: Bureau of Labor Statistics, 1970), p. 70.

[4] George Sayers Bain, *The Growth of White-Collar Unionism* (Oxford: Clarendon Pr., 1970), pp. 41–42.

[5] *White-Collar Unionization* (National Industrial Conference Board, No. 220, 1968), p. 28.

[6] Vignone, *Collective Bargaining Procedures*, p. 122.

[7] Bryan, *Public Librarian*, p. 272.

are female, and it's very easy to prove statistically that the lowest paid workers (even in libraries) are female, so until we organize we're going to remain at the bottom."

Although men represent a small proportion of librarians, they generally attain higher status in the profession. A 1970 study of public library administrators shows that men are greatly over-represented in the higher levels of the profession: 63 percent of the administrators were male, while 37 percent were female.[8] A recent article in *American Libraries*, entitled "The Disadvantaged Majority," complains that even though

> about four out of every five librarians are women, their salaries tend typically to be lower than those of men librarians. . . . A national study of academic librarians . . . showed . . . that the median salary for men was about $1500 higher than that for women, that men were about twice as likely as women to be chief librarians, and that men who were *not* chief librarians tended to earn more than women who *were*.[9]

These accusations are well founded. The survey of southern California librarians shows that inequalities do exist, at least with respect to earnings. When salaries of men and women with equivalent education, age, seniority, and years in the profession were compared, the men fared much better. The breakdown of salary levels by sex is shown in table 6.

TABLE 6
BREAKDOWN OF SALARY LEVELS
(In Percentages)

	Under $9,000	$9,000–11,000	$11,000–14,000	Over $14,000	Total
Male	8	39	40	13	100
Female	11	54	31	4	100

Observation of table 6 shows that a larger proportion of male librarians earn over $11,000. These differences alone are not significant at the .01 level of probability. But when salaries of males and females with equivalent education, age, number of years at the present library, and number

---

[8] Mary Lee Bundy and Paul Wasserman, *The Public Library Administrator, Technical Data Summary* (Washington, D.C.: Office of Education, Feb. 1970), preliminary analysis, p. 1.

[9] Anita R. Schiller, "The Disadvantaged Majority," *American Libraries* 1:345 (Apr. 1970).

of years in the profession were compared, a statistically significant difference was found to exist.

Data are not available to investigate sexual inequalities in the positions of these librarians. But, there was little variation between men and women in their attitude toward advancement. When given the statement, "There are many good positions here for those who strive to get ahead," a slightly larger proportion of men agreed than women, but the difference was not statistically significant. The proportions were as follows:

	Agreed	Disagreed
Male	60%	40%
Female	46	54

Despite the inequalities in salaries, however, union membership data reported for southern California do not suggest that women are *more* prone toward unionization. Similarly, Vignone did not find that female librarians in Pennsylvania were significantly more in favor of the model for collective bargaining.[10]

Arguments stating that women are less prone to join unions than men generally center on marital status more than sex alone as the crucial factor. For example, Bain hypothesized that women have less commitment to their work, and therefore are more indifferent toward unionism than men due to the fact that they "do not participate continuously in the labor market because of marriage and family responsibilities, and they generally are supplementary earners in the sense that their pay is not the family's main source of income but merely supplements the earnings of their husbands."[11]

Such arguments cannot be categorically applied to all occupations. Some vocations are obviously less career orientated and attract a higher proportion of married women, while others are highly career orientated and employ a smaller proportion of married women. Clerical, sales, and service occupations typify the former; while many of the so-called women's professions—teaching, nursing, social work, and library—are characteristic of the latter. While there is no definite index of the career orientations of these various occupations, it is clear that the former represent more married women. The *Manpower Report of the President* showed that in 1969, clerical, sales, and service workers accounted for 56 percent of the married women in the labor force. In contrast, only 15 percent of employed married women were professional or technical workers.[12]

[10] Vignone, *Collective Bargaining Procedures*, p. 152.

[11] Bain, *White-Collar Unionism*, p. 40.

[12] *Manpower Report of the President* (Washington, D.C.: Dept. of Labor, 1970), p. 248.

The majority of women librarians are not married. In 1950, the date of the most recent national survey, only one out of four was married.[13] The survey of southern California librarians shows that 46 percent are married; while 36 percent are single, 13 percent are divorced or separated, and 5 percent are widowed. At best, then, marital status could hinder the unionization of less than half of the profession.

Analysis of the union status of married librarians shows that they are not necessarily more difficult to unionize than nonmarried women. In the unionized libraries of southern California, 70 percent of the married women are union members as compared to 53 percent of the nonmarried women. In the nonunionized libraries, 41 percent of the married women said they would join a union, as compared with 35 percent among non-married women.

In addition, the survey also indicates that married women tend to be employed as librarians just as continuously as nonmarried women. As figure 1 shows, there exists little significant variation between married and nonmarried women in terms of length of time employed as a librarian; length of time employed at the present system; and number of library systems worked. These relationships existed regardless of whether or not the married woman's spouse was employed. A 1960 national study of public librarians shows that although women are more likely to leave the occupation, the difference between women and men is not significant.[14]

Although the evidence presented here is not conclusive, is does suggest that sex and marital status are not significant deterrents of unionization.

Age

Shister has written that younger workers will show a greater propensity to unionize than older workers. Kleingartner found the opposite to be true; unionized engineers and technicians were more likely to be over 40 years of age than nonunion members. Bain showed that there was no significant connection between the age of foremen in Great Britain and the degree to which they are unionized.[15]

Shister's hypothesis is based on three observations. First, younger workers usually have shorter tenure of service than older workers, which induces a greater degree of militancy since loyalty is not as developed. Sec-

[13] Bryan, *Public Librarian*, p. 35.

[14] Drennan and Darling, *Library Manpower*, p. 12.

[15] Joseph Shister, "The Logic of Union Growth," *Journal of Political Economy* 61:421 (Oct. 1953); Archie Kleingartner, "The Unionization of White-Collar Workers," Institute of Industrial Relations, University of California, Los Angeles, 1968, reprint no. 182, p. 86; Bain, *White-Collar Unionism*, p. 47.

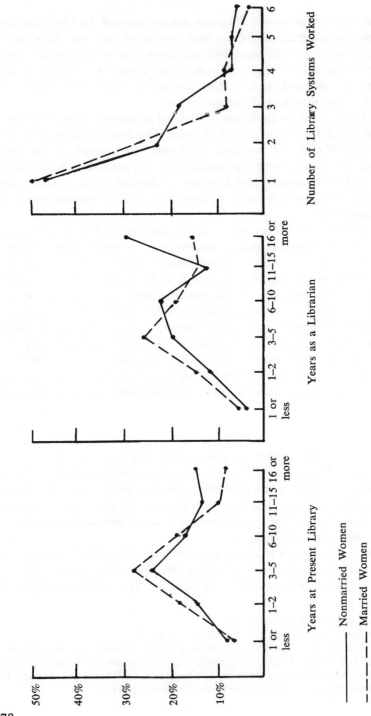

Figure 1. Comparisons of length of time of employment of married and nonmarried women

ond, younger workers are better educated than older workers, and as a result are more resentful of arbitrary treatment by management. Finally, younger workers have been reared in an age when unionism has been an accepted institution. They are more prone to think of unionism as the natural way of handling worker problems.[16]

If his hypothesis is correct, unionism should be a rarity among librarians. In 1960, the median age of most public librarians was nearly 50 years. The median for men was 40.5 years (13 percent of total); and for women, 49.2 years.[17] This partially coincides with figures for 1950, which show the median age of all professional librarians to be 42.3 years; for women, 42.6 years; and for men, 39.3 years.[18] In 1966, Howe found that 64 percent of the public librarians in Illinois were 50 years of age or older.[19] In 1971, Vignone found that 30 percent of the public librarians sampled in Pennsylvania were between the ages of 21 and 30; 10 percent between 31 and 40; 24 percent between 41 and 50; and 36 percent 51 years or older.[20] In southern California, 43 percent of the librarians are 45 years or older; the median age is about 40 years.

Shister's hypothesis is not supported by the southern California survey results. There is no statistically significant difference in the ages of union and nonunion librarians, nor between librarians who would choose union membership and those who would not. As table 7 shows, however, there is greater anti-union sentiment among older librarians.

TABLE 7
UNION SENTIMENT AMONG LIBRARIANS
(In Percentages)

Age	Pro-union	Anti-union	Total
Under 30	56	44	100
30 to 44	56	44	100
Over 45	47	53	100

Vignone obtained similar results among Pennsylvania librarians: the younger were more in accord with the collective bargaining model than

[16] Shister, "Logic of Union Growth," pp. 421–22.

[17] Drennan and Darling, *Library Manpower*, p. 2.

[18] Bryan, *Public Librarian*, p. 31.

[19] Mary Jane Ryan, "Career Development of Librarians," *Catholic Library World* 40:167 (Nov. 1968).

[20] Vignone, *Collective Bargaining Procedures*, p. 84.

the older librarians, although the differences were not significant. He did find significant differences between extreme age groups. Librarians between the ages of 21 and 30 showed markedly greater approval of collective bargaining than those who were 61 years of age and over.[21]

As is discussed in a later section, union membership was found to be significantly associated with attitude toward unions in general. Even though age and union membership are not significantly correlated (except at extreme age differences), it could be expected that younger librarians would have a more favorable attitude toward unionism than older librarians, thus making them more susceptible to unionization. The southern California survey only partially confirms this expectation. When the attitude distribution of individual age groups is considered, a larger proportion of younger than older librarians do express more favorable attitudes, although the difference is not statistically significant. Of those who are 30 years old and under, 83 percent hold favorable attitudes toward unions; while of those 45 years and older, 70 percent hold favorable attitudes. But, as the following figures show, when the distribution of attitude is analyzed across age groups, slightly more older librarians hold favorable attitudes, although a larger proportion also holds unfavorable attitudes. The differences are not significant.

	Under 30	30–44	Over 45	Total
Favorable attitude toward unionism	24%	38%	38%	100%
Unfavorable attitude toward unionism	17	27	56	100

Based upon the evidence provided by the southern California survey, it is concluded that age is not a significant determinant of union membership, except, as Vignone's survey implies, at very advanced age levels (61 years of age and over) where attitudes toward unions are likely to be negative.

Social Origin

It has been hypothesized by some that social origin is significant in determining union membership. Specifically, it is advanced that those whose father's occupation was laborer, farmer, or semiskilled worker are more likely to join unions than those whose father's occupation was white-collar, proprietor, or professional. There is considerable disagreement over the validity of this relationship. Lipset, and Goldstein and Indik found some

[21] Ibid., p. 120.

relationship to exist between social origin and union membership;[22] Kornhauser, Kleingartner, and Bain found no significant relationship to exist.[23]

Librarians tend to come from families whose fathers are professionals, proprietors, or white-collar workers; few have working class backgrounds where unionism is more influential. According to a 1962 national survey, approximately 46 percent of all public librarians come from social origins where the father's occupation is professional, technical, or proprietary in nature; a little over 27 percent come from origins where the father's occupation is white-collar or skilled worker; and close to 16 percent from where the occupation is farmer or unskilled laborer.[24] A 1950 national survey showed that 55 percent of professional librarians had fathers who were professionals, managers, or self-employed.[25]

The survey of southern California librarians indicates that social origin is not a significant factor in determining union membership. Of the 404 professional librarians sampled, 28 percent had fathers who were professionals; 29 percent, businessman or proprietor; 15 percent, white-collar worker; 23 percent, skilled laborer; and 5 percent, unskilled laborer. For testing purposes, these occupations were divided into two groupings: High: professional, businessman or proprietor, and white-collar worker; Low: skilled and unskilled laborer. There was no statistically significant difference with respect to father's occupation between union and nonunion librarians or between librarians who would choose unionization and those who would not. In both cases, "high" level occupations were only slightly more common in the nonunion groups. The figures are as follows:

Father's Occupation	Pro-union	Anti-union
Low grouping	54%	46%
High grouping	51	49

Another index of social origin often used is educational attainment, the hypothesis being that the higher the level of education, the higher the social origin and hence the less likely one is to join a union. Goldstein and Indik used this index in their study of engineers, and found no significant

[22] Seymour Martin Lipset, "White Collar Workers and Professionals–Their Attitudes and Behavior Towards Unions," in *Research Developments in Personnel Management* (mimeographed, Institute of Industrial Relations, Univ. of California, Los Angeles, 1962), pp. 31–54; Goldstein and Indik, "Unionism as a Social Choice," p. 366.

[23] Ruth Kornhauser, "Some Social Determinants and Consequences of Union Membership," *Labor History* 2:43 (Winter 1961); Kleingartner, "White-Collar Workers," p. 86; Bain, *White-Collar Unionism*, p. 45.

[24] Drennan and Darling, *Library Manpower*, p. 8.

[25] Bryan, *Public Librarian*, p. 34.

difference to exist between union and nonunion members. On the other hand, Kleingartner found unionized engineers to have a somewhat lower educational level than nonunionized engineers.[26]

The educational level of public librarians has risen in the past twenty years. In 1950, 58 percent had received a bachelor's degree, with the percentage of degree holders much higher among younger librarians than among those in more advanced age levels.[27] In 1962, 62 percent of male and 30 percent of female librarians held master's degrees; 63 percent of the females held bachelor's degrees.[28] In 1968, it was reported that the number of degrees earned in the field of library science (bachelors and masters combined) had nearly tripled since 1960, and that the percentage of library science degrees to all degrees had risen from a low of 42 percent in 1959, to 70 percent in 1968.[29] Among southern California librarians, 77 percent reported having a master's degree—71 percent in library science and 6 percent in other fields. A 1969 national survey sponsored by ALA shows that in large public libraries, 74 percent of the professionals have graduate degrees; in small to medium libraries, 53 percent have graduate degrees.[30]

The survey conducted for this study shows no statistically significant difference in the educational attainment of union and nonunion members; nor between those who would choose membership and those who would not. In fact, as the following figures show, a higher proportion of pro-union librarians hold master's degrees than anti-union librarians.

Degree	Pro-Union	Anti-union
M.S., M.L.S., or equivalent	54%	46%
Other (B.S., B.L.S., B.A., high school)	47	53

Vignone found that librarians with master's degrees were significantly more in agreement with the collective bargaining model than those who held less than a bachelor's and those who had only a bachelor's degree.[31] However, while in the former case the difference was highly significant, in

26 Goldstein and Indik, "Unionism as a Social Choice," p. 366; Kleingartner, "White-Collar Workers," p. 86.

27 Bryan, *Public Librarian*, pp. 57–58.

28 Drennan and Darling, *Library Manpower*, p. 3.

29 August C. Bolino, *Supply and Demand Analysis of Manpower Trends in the Library and Information Field* (Washington, D.C.: Office of Education, July 1969), p. 56.

30 "Opinions on Collective Bargaining," pp. 804–6.

31 Vignone, *Collective Bargaining Procedures*, p. 125.

the latter the difference was only passably significant at the .05 level of probability. This pattern suggests that the observed significance may be more a function of age than education. The southern California survey shows a highly negative correlation between age and education, such that the older the librarian, the less education he is likely to have received. This finding is substantiated by figures given earlier showing a rise in the educational level of librarians over the past twenty years. Since Vignone's greatest difference occurred among librarians with less than a bachelor's degree, it might be suspected that these respondents were the same individuals who comprised the oldest age group, which, as Vignone indicates, showed a highly significant difference from younger librarians in their attitude toward collective bargaining.

On the basis of these findings, it is concluded that neither father's occupation nor educational attainment are significant in determining union membership; and, as a result, there is no significant relationship between social origin and propensity to unionize.

Professionalism vs. Unionism

One commonly cited obstacle to unionization among professionals concerns the conflict between "professionalism" and unionism. Goldstein writes that most professionals view collective action as incompatible with professional status. They believe that ". . . an individual is entirely responsible for his own actions and that success and failure are objective criteria of competency . . . only the incompetent or those who lack ambition rely on group action and explicit rules concerning salaries and conditions of employment."[32] However, the growing extent of unionization among several of the salaried professions suggests that the conflict may not be as real as suspected.

Kleingartner conducted one of the few studies that directly examined the relationship between professionalism and attitude toward unionism. In studying two industrial firms where salaried engineers were unionized, he found that a high proportion of both union and nonunion members saw no inherent conflict between professionalism and union membership.

> The engineers showed surprising support for the idea of unionism, but this did not lead to a proportionate willingness to support the actions associated with unionism or to become members. They do

---

[32] Bernard Goldstein, "Unions and the Professional Employee," *Journal of Business* 27:280 (Oct. 1954).

not, to any great extent, view union membership as presenting a threat to the maintenance of professional standards in their work . . ."[33]

Jack Barbash verbally supports these findings by charging that many professionals have succumbed to a cultural myth that "unions and collective bargaining are fine for manual workers but they won't work for professionals."[34]

The incompatibility of unionism and professionalism is treated in most discussions of unionization among librarians. The issue is not new. During the 1930s, opponents of library unionization argued that collective action was not only detrimental to the profession but also impractical when applied to a service orientated occupation. An excerpt from an article written in 1937 states:

> Those who oppose unionization may argue . . . that such organization will have a tendency to destroy what professional prestige we now enjoy and that professional standards generally will suffer. They may also say that too much emphasis will be placed on gaining economic recognition and that the idealism, and spirit of public service . . . will pass into the discard . . . .[35]

Another article printed in 1939 stated, "A union applied to a library, especially a public library, just doesn't make sense. Public libraries were established and are maintained not primarily to provide work for librarians, but to render service to a community of readers."[36] The same article concluded, "A union in the public library, a social force established not for profit but solely for free public service, is ill-considered and illogical, and if introduced in an institution still struggling for adequate recognition and standing, might result in a very unpleasant adventure in hara-kiri."

Today, similar statements are heard. Here are reasons given by some southern California librarians for not joining library unions:

> I would not like to become a member of a [library] union. To me, professional people are no longer professional if they turn over their rights and freedom to a union.

---

[33] Archie Kleingartner, "Professionalism and Engineering Unionism," *Industrial Relations* 8:224–35 (May 1969).

[34] Jack Barbash, *Union Philosophy and the Professional*, pamphlet, released by the American Federation of Teachers, AFL–CIO, p. 4.

[35] Stewart W. Smith, "In Union—Is There Strength?" *Wilson Library Bulletin* 11:310–11 (Jan. 1937).

[36] Clarence E. Sherman, "The Unionization of the Profession as One Librarian Sees It," *Special Libraries* 30:40–41 (Feb. 1939).

I, personally, would not like to be a union member because they tend to herd you like sheep or cattle; you are not treated like a thinking *individual*.

As a city employee, I still seem to feel that I should remain nonunion.

I do not believe in unions for librarians. Ours is a *service* occupation and I would not go out on strike.

Library unions, in their recruiting efforts, have attempted to propitiate those who share these opinions. The first newsletter of the Los Angeles Public Library Guild contained the following excerpt written by the Guild president:

> ... A union of librarians is also a professional group. They will not have sold out their responsibility to the library and the community merely because they banded together in a union. In fact, their responsibility will undoubtedly increase as a result of union activities. They will become both more involved in and more knowledgeable about the library's problems. Involvement begets professionalism; professionalism is almost by definition responsible.[37]

In a later newsletter, the formation of the Guild was described as a "unique adventure—a search by a group of librarians for greater control over their own profession and an exploration of unionism as a vehicle for gaining that control."[38] The New York Public Library Guild newsletter, the *Voice*, argued in an editorial that the main features separating librarianship from the "revered" professions—medicine, law, and theology—are prestige, money, and respectability. "Any library employee knows that while we may not be lacking in respectability, of a sort, we certainly have none at all of the money and prestige we deserve. . . . Perhaps with a more interested, involved organization, we could obtain the prestige and the money we deserve."[39]

There is evidence to indicate that Kleingartner's conclusion that engineers perceive no inherent conflict between professionalism and union membership is also true of librarians. Vignone found that there was a general feeling among Pennsylvania librarians that collective bargaining by librarians would not be condemned by public sentiment as being unprofessional. Of the 207 librarians surveyed, 85 percent held "ambivalent," "high," or "very high" opinions in this respect.[40] A majority (80 percent)

---

[37] *Librarian's Guild Communicator*, Dec. 1968, p. 3.
[38] Ibid., July 1, 1969.
[39] *Library Guild Voice*, Brooklyn Library Guild Local 1482, 1:3 (July 1, 1967).
[40] Vignone, *Collective Bargaining Procedures*, p. 113.

of the 415 southern California librarians surveyed disagreed, as the following figures show, with the statement, "It is impossible for a librarian to belong to a union, and at the same time to maintain the standards of his profession."

	Pro-union	Anti-union
Agree	26%	74%
Disagree	61	39

The survey demonstrates that those librarians who do perceive a conflict are unlikely to be union members. A statistically significant difference is seen between pro-union and anti-union librarians in attitude toward the professionalism-unionism issue and there is a high probability that those who see a conflict between professionalism and union membership will not join unions. But, the survey also shows that the perception of no conflict does not necessarily imply that a librarian is or desires to become a union member. Of the 80 percent of the total sample who disagreed with the above statement, 39 percent were anti-union.

Attitude Toward Unionism

Although most librarians seem to perceive no conflict between being a professional and being a union member, statements such as the following, made by librarians, suggest that perceptions of unionism itself may hinder unionization.

> I would never join a labor union, as I resent the domineering and intimidating tactics of union leaders and organizers.

> They [unions] are too big to be democratic.

> I have a deep distrust of *modern* unionism. I have friends and relatives who have gone out on strike against their will because of their union's stand. . . .

> The reason I do not belong [to the library union] is my opposition to many of the programs of the parent union, AFL–CIO. . . . I am unalterably opposed to the AFL–CIO practice of using union dues money for partisan political purposes.

> Unions are too prone to include items in their bargaining packages which are not needed (however desirable) and not feasible. . . .

> When you present a package deal, as unions do, it's all or nothing. Therefore legitimate demands lose out.

> I cannot think about unionization of public employees without disgust and a taste of dust and ashes.

Goldstein suggests that unfavorable stereotypes of trade unions, such as the above, are important in deterring the rapid growth of unionism among professionals.[41] General public opinion polls lend support to this proposition. Gallup polls show that the majority of the American public approves of unions, *in principle*. In 1967, approximately 65 percent of the general public checked "approve" to the statement, "Do you approve or disapprove of trade unions?"[42] On the other hand, different sentiments are expressed regarding the *practices* of labor unions. Polls have consistently shown a "widely shared belief that unions help cause unnecessary strikes, that corruption is widespread, and that union leaders are more unreliable, self-interested, and insensitive to the general welfare than other highly influential figures in the society."[43]

In an attempt to test the effects of such attitudes on propensity to unionize, Goldstein and Indik developed a scale of attitude toward unionism. It incorporated six commonly held unfavorable stereotypes of trade unions. When the measure was administered to engineers, a statistically significant difference was found between union and nonunion members, with the former showing a more positive attitude toward unionism in general.[44]

A basically identical scale was given to southern California librarians. A statistically significant difference was found to exist between pro-union and anti-union librarians in attitude toward unionism *in general*. The results, given below, show a pattern similar to the results on the professionalism-unionism issue. A significantly higher proportion of librarians with favorable attitudes toward unionism are pro-union rather than anti-union; and there is a high probability that those with unfavorable attitudes will not become union members. The possession of a favorable attitude, however, does not necessarily mean the respondent will be a union member. Seventy-seven percent of the total sample showed favorable attitudes; of these, 34 percent are not, nor desire to be, union members.

	Pro-union	Anti-union
Favorable attitude toward unionism	66%	34%
Unfavorable attitude toward unionism	18	82

[41] Goldstein, "Professional Employee," p. 280.

[42] Bok, Derek, and John T. Dunlop, *Labor and the American Community* (New York: Simon and Schuster, 1970), p. 12.

[43] Ibid., pp. 18–19.

[44] Goldstein and Indik, "Unionism as a Social Choice," p. 368.

As would be suspected, a high correlation exists between perception of no conflict between professionalism and union membership, and attitude toward unionism. But when the effect of each factor is analyzed while "controlling" for the other, each continues to be statistically discriminatory of pro-union and anti-union librarians. Thus, it is concluded that perception of the professionalism-unionism issue and attitude toward unionism are both independently significant determinants of propensity to unionize. Their significance is such that those individuals with a negative attitude toward either are highly unlikely to become union members.

Do the same factors help explain long-term growth of library unionism? Only sketchy evidence is available to test this hypothesis. Table 8 shows four surveys covering the period 1940–70, which provide attitudinal measures of whether or not librarians would join library unions. Inspection of the results shows a moderate increase in the proportion who would join unions, and a corresponding decrease in the proportion who would not. It is not unreasonable to suspect this trend represents an increasing acceptance of unionism among librarians. Figure 2 traces general public

TABLE 8

ATTITUDE TOWARD MEMBERSHIP IN A LIBRARY UNION
(In Percentages)

	1940[a] Should librarians organize?*	1949[b] Nine attitudinal questions as to whether or not a librarian would join a library union.†	1968[c] If your library had a union, would you probably belong?‡	1970[d] Are you a member of a library union / Would you be likely to join if one were organized?§
Yes	32	31	43	52
No	61	61	49	48
No answer	7	..	8	..
	100	92	100	100

[a]Oscar C. Orman, "550 Librarians Speak," *Wilson Library Bulletin*, 14:572 (Apr. 1940).
[b]Alice I. Bryan, *The Public Librarian* (New York: Columbia Univ. Pr., 1952), p. 274.
[c]"Opinions on Collective Bargaining," *ALA Bulletin* 62:804 (June 1969).
[d]Southern California survey, 1971.
*Sample was national (N-550).
†Sample was national (N-2,395).
‡Sample was national (N-2,185).
§Southern California sample (N-415).

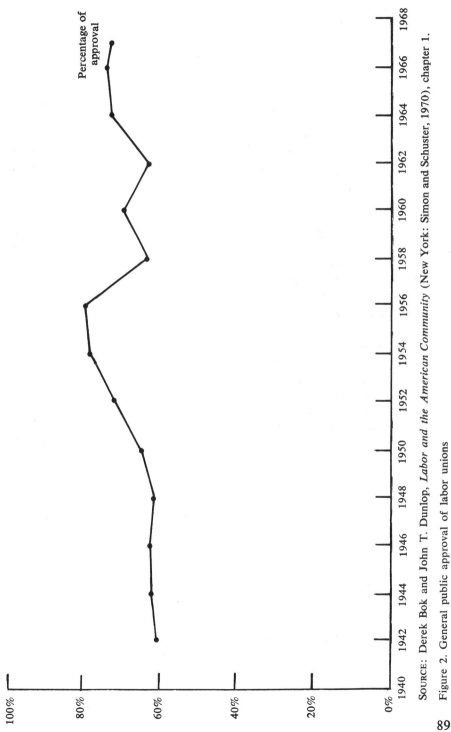

Percentage of
approval

SOURCE: Derek Bok and John T. Dunlop, *Labor and the American Community* (New York: Simon and Schuster, 1970), chapter 1.

Figure 2. General public approval of labor unions

opinion provided by successive Gallup polls of trade unions from 1940 to 1967. The question, "Do you approve or disapprove of trade unions?", was asked of national samples of the population. As can be seen, there has been a small increase in the percentage of approval of unions.

Several writers have hypothesized that public acceptance of trade unionism is important in influencing long-run growth of union membership. Bernstein states that "over the long run the trade union has become an increasingly accepted institution in American society—in the law, with employers, in the community, and, most important . . . with workers. Hence the act of joining has won growing respectability."[45] S. M. Miller, in discussing growth prospects of unions asserts, "The most basic thing affecting the possibility of unionization in new fields is . . . the general community attitude towards unions."[46] Bain reports that many of the employers he interviewed for his study on white-collar unionization in England argued that the " 'inability of the trade union movement to bring itself up to date and to present a better image of itself' was a major factor hindering its expansion among white-collar workers."[47] Although the evidence is by no means conclusive, it is sufficient to suggest that long-run positive changes in acceptance of unionism will cause an increase in the degree of unionization.

While attitude toward unionism has an important bearing on propensity to unionize, it has been argued by some that it is not an independent factor in the long run. For instance, S. M. Miller points out that, increasingly, white-collar workers are the offspring of manual workers. He concludes that those who "originated in manual families will be pro-union, because they have knowledge of what unions are and what they can do; but *some will be anti-union* because they also think they know what unions are like and therefore do not want any part of them."[48] Blackburn and Prandy argue that attitudes of white-collar workers are mainly related to such objective features of the work situation as employer behavior, bureaucracy, and the degree of control that an individual has over his work.[49] Shister states that climate of opinion is derived "in large measure, if not ex-

[45] Irving Bernstein, "The Growth of American Unions," *The American Economic Review* 44:314 (June 1954).

[46] S. M. Miller, "Discussion of 'The Occupational Frontiers of Union Growth,' " *Proceedings of the Industrial Relations Research Association*, 13th annual meeting, Dec. 1960, pp. 214–15.

[47] Bain, *White-Collar Unionism*, p. 88.

[48] S. M. Miller, "Occupational Frontiers," p. 214.

[49] R. M. Blackburn and Kenneth Prandy, "White-Collar Unionization: A Conceptual Framework," *The British Journal of Sociology* 16:116–18 (1965).

clusively, from the rate and pattern of economic change and from the structure of industry."[50]

The results of the southern California survey show a statistically significant correlation between attitude toward unionism and the following personal factors: length of time employed at respondent's library, perception of the professionalism-unionism issue, attitude toward the adequacy of material rewards, and opinion as to whether librarians should have some organization to protect their job and professional interests. The correlation between attitude and the professionalism issue was noted previously. The correlation with desirability of a protection organization is as expected and provides no new dimension to the analysis. The correlation between attitude toward unionism and material rewards is such that respondent's with a favorable attitude of the former will have an unfavorable opinion toward the adequacy of the latter. This relationship is discussed in a later chapter, where it is argued that attitude toward the adequacy of material rewards is a consequence of union membership. The correlation with length of service lies in the direction that those with longer tenure are likely to have more unfavorable attitudes toward unionism. The significance of this factor is explained by the fact that it is highly correlated with age.

Three other personal factors show a slight correlation with attitude toward unionism. Younger librarians tend to have more favorable attitudes than older librarians; respondents who are not married have more favorable attitudes than those who are married; and those whose father's occupation was low (laborer) view unionism more favorably than those whose father's occupation was high (white-collar worker, businessman, or professional). But in all three cases, the relationships are not significant at the .01 level of probability. Two other potential causal factors, structures of the industry (which, in the case of libraries, includes size of the library and bargaining power of the employees) and proximity to organized employees are considered later as well.

A finding in the southern California survey relevant to the preceding analysis is that librarians apparently desire some form of representation. Of the total sample, 97 percent agreed that, "It is good for persons in an occupation such as yours to have at least one organization which looks out for the job and professional interests of the members of the occupation." A smaller proportion (88 percent) agreed that, "The American Library Association should assume a more direct role in improving salaries and other conditions of employment for librarians." And, as noted above, 80 percent disagreed that union membership was inconsistent with maintaining professional standards. These results are given in table 9.

[50] Shister, "Logic of Union Growth," p. 414.

TABLE 9

RESPONSES TO QUESTIONNAIRE ITEMS MEASURING
ATTITUDE TOWARD REPRESENTATIVE ORGANIZATIONS
(In Percentages)

	Agree	Disagree
It is good for persons in an occupation such as yours to have at least one organization which looks out for the job and professional interests of the members of the occupation. (N = 400)	97	3
ALA should assume a more direct role in improving salaries and other conditions of employment for librarians. (N = 393)	88	12
It is impossible for a librarian to belong to a union and at the same time to maintain the standards of his profession. (N = 391)	20	80

Cross tabulations show, that for the most part, the same individuals responded favorably to all three statements. A scalogram analysis shows, however, that the statements do not fall along a single continuum. Since perception of professionalism vs. unionism is the most discriminatory statement, it might be expected that respondents who perceive no conflict would also respond favorably to the other two statements. This is the case for approximately 70 percent of the sample. These individuals apparently have no strong preference as to whether the representing organization is a union, a professional association, or an organization combining the elements of each. As shown in table 10 and explained below, these individuals are likely to be union members. The remaining 30 percent are almost equally divided between two schools of thought: those who believe the representing organization should be a union (11 percent) and those who believe it should be a more aggressive ALA (19 percent).

The category in which an individual falls is generally discriminatory of whether he is or would choose to be a union member, and his attitude toward unionism. Table 10 shows the percentages for each category. As can be seen, respondents with a strictly ALA or professional association orientation responded unfavorably to union membership and attitude toward unionism, and hence are unlikely to become union members. On the other hand, a majority of librarians desire some form of representation, and apparently are willing to accept unionism in order to obtain it.

TABLE 10

DISCRIMINATORY POWER OF QUESTIONNAIRE ITEMS MEASURING
ATTITUDE TOWARD REPRESENTATIVE ORGANIZATIONS
(In Percentages)

	Union Member	Would Choose Union Membership	Favorable Attitude Toward Unionism
Respondents with favorable attitude toward all three statements.	69	47	86
Respondents with favorable attitude toward first and third statements (union orientation).	54	60	84
Respondents with favorable attitude toward first two statements (ALA orientation).	41	12	49

Conclusion

Several occupational characteristics generally thought to be obstacles to professional unionization seem to have little relevance in influencing librarians' propensity to unionize. The large proportion of females, the advanced median age, and the higher social origins were not found to be significant deterrents of union membership. On the other hand, two attitudinal characteristics demonstrated high significance in impeding union membership. Librarians who perceive an inconsistency between membership and their professional standards, and who adversely view unionism in general are highly unlikely to become union members. These opinions are not typical of the profession, however. In fact, most librarians desire some organization to represent their job and professional interests, and at least in attitude are willing to accept unionization as a plausible choice.

Chapter 5

Economic Position

One variable which may have an affect on unionization is economic position of the profession. It is often assumed that employees will join labor unions if they are dissatisfied with their terms and conditions of employment, or refrain from joining if they are not. Important aspects of librarians' economic position are examined here in order to ascertain their influence on propensity to unionize.

Earnings Position

Absolute and relative earnings data for librarians are presented in this and the next three sections. The discussions and analyses will attempt to determine the importance of earnings position in promoting library unions.

A historical analysis of earnings position and unionization is limited because earnings data prior to 1957 are difficult to gather. Table 11 presents average annual salaries for years in which data are available. Salaries for the majority of the years are computed averages from surveys giving minimum and maximum salaries actually being paid in large public libraries. The frequency at which the minimum and maximum rates apply were not generally given so it cannot be ascertained whether the averages over or underestimate true average salaries. More than likely, the averages in table 11 are slightly higher than true averages. No salary surveys were conducted during the 1940s from which data can be used.[1] In order to have an estimate for that decade, the ALA standard salary schedule was used. As explained previously, in 1939, 1946, 1948, and 1952, ALA published minimum salary standards for public libraries. The standards for

---

[1] The Bureau of Labor Statistics published a salary survey in 1949, but the nature of the statistics does not make them comparable with other figures contained in table 11.

94

TABLE 11

AVERAGE ANNUAL SALARIES FOR LIBRARIANS EMPLOYED AT LARGE PUBLIC LIBRARIES, 1923–69

	1923[a]	1928[a]	1933[b]	1939[c]	1946[d]	1952[e]	1957[f]	1965[g]	1969[h]
					Position				
Beginning professional	$1,282	$1,434	$1,356	$1,599	$2,340	$3,317	$4,258	$6,269	$8,628
Beginning subprofessional	973	1,023	991	1,100	1,740	2,519	3,497	4,804	7,263
					Percent Increase				
Beginning professional	—	11	−5	17	46	42	28	47	37
Beginning subprofessional	—	5	−3	10	58	45	38	37	51
Average	—	8	−4	13.5	52	43.5	33	42	44

[a]"Trends in Library Salaries," *ALA Bulletin* 22:805 (1928).
[b]Based on figures in "Public Library Salaries in Cities of More Than 200,000 Population," *ALA Bulletin* 27:246–47 (1933).
[c]Based on figures in "General and Salary Statistics—Public Libraries," *ALA Bulletin* 34:271–72 (1940).
[d]"ALA Salary Standards for 1946," *ALA Bulletin* 45:102 (1951).
[e]*Salaries of Library Personnel, 1952*, (Chicago: American Library Assn., 1953).
[f]Based on figures in *American Library Annual, 1958* (New York: Bowker, 1958), pp. 72–3.
[g]Based on figures in *Bowker Annual* (New York: Bowker, 1966), pp. 20–21.
[h]Based on figures in *Bowker Annual, 1970*, pp. 162–65.

the years 1939 and 1952 were close enough to the average salaries computed from surveys for those years that the 1946 standard was used to provide a reasonable estimate of actual average salaries.[2]

Salary data are consistently available for two positions: library assistant and junior library assistant. The former is a beginning professional position requiring graduation from a library school; the latter is a beginning subprofessional position requiring a college degree. Observation of table 11 shows that salary increments for both positions fluctuated widely between 1923 and 1969. From this, it can be postulated that interest in unions should have been the strongest during periods when changes in absolute earnings were minimal; and union activity should have been at a minimum during periods when changes in earnings increased the most. To test this, the percentage changes in earnings are compared with periods of union activity. Keeping in mind that the percentages are not strictly comparable due to the varying year intervals, the data lend only partial support to the proposition.

The two lowest intervals for salary movements are 1923–28, and 1928–33. No library unions were in existence during either period. The third lowest period, 1933–39, was accompanied by a relatively high degree of union activity. The fourth period, 1952–57, was associated with little union activity. Salaries for the years 1946–52 and 1957–65 rose modestly, and there was little union activity. The two highest periods during which salaries rose, 1939–46 and 1965–69, are associated with marked increases in library union activity. During the former period, however, there is evidence that significant salary increases came during the latter part of the period, whereas the majority of union activity occurred between 1940–44.

Accounting for this last discrepancy, in only four out of the eight periods did the growth of unionism correspond with the tested proposition. The limited scope of library unionism during all eight periods suggests that library unions did not affect the level of salaries.

Although the evidence shows no significant relationship between changes in the absolute level of earnings and unionization, there may exist a relationship between unionization and changes in relative earnings as compared with other employees. This proposition is more likely to hold since wage earners more often judge their earnings not on absolute levels, but in relation with other wage earners. In the case of librarians, the comparative groups are likely to be librarians in other geographical regions; nonprofes-

[2] The average ALA minimum salary standard in 1939 for library assistants was $1,560; for junior library assistants, $1,200. The average salary for each position according to a 1939 survey was $1,599 and $1,100, respectively. The average ALA standard in 1951 for each position was $3,297 and $2,478; the average salary for each position in 1952 was $3,317 and $2,519.

sional library employees; other professionals, including other types of librarians; and other public employees.

Earnings: Regional Comparisons

If regional variation is an important factor of union formation, unions can be expected to form in those regions with the lowest relative earnings. Table 12 shows average salaries in 1968 for professionals in large public libraries for nine regions of the United States. To test whether variations in regional earnings are associated with unionization, the variance between the region's average salary and the national average salary was computed.

In 1968, three regions paid starting salaries 4 percent or more than the national average; and three regions paid salaries 4 percent or less than the national average. Table 1 (pp. 12–15) shows that library unions are heavily concentrated in three regions: middle Atlantic, Great Lakes, and Pacific; and that four regions have no unionization at all: Southeast, Middle West, Southwest, and mountain regions. Comparing table 1 with table 12 shows that unionism is concentrated in those regions having the highest relative salaries; and, except for one case, regions having no unionism pay salaries below the national average.

Within the middle Atlantic region, the majority of unions are located in New York. Comparing the average salary of that state with the national average shows that the former is still 6 percent higher.[3] The unions in the Great Lakes region are distributed among all six states of the region. Unions in the Pacific region are all located in California. Comparison of that state's average with the national average shows that California salaries are approximately 5 percent higher.[4] Hence, the evidence suggests that unionization cannot be explained by relatively lower earnings within a given geographical region.

It could be argued that earnings are higher in the unionized regions due to the unions' successes in improving salaries. To account for this, average salaries in 1952 are given in table 12 for each region. This was a time when library unionism was inactive throughout the country, and therefore it is safe to assume that the 1952 salaries are free of any union effect. Comparing the averages for 1952 and 1968 shows that with one exception the same regions were above, or below, the national average for both years. This indicates that those regions with unionization tend to have higher salaries even in the absence of unions.

---

[3] The 1968 average salary for New York was $7,232.
[4] The 1968 average salary for California was $7,153.

TABLE 12
REGIONAL AVERAGE SALARIES OF LARGE PUBLIC LIBRARIES, 1952 and 1968

	All Regions	New England[a]	Middle Atlantic[b]	Border States[c]	Southeast[d]
1968	$6,800	$6,750 (−0.7%)	$7,150 (+5%)	$7,025 (+3%)	$6,202 (−9%)
1952	3,644	3,193 (−12%)	3,650 (+0.2%)	3,660 (+0.4%)	3,166 (−13%)

SOURCES: Ruth Boaz, *Statistics of Public Libraries Serving Areas with at Least 25,000 Inhabitants, 1968*, (Washington, D.C.: Office of Education, 1970), pp. 47–64. *Salaries of Library Personnel, 1952* (Chicago: American Library Assn., 1953).
NOTE: Figures in parentheses indicate variance between region's average salary and national average salary.
[a]New England: Connecticut, Maine, Massachusetts, New Hampshire, Rhode Island, Vermont.
[b]Middle Atlantic: New Jersey, New York, Pennsylvania.
[c]Border states: Delaware, District of Columbia, Kentucky, Maryland, Virginia, West Virginia.
[d]Southeast: Alabama, Florida, Georgia, Mississippi, North Carolina, South Carolina, Tennessee.

It should be pointed out that care must be taken in analysis of regional differences since erroneous conclusions can easily be made. In order to make valid comparisons, the same situation should exist in all regions. One main variable which distinguishes the regions considered above is population, with the three regions in which unionism is concentrated being the most populated. With heavier population and many large cities, libraries in these regions tend to be larger. The larger libraries generally demand more departments and a larger number of positions with duties and responsibilities in higher grades than the smaller libraries in the less populated regions. The regional differences in average salaries, therefore, might be due largely to the differences in the number of higher grade positions rather than to the speculation that some regions pay higher salaries for positions having the same level of duties and responsibilities.

To account for this, salaries of unionized and nonunionized libraries of comparable size and within the same region were compared. In the middle Atlantic region, the average salary in 1968 for the unionized Philadelphia, Queens Borough, and Brooklyn public libraries was $7,583, or 6 percent above the regional average. The average salary for the nonunionized libraries in Newark, Rochester, and Pittsburgh was $7,057, or 1 percent below the regional average. In the Great Lakes region, the average salary for the unionized Detroit, Minneapolis, Cleveland, and Milwaukee libraries was $7,241, or 3 percent above the regional average; for the nonunionized libraries in Fort Wayne, Indianapolis, Flint, Cincinnati, and Dayton,

TABLE 12 (Continued)
REGIONAL AVERAGE SALARIES OF LARGE PUBLIC LIBRARIES, 1952 and 1968

Great Lakes[e]	Middle West[f]	Southwest[g]	Mountain[h]	Pacific[i]
$7,049 (+4%)	$6,930 (+2%)	$6,530 (−4%)	$6,363 (−6%)	$7,201 (+6%)
3,967 (+9%)	3,425 (−6%)	2,874 (−21%)	2,867 (−21%)	3,769 (+3%)

[e]Great Lakes: Illinois, Indiana, Michigan, Minnesota, Ohio, Wisconsin.
[f]Middle West: Iowa, Kansas, Missouri, Nebraska, North Dakota, South Dakota.
[g]Southwest: Arkansas, Louisiana, Oklahoma, Texas.
[h]Mountain: Arizona, Colorado, Idaho, Montana, New Mexico, Utah, Wyoming.
[i]Pacific: California, Nevada, Oregon, Washington.

$7,182 or 2 percent above the regional average. In the Pacific region, the average salary for the unionized libraries in Los Angeles, San Francisco, and Santa Monica was $7,065, or 2 percent below the regional average; for the nonunionized libraries in Orange County, Sacramento, San Diego, and San Jose, $7,362, or 2 percent above the regional average.[5]

The evidence varies somewhat, but it tends to support the conclusion reached previously that although regional differences in salaries exist, they do not appear to explain the pattern of union formation. To check for the effect of union influence on the salaries in the above comparisons, 1960 and 1965 average salaries were studied for the same libraries. In 1960, unions were not active in any of the above libraries; and in 1965, unions were active in not more than two or three of the libraries. The data support the same conclusion. In both the middle Atlantic and Great Lakes regions, libraries with unions in 1968 had higher salaries in 1960 and 1965 than libraries without unions in 1968. In the Pacific region, nonunion libraries' salaries were slightly higher in 1960, but by 1965 the union libraries were higher.[6] It can be concluded, then, that although regional salary differen-

[5] Salary figures for these comparisons are from: Ruth Boaz, *Statistics of Public Libraries Serving Areas with at Least 25,000 Inhabitants, 1968* (Washington, D.C.: Office of Education, 1970), pp. 47–64.

[6] Average salary for public librarians, 1960 and 1965, by region:

	1960	1965
Middle Atlantic		
Libraries with unions in 1968	$5,096	$6,115
Libraries without unions in 1968	4,624	5,997
Great Lakes		
Libraries with unions in 1968	4,975	6,335
Libraries without unions in 1968	4,751	5,959
Pacific		
Libraries with unions in 1968	4,911	6,364
Libraries without unions in 1968	4,941	6,111

tials do exist, they do not appear to have a significant effect on union formation.

Earnings: Comparison with Nonprofessional Library Employees

Another aspect of earnings that may offer an explanation of unionization are changes in earnings differentials between professional and nonprofessional library employees. Table 13 shows the average annual earnings

TABLE 13

AVERAGE ANNUAL EARNINGS OF PROFESSIONALS AND NONPROFESSIONALS
EMPLOYED AT LARGE PUBLIC LIBRARIES, 1957–69

	1957	1958	1960	1962	1964	1966	1968	1969
Professionals								
Senior librarian	$4,714	$4,936	$5,519	$6,575	$6,665	$7,448	$9,303	$10,066
Junior librarian	4,258	4,501	4,884	5,656	5,960	6,464	7,892	8,628
Nonprofessionals								
Senior clerk	3,834	3,981	4,184	4,804	4,743	5,162	6,498	6,985
Junior clerk	2,979	3,075	3,330	3,646	3,680	4,017	4,959	5,463
Average	3,407	3,528	3,757	4,225	4,212	4,590	5,729	6,224

NOTE: Data were computed from figures in the *Bowker Annual*, 1958, 1959, 1961, 1963, 1965, 1967, 1969, 1970.

in large public libraries for two professional and two nonprofessional positions from 1957 to 1969. Senior librarian is an advanced position requiring a fifth year library degree and experience; junior librarian is a beginning professional position requiring a fifth year library degree. Senior clerk is an advanced, nonsupervisory, nonprofessional position; and junior clerk is a beginning nonprofessional position.

Although professionals have consistently earned more than nonprofessionals, changes in the earnings differential between the two which favor the latter may prompt the professionals to seek means to increase or maintain their relative earnings position. Table 14 shows the change in the average earnings of the two professional positions relative to the change in the average earnings for the nonprofessional positions. As can be seen, professionals were in a better position in 1969 than in 1957, relative to the nonprofessionals. In 1957, junior librarians were earning 25 percent more, and senior librarians 38 percent more than the nonprofessionals. In

TABLE 14

INDEX OF AVERAGE EARNINGS OF PROFESSIONALS RELATIVE TO
EARNINGS OF NONPROFESSIONALS, 1957–69

	1957	1958	1960	1962	1964	1966	1968	1969
Senior librarian	138	140	147	156	158	162	162	162
Junior librarian	125	128	130	134	142	141	138	139
Nonprofessional	100	100	100	100	100	100	100	100

1969, the percentages were, respectively, 39 and 62. Between 1964 and 1966, both professional positions reached their highest earnings relative to the nonprofessionals. Since that period, the relative earnings of senior librarians have held steady, and those of junior librarians have declined slightly. Between 1964 and 1969, nonprofessional earnings increased by 48 percent while junior librarians' earnings increased by 46 percent. It must be concluded, then, that the general earnings position of professional librarians has declined so slightly relative to that of nonprofessionals that the effect on current union formation is probably minimal.

Earnings: Comparison with Other Professional and Public Employees

Earnings of public librarians tend to be lower than those of other professionals with equal education, lower than other professions predominated by women, lower than other state and local government employees, and the lowest when compared with other types of professional librarians.

PROFESSIONAL LIBRARIANS. Table 15 shows the average salaries of public, public school, academic, and special librarians from 1952 to 1970. The lack of available data does not permit a complete analysis of earnings within the library field; and even a partial analysis is hindered by the fact that some of the salaries reported in table 15 are averages, some medians (1968), and some for ALA members only (1970). In order to obtain a rough comparison, however, indices were computed for salaries of public school, academic, and special librarians *relative to* salaries of public librarians. These are shown in table 16.

Since 1952, academic and special librarians have consistently received higher earnings than public librarians. Although the data show that in 1970, public school librarians earned slightly less than public librarians, it should be noted that the former are employed for nine to ten months while public librarians usually work eleven to twelve months. Thus, it is

101

TABLE 15
AVERAGE SALARIES BY TYPE OF LIBRARIAN, 1952–70

	1952[a]	1959[b]	1961[b]	1962[b]	1965[b]	1967[b]	1970[c]
Public librarian	$3,644	$4,862	$5,625[e]	$6,042[e]	$6,269	$7,305[f]	$11,135[h]
Public school librarian	5,012	[d]	5,520	6,264[e]	6,670	7,158[g]	10,623[h]
Academic librarian	3,664	6,901[e]	[d]	8,768	[d]	9,060	11,988[h]
Special librarian	[d]	6,099	[d]	[d]	[d]	9,620	12,084[h]

[a]*Salaries of Library Personnel, 1952* (Chicago: American Library Assn., 1953), p. 16.
[b]"Trends in Library Manpower," *Wilson Library Bulletin* 43:275 (1968).
[c]"ALA Salary Survey: Personal Members," *American Libraries* 2 (Apr. 1971).
[d]Data not available.
[e]Median salary.
[f]Beginning salary.
[g]Adjusted median salary.
[h]Salaries for ALA members only.

TABLE 16
INDICES OF SALARIES OF OTHER LIBRARIANS RELATIVE TO
SALARIES OF PUBLIC LIBRARIANS, 1952–70

	1952	1959	1961	1962	1965	1967	1970
Academic librarian	101	142	—*	145	—	124	108
Special librarian	—	125	—	—	—	132	109
Public school librarian	138	—	98	104	106	98	95
Public librarian	100	100	100	100	100	100	100

*Data not available for computation.

concluded that public librarians are the lowest paid type of librarian. This is supported by the *Occupational Outlook Handbook* which states, "The highest paying positions are found in school, college and special libraries rather than in public libraries."[7]

PROFESSIONALS WITH EQUIVALENT EDUCATION. The average earnings of all librarians as a group are generally lower than earnings of other pro-

[7] *Occupational Outlook Handbook* (Washington, D.C.: Bureau of Labor Statistics, 1969), p. 216.

fessionals with equivalent education. In 1966, the average starting salary for librarians after graduation from an accredited library school was $6,765. Starting salaries in the same year for school counselors was $8,000; engineers, $8,112; accountants, $7,128; personnel workers, $7,100; mathematicians, $7,300; and chemists, $7,500. In 1967, the starting salary for librarians was $7,305; while that for new college graduates in general was $7,500.[8] When comparison is made between graduates of library schools and other master's degree holders, the discrepancy is much wider. The average beginning salary for those with a master's in library science was $5,661 in 1962, and $7,305 in 1967; while beginning salaries for those with a master's degree in other fields were $7,482 and $9,996, respectively.[9]

The lower salaries of librarians is explained largely by the dominance of women in the field. But even when compared with women in other occupations, librarians fare little better. Table 17 shows average annual sal-

TABLE 17

AVERAGE ANNUAL SALARY IN 1964 OF WOMEN WHO GRADUATED IN 1957

Occupation	Salary
Librarians	$5,658
Chemists, mathematicians, statisticians	8,039
Clerical	4,813
Dieticians and home economists	6,110
Editors, copywriters, reporters	6,274
Managers, officials	7,466
Nurses	6,078
Professional workers (miscellaneous)	6,490
School workers (miscellaneous)	6,744
Secretaries, stenographers	4,527
Social, welfare, recreational workers	6,137
Teachers	5,890
Technicians (biological)	5,843

SOURCE: *College Women Seven Years after Graduation* (Washington, D.C.: U.S. Dept. of Labor, 1960), p. 54.

[8] "Trends in Library Manpower," p. 272; Bolino, *Supply and Demand Analysis*, p. 48.

[9] Bolino, *Supply and Demand Analysis*, p. 45.

103

aries in 1964 of women in various occupations who graduated from college seven years previously. As can be seen, only clerical and secretarial employees received earnings lower than librarians.

PROFESSIONS PREDOMINATED BY WOMEN. Looking only at professional occupations predominated by women shows the relatively lower earnings position of librarians. Women largely predominate the nursing, dietitian, librarianship, teaching (except college), and social and welfare work professions.[10] Table 18 gives the salaries of four of these professions from

TABLE 18

AVERAGE SALARIES FOR PROFESSIONAL OCCUPATIONS PREDOMINATED
BY WOMEN, 1956/57–68

| | | Teachers | | | |
	Librarians*	Primary	Secondary	Nurses	Social Workers†
1956–57	$4,250	$3,450	$3,600	$3,276*	—
1960	5,083	4,835	5,334	3,640	$4,230
1962–63	5,661	5,560	5,995	3,900	—
1964	6,145	6,035	6,503	4,498	4,700
1966	6,765	6,609	7,095	5,226	5,100
1968	7,500	7,676	8,160	6,400*	8,500

SOURCE: *Occupational Outlook Handbook* (Washington, D.C.: Bureau of Labor Statistics), 1956–70.
*Figures represent average starting salary.
†Figures represent median salary.

1956–57 to 1968.[11] (Dietitions were excluded due to unavailable data.) In 1956–57, librarians were in an advantageous position. Their starting salary was higher than the average salaries for both types of teachers, and higher than the starting salary for nurses. In 1960, librarians lost ground to secondary teachers, but still remained higher than the other three professions. By 1968, only the nurses received a starting salary lower than that of the librarians; the starting salary of social workers and the average salary of primary teachers surpassed the starting salary of librarians.

[10] *Manpower Report of the President*, p. 186.

[11] The discrepancy in earnings of librarians and nurses between tables 17 and 18 illustrates the difficulty in making salary comparisons. The salary of nurses given in table 17 represents the average for all nurses, whereas the figure in table 18 is for municipal nurses only, who generally receive a salary lower than the national average. The salary of librarians in table 17 is an average for all librarians, whereas, the figure in table 18 is for graduates of library schools only.

Of course these comparisons are obscured by the fact that starting salaries are being compared with average salaries. This can be partially controlled by analyzing percentage changes. By converting the average earnings figures in table 18 into index numbers, and then taking the indices for primary and secondary teachers, nurses, and social workers for each year as a percentage of the librarians' index for that year, it is possible to show the change in average earnings for the four professions relative to the change in the average earnings of librarians. This is shown in table 19. As

TABLE 19

Change in Average Annual Earnings for Professional Occupations Relative to Change in Average Annual Earnings of Librarians, 1956/57–68

| | Teachers | | | |
	Primary	Secondary	Nurses	Social Workers
1956/57*	100	100	100	—
1960	117	123	93	100†
1962/63	121	126	89	—
1964	121	125	94	92
1966	121	124	101	90
1968	126	129	111	138

*Base year.
†Base year for social workers is 1960.

can be seen, between 1956 and 1968, the relative earnings position of librarians has decreased. Earnings of primary and secondary teachers, nurses, and social workers relative to earnings of librarians increased by 26 percent, 29 percent, 11 percent, and 38 percent, respectively.

PUBLIC EMPLOYEES. The last major group to which librarians are likely to compare salaries are other state and local government employees. Here again the evidence shows the relatively low economic position of the public librarian. Table 20 gives average earnings of full-time employees of state and local governments for various functions (other than education) for the years 1957 and 1967. As the table shows, only one function received a salary lower than that paid at local libraries. The average earnings of full-time state and local government employees (other than education) for 1967 was $519, or 21 percent above the average for local library em-

TABLE 20

AVERAGE EARNINGS OF FULL-TIME GOVERNMENT EMPLOYEES, 1957 AND 1967

| Category | Median state earnings, April 1957 | Earnings, October 1967 | | |
		Average for State and Local Governments	State	Local
Local fire protection	$350	$633	—*	$633
Local utilities, total	315	625	—	625
Water transport and terminals	—	621	575	659
Police protection	313	598	613	596
Employment security: administration	—	587	587	—
Local airports	—	577	—	577
Correction	280	562	561	564
Housing and urban renewal	324	558	—	558
Health	316	552	592	530
Natural resources	308	551	566	460
General control	299	544	738	511
Sewerage	282	510	—	510
Financial administration	—	505	527	487
State liquor stores	—	500	500	—
Highways	294	497	530	461
Public welfare	276	483	503	470
Local parks and recreation	267	458	—	458
Sanitation other than sewerage	—	458	—	458
Local Libraries	238	429	—	429
Hospitals	225	423	444	400

SOURCES: *Census of Governments* (Washington, D.C.: Dept. of Commerce, 1957), p. 7; *Census of Governments, Compendium of Public Employment* (Washington, D.C.: Dept. of Commerce, 1967), p. 7.
*Data not available.

ployees.[12] The position of professional librarians is understated in these figures since average librarians' salaries cover all library employees. The earnings position of professional librarians alone would be somewhat better, but data are not available to determine how much.

CONCLUSIONS. The following conclusions can be drawn from the preceding analyses. The relative earnings position of professional public librarians is slightly below that of professional librarians in general, and the relative position of all librarians is noticeably below that of other professional occupations, other professional occupations also predominated by women, and other public employees. The relative position of professional public librarians is favorable when compared with the nonprofessional library staff. In general, the earning positions of public librarians could not operate to hinder unionization, and could be significant in promoting union formation.

Other Terms of Employment

In addition to salary, economic position is influenced by other terms of employment. These fall into the broad category of fringe benefits, and primarily include vacations, holidays, and other types of paid leave; protection against economic hardship resulting from unemployment, retirement, disability, illness; and premium pay for overtime work.[13] Salaried employees have generally enjoyed a superior position to blue-collar workers in relation to fringe benefits, but since World War II, with the aid of industrial unions, benefits of industrial employees have increased to the point where it appears that the differential has been eliminated.[14]

Historically, librarians too have been in a favorable position. According to a national study of large public libraries made in 1926, the average work week of librarians was 41.7 hours. Almost half of the libraries paid extra for work on Sundays and holidays; the majority of libraries granted paid vacations varying from two weeks to one month annually; only a few libraries did not grant sick leave; and although few libraries had pension plans, several had group insurance plans generally paid entirely by the employee, but at relatively low rates.[15] Another survey covering both

---

[12] *Census of Governments: 1967, Compendium of Public Employment* (Washington, D.C.: Bureau of the Census, 1967), p. 7.

[13] Alvin Bauman, "Measuring Employee Compensation in U.S. Industry," *Monthly Labor Review* 93:17 (Oct. 1970).

[14] Goldstein, "Professional Employee," p. 282.

[15] *A Survey of Libraries in the United States*, vol. 1 (Chicago: American Library Assn., 1926), pp. 138–43. *See also* Arthur E. Bostwick, *The American Public Library* (New York: Appleton, 1929), pp. 223–40.

large and small libraries conducted by the Bureau of Labor Statistics in 1949 showed that the most usual work week for library employees was forty hours; that they typically received holidays with pay, with a substantial number of libraries reporting six or eight holidays a year; and that almost all employees were entitled to paid vacations and sick leave, with average vacation provisions allowing four weeks for professionals and two weeks for nonprofessionals, and average sick leave from ten to twelve days a year. About three-fourths of the professional and two-thirds of the nonprofessional workers received coverage by some type of retirement pension plan; and one out of four employees received coverage by some other type of insurance (accident, hospitalization, and life) paid at least in part by the library.[16]

The current position of librarians is reflected in a national study conducted in 1967. Unfortunately, this study is not strictly comparable with the 1949 study because professional and nonprofessional employees were considered together. The 1949 survey showed that professionals receive somewhat better benefits; hence, the 1967 study understates the current benefit position of the professionals. According to the 1967 survey, which covered both large and small public libraries, 94 percent of the nation's libraries grant vacations, with an average time of 13.6 days annually. Sick leave is granted by 84 percent of all libraries, with a mode of 12 days, which suggests a widespread practice of one sick leave day per month employed. Slightly less than half of the public libraries provide for a retirement plan. Among those with retirement plans, the cost is shared by the staff and the library in approximately 80 percent of the libraries.[17]

Thirty-eight percent of the libraries offer medical insurance; and of these, only about 32 percent of the libraries share the cost with the staff. The cost is paid fully by the staff in over 40 percent of the libraries. Health insurance is offered in 29 percent of the libraries. Health insurance provides income in case of illness or medical and hospital expenses, or both; whereas medical insurance provides specifically for the payment of hospital expenses and physician's fees. In slightly less than 50 percent of the libraries, health insurance is paid by the staff. Life insurance is offered in 21 percent of the libraries, and in slightly half of these the costs are shared jointly by the library and the staff.[18]

Since 1926, there has been growth in the areas of retirement; and medical, health, and life insurance benefits. But the growth in these areas since

[16] "Salaries and Working Conditions of Library Employees, 1949," *ALA Bulletin* 43:297–98 (1949).

[17] Peter Spyers-Duran, *Public Libraries: A Comparative Survey of Basic Fringe Benefits* (Rochester, N.Y.: Libraries Unlimited, Inc., 1967), pp. 12–16.

[18] Ibid.

1949 has been slight. The extension of benefits in other areas since 1949 also appears to be slight. When retirement and other insurance benefits are compared with those received by employees in the private sector, librarians are in a relatively unfavorable position. According to a survey conducted in 1965–66 by the Administrative Management Society, covering 600,172 clerical workers in 8,486 American and Canadian companies, 89 percent of the companies offered life insurance, 97 percent offered health insurance, and 96 percent offered medical-surgical insurance. In half of the companies the benefit cost was paid jointly for each type of benefit.[19] Another survey conducted by the Bureau of Labor Statistics shows that in 1957, from 61 to 85 percent of all office employees in industry were covered by a pension plan which was separate from federal Social Security.[20]

In the area of sick leave, librarians have a more liberal policy. Although policies vary, the norm in 1970 was five to six sick leave days per year. In the area of vacations, librarians again appear to be in a favorable position. According to a 1970 study of office and technical employees in manufacturing firms in the four-county area of Los Angeles, 75 percent of the defense firms did not grant 15 days of vacation until after 10 years of service; and 55 percent of the nondefense firms until after 10 years of service.[21] Average weekly hours are fairly equal between librarians and factory production workers. In 1962, the median work week for librarians was 40.1 hours.[22] Average weekly hours for production workers vary with economic activity, but during 1961, they ranged from 39.2 to 40.4 hours.[23]

When compared with school teachers in cities of 100,000 population or greater, librarians appear to be at a disadvantage. In 1959, the mean sick leave allowance for teachers was 13.2 days a year, as compared with a mode for librarians of 12 days a year in 1967.[24] Vacation allowances for teachers in 1959 ranged from an average of 11.3 days the first year to 17.4 days after 25 years of service. In 1967, the average vacation allowance for librarians was 13.6 days. Retirement was the most common insurance provided by school districts in 1959, with 69.2 percent providing retirement plans. The provision of hospitalization and medical and life

---

[19] Donald R. Herzog, "Fringe Benefits: The Federal Government v. Private Industry," *Labor Law Journal* 22:91 (Feb. 1971).

[20] Ibid., p. 92.

[21] Ibid., p. 94.

[22] Drennan and Darling, *Library Manpower*, p. 11.

[23] Hazel M. Willacy, "Changes in Factory Workweek as an Economic Indicator," *Monthly Labor Review* 93:28 (Oct. 1970).

[24] Edgar C. Egly, *Fringe Benefits for Classified Employees* (Association of School Business Officials of the U.S. and Canada, 1959), Bulletin No. 19, p. 33.

insurance was not a general practice among large-city school districts in 1959.[25] Considering the differences in years of the data, plus the fact that teachers are employed only nine to eleven months of the year while librarians are employed eleven to twelve months, it must be concluded that librarians have a less favorable economic position. Comprehensive data are not available concerning various benefits provided by local and state governments to permit a comparison between librarians and other government employees. It could be expected, however, that benefits are fairly comparable, particularly in libraries under civil service.

There are a host of other benefits that have not been considered. For example, workman's compensation, severance pay, military leave, and terminal leave on retirement are fairly common benefits in private industry, but are not generally granted to librarians.[26] On the other hand, many librarians enjoy such benefits as cleaner working surroundings, autonomy to arrange working schedules, and time off to attend professional meetings. While an exhaustive comparison of benefits is not intended, the limited data presented above permit drawing two conclusions. First, librarians have shared the plight of most other salaried employees in having their historical advantage in fringe benefits reduced somewhat since the postwar period. Second, retirement and various insurance benefits offered by the majority of libraries are not comparable with benefits received by employees in the private sector, nor those received by most teachers. In the areas of sick leave, vacations, and weekly hours, librarians are in a farly comparable position.

What impact this aspect of librarians' economic position has had on library union formation is difficult to say with any exactness. Table 3 (page 40) shows that all current union agreements, except one, contain provisions relating to fringe benefits. Based on the data analyzed thus far, this aspect of librarians' economic positions is retained as a potential factor in promoting unionization.

Employment Security

The last facet of economic position considered is employment security. Goldstein has argued that in the last two decades professional employees have experienced a weakening of their traditional security of employment, and attributes that as an important factor tending to make professionals more prone to accept unionism.[27]

[25] Ibid., p. 46.
[26] Spyers-Duran, *Public Libraries*, p. 45.
[27] Goldstein, "Professional Employee," p. 282.

Professional librarians have historically enjoyed security of employment. The only period in which there existed a significant loss of security was during the depression of the 1930s, when librarians as well as other professional employees experienced considerable unemployment for the first time on a wide-scale basis.[28]

Since 1940, the profession has witnessed a shortage of professionally trained personnel.[29] As a result, there has been a general abundance of job security. The job market for the 1960s is reflected in the data contained in table 21, which shows vacancy rates for professional public librarians from

TABLE 21
VACANCY RATES IN PUBLIC LIBRARIES, 1960–65

Year	Number of Unfilled Professional Vacancies	Vacancy Rate
1960	812	7.0%
1962	965	7.2
1965	1,015	7.1

SOURCE: August C. Bolino, *Supply and Demand Analysis of Manpower Trends in the Library and Information Field* (Washington, D.C.: Office of Education, July 1969), p. 66.

1960 to 1965. Although vacancy rates are not an exact measure of manpower shortages since vacancies are real only if funds are available to fill them, they provide an indication of the rather favorable labor market for librarians.

In the past few years, there has been growing alarm over a reversal of the favorable labor market. Frarey points out, "For the first time in 19 years, we can observe marked reduction in the number of openings available to . . . beginning librarians, strong evidence that the disparity between supply and demand that we have considered commonplace for the last two decades is at last beginning to narrow significantly."[30] But cries of "job crises" and "death of the manpower shortage" seem to be an overstatement of the situation,[31] and there is no evidence to indicate that librarians should fear a significant degree of unemployment in the near

[28] Charles H. Compton, "Salary and Employment Conditions," *ALA Bulletin* 27:12 (1933).

[29] "Trends in Library Manpower," p. 272.

[30] *Bowker Annual*, 1971, p. 162.

[31] *See*, for example, "Death of the Manpower Shortage," *Library Journal* 95:3735–44 (Nov. 1, 1970).

future. Frarey concludes, "There are still more jobs than there are people to fill them . . . there were still positions available in 1969 for all new graduates [of library schools] who wanted them."[32]

In addition to the labor market situation, many librarians have the security from arbitrary dismissal provided through civil service systems. Exact figures are not available on the percent of librarians under civil service, although the majority of employees working for libraries in large cities are covered. For libraries in cities with populations of 250,000 or more, approximately 65 percent operated under civil service in 1962.[33] These librarians are entitled to an appeal before a civil service commission in the event of dismissal after a probationary period. There is no correlation between libraries not under civil service and union formation. Of the twenty-six current unionized libraries, eight do not operate under civil service.

The survey of librarians in southern California shows that employment security is not a factor influencing unionization. Of the librarians sampled, 89 percent agreed with the statement, "I can feel secure about my position as long as I do good work." Fewer pro-union librarians agreed with the statement than anti-union librarians, but the difference is negligible: of the former, 88 percent agreed; and among the latter, 90 percent indicated agreement.

Although the severe unemployment during the 1930s may have been instrumental in promoting unionization during that decade, there is no evidence to indicate that concerns of unemployment or other matter of employment security are important in promoting unionization during the current period. In fact, since one important function of labor unions is to obtain job security for its members, the employment security which has characterized the library profession could operate to hinder union formation.

Economic Position and Unionization

The relationship between economic position and unionization will be analyzed first with respect to periods of union activity prior to 1960. The preceding sections showed that little comparative economic data are available on the early periods of library unionism. Nevertheless, several con-

---

[32] *Bowker Annual*, 1971, p. 162.

[33] The percentage of libraries in large cities under civil service is based on data in the 1962 *Municipal Yearbook* (Chicago: The International City Managers' Association, 1962), pp. 199–200.

siderations make it possible to hypothesize that economic matters were instrumental to the formation of most early unions.

First, the economic data which are available support this proposition. Inspection of table 11 (page 95) shows that the smallest percentage increases in absolute earnings of librarians occurred between 1923 and 1939; and it was noted earlier that the greatest proportion of the 46 percent salary increase between 1939 and 1946 occurred during the latter part of the period. Therefore, from 1923 until after 1944, there was not a marked increase in librarians' salaries. Significantly, only two unions were formed between 1944 and 1960, and neither showed specific attention toward achieving economic gains. The Minneapolis union was organized in 1945 at the instigation of the chief librarian; and the Detroit union was formed in 1949 in order to provide a vehicle of communication between the administration and the staff.

Second, except for the two unions just mentioned, the formation of most unions prior to 1960 is accredited as being an effort to improve salaries and working conditions. Berelson states that "the first movement toward library unionization . . . came in the years just before 1920 when economic forces . . . were stimulating organization of workers in all fields."[34] Of the unions organized during the 1930s, Berelson states, "Librarians have sought to organize . . . to counteract the effect of the depression upon salaries and other working conditions. . . ."[35]

Accordingly, the primary and often sole preoccupation of most early unions was with improvements in salaries and working conditions. A cursory survey of unions cited earlier shows most were engaged in two types of activities: securing better wages and working conditions, and improving personnel policies. Of the thirteen unions for which activities were sufficiently available, twelve were involved in obtaining better salaries and working conditions, and five with improvements in library personnel policies. Bryan wrote of the seven library unions she studied in 1949, "None of the unions attempts to help regulate conditions of employment as they affect appointments and terminations, and none assists in securing retirement pensions, only one union interests itself in promotions, three in hours of work and in collective bargaining, and five in wage scales and working conditions."[36]

Finally, during the 1930s and early 1940s, when the majority of early unions were formed, librarians were operating under the most severe budgetary constraints in history. This accounts for the low salary levels

[34] Berelson, "Library Unionization," p. 492.
[35] Ibid., p. 497.
[36] Bryan, *Public Librarian*, pp. 271–73.

during these periods, and justifies the unions' preoccupation with economic concerns. The public library situation is reflected in a 1932 survey of 227 libraries which showed that 72.9 percent had made salary cuts during that year ranging from 1 percent to 34½ percent.[37] In 1940, a national sample of 550 librarians was asked, "What do you regard as the most vital library problem today?" The reply most often given was "need of funds."[38]

The concern among librarians over economic conditions during the 1930s and 1940s is reflected not only by the emergence of unions, but also by the increase in local staff associations. Berelson points out that "as many staff associations were formed in the six years following 1930 as in the fourteen years preceding 1930, and nearly half of those formed from 1930 through 1936 were founded in 1939."[39] The activities of the associations were not recorded, but a 1949 survey shows their members' desire to work toward economic improvement. Of 2,395 librarians sampled, 95 percent thought staff associations should work toward "improved economic welfare of the staff."[40]

Economic matters have been much less important in promoting current library unions. The economic data presented in the preceding sections suggest that some dissatisfaction over relatively low earnings and fringe benefits undoubtedly exists among librarians, but other considerations indicate that dissatisfaction has not been sufficient in and of itself to cause union formation.

In contrast to earlier periods, economic concerns are rarely cited in current literature as a singular cause of library unionization. Hopkins writes, "Employee interest in unions has been attributed to unsettling influences brought about by broad social and technological change, favorable legislation, union successes, and professional failures."[41] A library administrator stated that professional librarians have organized ". . . to have a voice in the decision-making process regarding conditions of employment."[42] A union official stated professional librarians have organized "to establish professional standards, salaries, and working conditions; to codify professional, educational, and social policies and ethics."[43]

In addition, economic concerns have been only a part of the total program of most current unions. In a review of the current library union

---

37 "Salaries and Unemployment," p. 94.

38 Oscar C. Orman, "550 Librarians Speak," *Wilson Library Bulletin* 14:573 (Apr. 1940).

39 Berelson, "Library Unionization," p. 497.

40 Bryan, *Public Librarian*, p. 270.

41 Joseph A. Hopkins, "Unions in Libraries," *Library Journal* 63:3407 (Oct. 1969).

42 "Collective Bargaining: Questions and Answers," p. 1385.

43 Ibid., p. 1386.

movement, Boaz writes, "Many of the library union issues have been focused not so much on salary as on staff efforts to participate in managerial decisions."[44] Analysis of the activities conducted by unions described earlier proves that unions are giving attention to library personnel policies and "professional" matters that is at least equal to purely economic issues.

This is not to suggest, however, that economic matters are of little consequence to today's unions. Table 3 shows that salaries and fringe benefits are the most frequently mentioned issues in collective agreements of library unions. But for several reasons it cannot be implied that they are necessarily of paramount concern. First, most current agreements represent first efforts at negotiations. Hence, many agreements contain *pro forma* demands usually made in the first contract. Second, collective bargaining is a new phenomenon for both unions and administrators. The latter are likely to be overzealous in protecting their "management prerogatives," while the unions are likely to be hesitant in creating pointed conflict at the bargaining table over policy and "professional" matters. As both become more mature in the process of negotiations, bargaining over noneconomic issues is likely to become more common. Third, it should be remembered that "collective bargaining" is a much broader concept than contract negotiations alone. It also includes day-to-day discussions of grievances and administrative decisions and actions affecting employees. Many of the daily interactions undoubtedly involve professional matters. For instance, the library commission of the Los Angeles Public Library was recently seeking a successor for the position of head librarian. When it announced that the new director need not be a librarian, the Library Guild violently opposed the decision as being detrimental to the operation of the library, and the commission later reversed itself. The action by the union will not be reflected in a collective agreement, but it clearly involved interaction with the administration over a professional concern. Finally, informal agreements are often reached between administrators and unions which are outside and independent of the collective agreement. For example, several unions and administrators have informally agreed on periodic meetings for the purpose of discussing matters of mutual concern. One union leader expressed the opinion that the library administration has become much more receptive to opinions of the staff since the union was formed, "as a result of frequent meetings between the chief librarian and union officials."

Even though the economic data given in the preceding sections reflect a relatively unfavorable position for public librarians, it must be remem-

[44] Martha Boaz, "Labor Unions and Libraries," *California Librarian* 33:105 (Apr.–July 1971).

bered that it is not certain who librarians use as their comparative reference group on questions of earnings. If comparison is made with other professionals, then librarians should feel relatively deprived of adequate earnings. If comparisons are made with nonprofessional employees in the same library, and with other types of professional librarians, tables 13 (page 100) and 15 (page 102) show that public librarians will not feel relatively deprived because their earnings have been only slightly reduced relative to those for these groups. Unfortunately, there is no evidence to substantiate who the primary reference group is likely to be.

The survey of southern California casts doubt on whether a high degree of earnings dissatisfaction actually exists among librarians; the survey shows that most librarians have a favorable attitude toward the adequacy of their earnings. Librarians were asked to respond to the following statements: (1) "I am very much underpaid for the work that I do." (2) "My salary is enough to live on comfortably." (3) "The library's (city's) employee benefit program is adequate." The first statement was purposely chosen to ascertain the proportion of librarians who believe their salary is at a critically low level. Of the librarians sampled, 78 percent disagreed with the statement. The second is more moderately worded, but produced a similar response: 77 percent agreed. The third statement was intended to measure attitude toward adequacy of fringe benefits, and it yielded the greatest degree of dissatisfaction: only 57 percent of the librarians agreed that employee benefits were adequate.

Comparing the responses of librarians employed at libraries with unions and those employed at libraries without unions shows that the latter have a more favorable attitude toward adequacy of material rewards. Table 22 shows that a large majority of librarians in both types of

TABLE 22

FAVORABLE RESPONSES TO QUESTIONNAIRE ITEMS MEASURING
SATISFACTION TOWARD MATERIAL REWARDS
(In Percentages)

1. I am very much underpaid for the work that I do.	
Libraries with unions	81
Libraries with no unions	83
2. My salary is enough to live on comfortably.	
Libraries with unions	69
Libraries with no unions	83
3. The library's (city's) employee benefit program is adequate.*	
Libraries with unions	50
Libraries with no unions	74

*Statistically significant at .01%.

116

libraries do not agree with statement 1, that salaries are at a critically low level. Responses to statements 2 and 3 show that a higher degree of dissatisfaction exists with material rewards in the libraries with unions, and in the case of fringe benefits, the difference is statistically significant.

These differences would appear to indicate that dissatisfaction with adequacy of material rewards is important in promoting union formation. But it is hypothesized that the greater degree of dissatisfaction among librarians in the libraries with unions is a consequence of the existence of a union rather than a determinant of its formation. That is, the propaganda and programs of the library unions have influenced attitudes toward adequacy of material rewards held by librarians in the unionized libraries.

First, salaries in the three sampled libraries with unions are higher than those of the three sampled libraries without unions even though only one union has succeeded in bargaining for higher salaries. The figures in table 23 give the percentage breakdown of salary groups for professional

TABLE 23

BREAKDOWN OF SALARY GROUPS FOR PROFESSIONAL LIBRARIANS IN
SIX SAMPLE LIBRARIES
(In Percentages)

Salary	Libraries without Unions			Libraries with Unions		
	A	B	C	D	E*	F
Under $9,000	23	16	24	2	20	4
$9,000–11,000	32	56	49	66	47	52
$11,000–14,000	40	21	22	30	33	37
Over $14,000	5	7	5	2	0	7

*Union has negotiated a wage contract.

librarians in each of the six libraries. It can be seen in table 23 that a larger proportion of librarians in libraries without unions earn salaries of $11,000 or less, although the differences are not statistically significant. Hence, lower salaries do not explain the higher degree of dissatisfaction toward earnings within the libraries with unions.

In addition, the fringe benefits granted by each of the sampled libraries are almost equal, despite the fact that in the libraries with unions, the unions have not gained improvements in this area. Table 24 compares vacation, sick leave, and holiday allowances for each of the six libraries. Other benefits, such as retirement and medical insurance plans, are also similar in each of the libraries (the specific plans are too lengthy to be

TABLE 24

COMPARISON OF FRINGE BENEFITS IN SIX SAMPLE LIBRARIES

Benefit	Libraries without Unions		
	A	B	C
Paid vaca- tions	First year: 10 days 5 years: 15 days 15 years: 20 days	First year: 10 days 5 years: 15 days 10 years: 20 days	First year: 12 days 5 years: 13 days 20 years: 20 days
Paid sick leave	13 days per year	First year: 9 days 3 years: 12 days	12 days per year
Paid holi- days	9 per year	11 per year	14 per year

shown here). Hence, lower fringe benefits do not explain the higher degree of dissatisfaction toward earnings among librarians in libraries with unions.

Table 22 shows that librarians employed at libraries with unions are significantly more dissatisfied with the adequacy of fringe benefits than librarians employed at libraries with no unions. This significance can be explained by at least two important factors. When responses are compared while controlling for respondents' attitude toward unionism, the significant difference fails to appear. The same result occurs when respondents' attitude toward the library administration and organization is controlled. Both of these factors are proven in other chapters to have a significant and independent affect upon propensity to unionize. Hence, it is concluded that dissatisfaction with adequacy of fringe benefits is not by itself significant in promoting unionization, but rather is a reflection of other factors which have a more direct influence.

Second, if earnings are important in promoting unionization, dissatisfaction would be expected to occur primarily among librarians with the lowest salaries. But several factors which would indicate that dissatisfaction in libraries with unions is concentrated among these librarians fail to be significantly correlated with attitude toward material rewards. For instance, salary, sex, age, education, length of time employed at the library, and length of time employed as a librarian were found to be unrelated to each of the three measures of attitude toward material rewards.

Third, librarians in the libraries with no union who indicated that they would join a union if one existed do not differ significantly with respect to attitude toward adequacy of material rewards from those in the same

TABLE 24 (Continued)
COMPARISON OF FRINGE BENEFITS IN SIX SAMPLE LIBRARIES

| Benefit | Libraries with Unions | | |
	D	E	F
Paid vacations	First year: 10 days 5 years: 15 days 10 years: 20 days	First year: 10 days 5 years: 15 days 17 years: 20 days	First year: 12 days 10 years: 18 days
Paid sick leave	12 days per year	12 days per year	12 days per year
Paid holidays	11 to 12 per year	10 per year	11 per year

libraries who would not choose union membership. Here is the percentage of favorable responses for each group to the three statements:

	Would join a union	Would not join a union
Favorable replies to statement 1	85%	81%
Favorable replies to statement 2	85	82
Favorable replies to statement 3	63	77

These results provide evidence that among those who would join a library union, dissatisfaction with salaries and fringe benefits is not a statistically significant contributing factor.

At the same time, as the following figures show, there is no statistically significant difference in attitudes between union and nonunion members in the libraries with unions, although the pro-union and anti-union differences are greater than existed in the libraries with no unions.[45]

	Union member	Nonunion member
Favorable replies to statement 1	78%	88%
Favorable replies to statement 2	68	82
Favorable replies to statement 3	48	55

[45] In one of the unionized libraries, a statistically significant difference does appear between union and nonunion members when all three statements are combined into one measure, but the significance disappears when attitude toward unionism is controlled.

The higher degree of dissatisfaction among union members conceivably can be due to their contact with union leaders and other members, and their exposure to union newsletters and programs. For instance, the newsletter of the Los Angeles Public Library Guild frequently compares earning positions of librarians with those of other workers.

A fourth reason which supports the hypothesis that the existence of library unions influences librarians' attitudes toward adequacy of material rewards is found in statements made by the librarians themselves. The total sample was asked to indicate why they are, or would like to become, a union member. The replies from forty-three librarians who directly responded to the question are given in table 25. As can be seen, few

TABLE 25

REASONS GIVEN FOR JOINING, OR FOR DESIRING TO JOIN, LIBRARY UNIONS

To be protected from arbitrary decisions and actions by administrators (administrators	15
are isolated from library staff).	4
To be represented in order to improve professional aspects of the occupation.	8
To gain improvements in salaries and working conditions.	5
To be represented because ALA and other professional associations show little concern for the librarian.	5
Others.	6

NOTE: Figures represent sample of forty-three librarians.

librarians specifically indicated that displeasure over salaries and fringe benefits was a central reason for joining a union. Although it cannot be inferred from these statements that librarians consider salary matters to be unimportant, they show that such matters are not of paramount concern in instigating union membership.

The proposition that unions can affect attitudes is not without precedent. In a study of male manual workers, Kornhauser demonstrated the ability of unions to influence attitudes of its members toward certain subjective issues (party preference and perception of the relevance of economic group membership to voting behavior) on which unions take stands.[46] She did not apply the analysis to attitude toward material rewards, and confines the findings to cases where unions have become an accepted institution. The newness and precariously established position of library unions cast

[46] Kornhauser, "Consequences of Union Membership," pp. 30–61.

doubt on their ability to influence a variety of their members' attitudes. But, as the reasons in table 25 suggest, it is conceivable that even newly formed library unions could influence a relatively oscillatory issue such as attitude toward adequacy of material rewards, an issue on which most library unions take a clear and early strong stand.

Conclusion

Economic position has had a differential effect in influencing library union formation. The prevalent activity among early library unions of working toward improvements in salaries and conditions of employment, and the concern within the entire profession over economic welfare, suggest that unions formed prior to 1945 emerged primarily as a reaction to poor economic conditions. After 1945, the emphasis of unions has centered on noneconomic as well as economic issues. This observation, the current literature on library unionization, and the findings of the southern California survey suggest that economic position is less significant in promoting current unionization. Librarians' salaries and fringe benefits are relatively low when compared with many other employees, but it is concluded that dissatisfaction with economic position is not singularly sufficient in explaining current library unionization.

Chapter 6

Employment Environment

Certain variable features of the employment environment can explain union formation in one library and not in another. These features are generally out of the control of individual librarians, but nevertheless can affect their propensity to unionize. Three relevant characteristics of librarians' employment environments will be analyzed here. First, the effect of library size is examined. Attention is given to the degree of bureaucratization and bargaining power as factors of unionization. Second, the effect of working in a highly unionized environment is studied. Of paramount interest is whether librarians in union areas are more prone to organize than those in areas with relatively little union tradition. Finally, the effect of labor legislation in promoting unionization is investigated.

Employment Concentration

The patterns of library unionism described earlier show a concentration of unions in large public libraries. Numerous writers have called attention to the greater propensity of both manual and white-collar workers to organize when the degree of employment concentration is high. This phenomenon is generally explained by the effects of bureaucratization. For instance, Lipset notes Kark Marx's observation that "workers in small shops were markedly less class-conscious and less involved in working class organizations than those in larger plants. He accounted for this difference by the fact that the former were much more likely than the latter to associate informally with their employees and to develop personal ties to them."[1] Shister states that, "the propensity of workers to unionize is less in the small firm than the large one, *ceteris paribus* [other things being

---

[1] Lipset, "White Collar Workers," pp. 31–54.

equal], the difference stemming from closeness to management, work conditions, etc."[2] Blackburn and Prandy attribute the high degree of unionization of government white-collar workers in England to the "higher degree of bureaucratization which they [the government bodies] manifest."[3] Bain notes that larger groups of employees are probably more favorably disposed toward trade unionism because of the bureaucratic manner in which they are administered.[4]

In addition to bureaucratization, unionization is more likely to occur in large organizations because employees possess more bargaining power. This refers to the extent to which workers can exert pressure upon the employer. If employees have no bargaining power, it is impossible for them to provide inducement for employers to concede to organized demands. The most common source of bargaining power for employees is the strike. But other factors, such as political pressures, negotiating skills, and psychological elements may also be important sources in specific situations.[5]

The lack of bargaining power is undoubtedly a significant deterrent to unionization in some small libraries since the staffs question their power to influence administrators and legislative bodies through their own organized efforts. Most unions, in large and small libraries, have undoubtedly sought labor affiliation for this very reason. Berelson writes that during the 1930s, librarians formed unions and "sought labor affiliation to strengthen their position."[6] A prime example is the small library in Butte, Montana. Employees there organized in 1934 for the purpose of raising funds to keep the library from closing. They decided to unionize "in order to gain the active support of organized labor."[7] The president of the newly formed San Francisco union observed that librarians had little power to affect change as long as they remained an independent organization. Another union leader agreed, "Alone we would be much weaker, as we were."[8]

The degree to which bargaining power has hindered unionization in small libraries cannot be measured. Obviously, if employees of these libraries are willing to affiliate with national unions or employee associations, some form of power is available. This decision is dependent upon other factors considered in this study (primarily attitude toward unionism and prox-

---

[2] Shister, "Logic of Union Growth," p. 419.

[3] Blackburn and Prandy, "White Collar Unionization," p. 117.

[4] Bain, *White-Collar Unionism*, pp. 73–74.

[5] Myron Lieberman and Michael H. Moskow, *Collective Negotiations for Teachers* (Chicago: Rand McNally, 1966), p. 288.

[6] Berelson, "Library Unionization," p. 497.

[7] Ibid., p. 499.

[8] "Collective Bargaining: Questions and Answers," p. 1388.

imity to organized employees). Hence, the significance of bargaining power in explaining the concentration of unions in large libraries is questionable. Evidence is provided to this effect by a recent survey of large (71–400 staff members) and small to medium (4–70 staff members) public libraries in which employees were given a list of nineteen items related to salaries and fringe benefits, and asked to indicate whether they thought the library's having collective bargaining would result in "positive improvement," "negative effect," or "little difference" in these items.[9] The averaged responses from the professional staffs are shown in table 26. Employees of

TABLE 26
PROFESSIONAL STAFF RESPONSES ON PROBABLE RESULTS OF COLLECTIVE BARGAINING
(In Percentages)

	Positive Improvement	Negative Effect	Little Difference	No Reply
Large libraries (N = 1047)	20	5	67	8
Small/Medium libraries (N=614)	18	4	58	20

small to medium libraries were not less optimistic about the probable effects of bargaining than employees of large libraries. The most significant variation between the two groups is the markedly higher proportion of small to medium library employees who failed to reply to the question. This probably indicates that they have given less thought to the likelihood of collective bargaining; which, in turn, implies they do not perceive as great a need for collective bargaining as employees of large libraries. The same librarians were asked, "Does it appear likely that your library will have collective bargaining contracts within the next five years?" In the large libraries, 8 percent said "yes," and 81 percent said "no"; in the small to medium libraries, 3 percent said "yes," and 90 percent said "no."

A third reason employees in large organizations are more likely to unionize is that unions tend to concentrate recruiting efforts in larger establishments. This is largely a result of the higher potential return. Bain states, "Trade union recruiting is characterized by economies of scale: in general, the larger the group recruited the lower the *per capita* costs."[10]

[9] "Opinions on Collective Bargaining," pp. 805–7.
[10] Bain, *White-Collar Unionism*, p. 74.

But, for this very reason, librarians are not likely to be actively recruited. With a wide field of other professional employees available for unionization, the potential return of concentrating on librarians is minimal. Hence, if library size is an important factor of unionization, it is safe to venture that bureaucratization, more than recruiting efforts or bargaining power, is the central cause.

Relation between Library Size and Union Formation

It is relatively simple to demonstrate the relationship between library size and unionization. To do this, the number of full-time professional positions employed by libraries is used as a measure of library size. For clarification, it should be mentioned that the measure does not imply that a given number of professionals work at the same locality. In almost all large library systems, professionals are distributed among branches. For example, the Los Angeles Public Library employs close to 300 professionals, many of whom work at some 60 branch libraries. This does not reduce the validity of the measure, however. Librarians within a system are administered by one central agency, not by individual branches.[11]

Earlier it was shown that prior to 1960, unions were organized in fourteen public libraries. Statistics on the number of professional positions in these libraries are available for 1940 (two of the libraries, Grand Rapids and Wayne County, Michigan, are not reported). Unions were organized in eleven of these fourteen libraries between 1936 and 1945, so the 1940 data provide a reasonable indication of size at the time of unionization. The Washington, D.C., and Philadelphia libraries were unionized in 1918 and 1919, respectively, and since both are long established libraries, they were undoubtedly among the largest in the country then as well as in 1940. The remaining library, Butte, Montana, was one of the smallest in the country at the time of its unionization.

According to the 1940 statistics, eleven of the fourteen unionized libraries were grouped in a category representing the country's largest libraries. Within this category, sixteen libraries had professional staffs of one hundred or more. Eight of these libraries were unionized.[12] Thus, not

---

[11] Supervisory librarians at branch libraries do handle many personnel decisions, such as scheduling, employee evaluation, and employee recommendations for promotions or transfers; and may make some administrative decisions subject to central agency guidelines and approval. Decisions affecting library operating policies, such as operating hours or book selection, are made by the central agency.

[12] "General and Salary Statistics—Public Libraries," *ALA Bulletin* 34:271, 285 (Apr. 1940).

only were eleven of the fourteen unionized libraries among the largest in the country, but half of the largest sixteen libraries had unions.

Analysis of current libraries gives similar results. The 1968 *Library Statistics* shows that there are fourteen libraries in the country with one hundred or more positions filled by employees holding a fifth-year degree in librarianship. Union activity exists in twelve of these libraries. Thirty-three libraries have fifty or more fifth-year degree positions, of which fifteen—or slightly less than half—are unionized.[13]

Table 27 shows for each of the current unionized libraries the number of positions filled by employees holding a graduate degree in librarianship in 1968. As can be seen, only eight of the twenty-six libraries have fifty or fewer professional positions. The evidence proves, then, that throughout the history of library unionism, there has existed a strong correlation between union formation and library size.

Effect of Library Size

In this section, bureaucratization is analyzed as a potential factor promoting unionization. The approach taken in the ensuing analysis is determining the extent to which library union activities, statements giving causes of union formation, and literature on library unions are responsive to, and reflective of, elements of bureaucratic administration.

It has been noted earlier that the main activities of early unions centered around improvements in wages and working conditions. But there is also evidence that dissatisfaction existed with library administration, particularly with respect to personnel policies. For instance, Berelson states that the Cleveland union was formed in 1937 "specifically because of low salaries and 'undesirable methods of administration,' including unsystematic procedure in promotions and vacations and undue concentration of authority."[14] The 1940 program of the Chicago union included "adjustment of employee grievances through the adoption of a modern, democratic personnel policy."[15] It is a matter of record that during the 1930s and 1940s most of the country's libraries operated under archaic personnel practices. In 1937, the following observation was made:

> Personnel management in the public service is literally leagues behind the standards that are accepted as sound by progressive managers in private enterprise. . . . library service would stand below,

[13] Ruth Boaz, *Statistics*, pp. 47–64.
[14] Berelson, "Library Unionization," p. 500.
[15] "Letters to Editor, 'Chicago's Union Program,'" *ALA Bulletin*, 34:420 (June 1940).

126

TABLE 27

SIZE OF PROFESSIONAL STAFF OF CURRENT UNIONIZED LIBRARIES

Library	Positions Filled by Employees Holding a Fifth-Year Degree in Librarianship
Berkeley PL	100
Bloomfield PL	150
Boston PL	21
Brooklyn PL	209
Buffalo and Erie County PL	101
Chicago PL	†
Cleveland PL	172
Contra Costa County PL	22
Detroit PL	9
District of Columbia PL	86
Enfield PL	329
Enoch Pratt Free Library	141
Los Angeles PL	300
Los Angeles County PL	133
Milwaukee PL	86
Morris County PL	6
New York PL	698
Newark PL	60
Oakland PL	105
Oshkosh PL	5
Philadelphia Free Library	193
Queens Borough PL	276
San Francisco PL	110
Santa Monica PL	22
Youngstown and Mahoning County PL	27

SOURCE: Ruth Boaz, *Statistics of Public Libraries Serving Areas with at Least 25,000 Inhabitants, 1968* (Washington, D.C.: U.S. Office of Education, 1970), pp. 47–64.

*Figures are for 1960.

†Figure is not available for either 1960 or 1968, but the number of professional positions is under fifty.

127

rather than above, a median position with respect to the attitude toward, and treatment of, library employees.[16]

Activities of current unions depict a high regard toward seeking changes in library administration and participating in policy making. The Detroit union, organized in 1949, was the first to establish this pattern. According to a union brochure, the need for an organization to bridge the distance between administrators and employees at Detroit was created as the library staff increased in size and personal ties between the two were weakened. Cursory review of union activities described earlier illustrates that many current unions are negotiating for greater participation in certain personnel procedures, especially areas relating to promotion, transfers, and employee grievances; and urging better communication between administrators and staff. Undoubtedly, part of the concern revolves around the desire on the part of librarians to fulfill their professional expectations. The Los Angeles Public Library Guild has expressed this concern:

> Professional involvement, exposure to new ideas in the field, freedom to be creative and to experiment, [and] the opportunity to improve services offered to the public . . . are all characteristics of a profession and within the field of librarianship, [and] are normally only available to or experienced by library administrators.[17]

Activities of current unions confirm reasons often advanced for their formation. For instance, one library administrator commented,

> Professional librarians . . . organize into unions to permit them to have a voice in the decision-making process regarding conditions of employment. Such matters as job security, salary, and promotion policies and procedures are of immediate and intense concern for professional librarians. No matter how benign or benevolent the administration of a library organization purports to be or appears to be, professional staff of the library frequently wish to play a role in the decision-making process with regard to their conditions of employment.[18]

In addition, table 25 (page 120) showed that the reason most often cited by southern California librarians for joining or desiring to join a union

---

[16] W. E. Mosher, "Implications of an Enlightened Personnel Policy," *Library Journal* 62:849 (1937).

[17] Darryl Mleynek, "Professional Unions," *California Librarian* 31:110 (Apr. 1970).

[18] "Collective Bargaining: Questions and Answers," p. 1385.

concerned library administration. The following statements are illustrative of the sources of dissatisfaction:

> I became a union member because of morale problems. Our librarians are treated like mindless children, incapable of doing professional work, yet, at the same time, absolute perfection on the job is demanded.

> . . . I support the union because management has not been sensitive to the needs of library personnel. . . .

> The arrogance of administration and the "father knows best attitude" were directly responsible for the success of the unionization of our system. If any real effort had been made to solicit ideas, communicate plans, enlist cooperation and engage in discussion with the professional staff, there would have been less dissatisfaction and disenchantment.

> I believe that unions are more needed than ever. It seems as if the administrators are more and more isolated from the librarians. . . . The isolation seems more prevalent now than when I started working three years ago. . . .

Current literature on library unionism further substantiates the importance of administration concerns. Jack Golodner, an AFL–CIO executive, in discussing library unionization states,

> By joining together in union with their professional colleagues and with other employees, they [librarians] are lengthening their shadow to match the growing size and scale of their employer institutions. They are insisting that they will have a voice in the shaping of their profession and that control of their profession should not be the sole province of employers. . . .[19]

Eldred Smith commented on the current division between administrators and librarians. He explained that with the recent growth in the size of libraries and library systems, administrators are assuming characteristics of managerial elite whose duties separate them from their professional staff. "The community of interest among administrative and nonadministrative librarians is being eroded and an employer-employee situation is being created in which the functions, economic interest, and social position of one group is coming into opposition to the other."[20]

[19] Jack Golodner, "The Librarian and the Union," *Wilson Library Bulletin* 42:390 (Dec. 1967).
[20] Eldred Smith, "Librarians and Unions," p. 718.

The statements in the preceding paragraphs are representative of opinions on the current library union movement. There is no question that they depict disenchantment with library administration and detachment from administrators as important underlying causes of current unionization. The major concerns of today's union members can be summarized as follows:

1. Librarians want a greater voice in personnel policies affecting them.
2. Librarians want more control over their profession, particularly in regard to professional policies of the library.
3. Librarians want closer contact and more communication with administration.

There are at least three relevant characteristics of bureaucratization which account for the above concerns. The first is that in bureaucracies, conditions of employment, promotion prospects, and other personnel matters are determined by formal policies which apply impersonally to all members of the organization. This can be contrasted with paternalistic administration, which is generally associated with small organizations, although certain of its features can be produced in large ones. The distinguishing feature of paternalism is that many personnel matters are determined by the personal relations of the administrator and the employee. As a result, there is a lack of uniformity in working conditions throughout the entire staff.

A second characteristic of bureaucracies is the well-defined hierarchy of authority, which differs greatly from that employed in the professions. Blau and Scott point out that one distinguishing characteristic of the professions is their control structure. "Professionals typically organize themselves into voluntary associations for the purpose of self-control. . . . Professionals in a given field constitute a colleague group of equals. Every member of the group . . . is assumed to be qualified to make professional judgments."[21] In contrast, the source of decision-making and control within a bureaucracy is not the colleague group but the hierarchy of administrative authority.[22] Scott states further that a number of studies indicate that professionals are uncomfortable with bureaucratic authority, at least to the extent of expressing dissatisfaction with the management.[23] Arensberg and MacGregor (1942) found that engineers in an electrical equipment company felt that management sometimes made decisions which were arbi-

[21] Peter M. Blau and Richard Scott, *Formal Organizations* (San Francisco: Chandler, 1962), pp. 62–63.

[22] Ibid.

[23] W. Richard Scott, "Professionals in Bureaucracies—Areas of Conflict," in *Professionalization*, eds. Howard M. Vollmer and D. L. Mills (New Jersey: Prentice-Hall, 1966), p. 273.

trary, inconsistent, or interfered with their prerogative to make technical decisions. In a survey of 587 engineers and natural scientists employed in nineteen separate work groups, Moore and Rench (1955) found that, compared to the average employee, both engineers and scientists had a low opinion of the general effectiveness of the administration. Becker (1953) in a study of public school teachers reports that "conflict arises when the principal ignores his teachers' need for professional independence. . . ." Ben-David (1958) found that physicians employed by Israeli medical care organizations showed high dissatisfaction, complaining about administrative inefficiency and interference.[24]

Third, a basic ingredient of bureaucracy is hierarchical organization. This, in turn, restricts communication. Bennis cites as one of the criticisms of bureaucracy, "Communication (and innovative ideas) are thwarted . . . due to hierarchical divisions."[25] Studies show that plant size is inversely related to personal communications between supervisors and subordinates.[26]

Although the discussion has been oversimplified, it lends support to the studies cited at the beginning of this chapter which attribute the higher degree of unionization in large organizations to bureaucratization.

In an attempt to quantify the significance of bureaucratization, the survey of southern California librarians included a measure of respondents' attitudes toward the library and its administration. The sample was given Likert-type questionnaire items (shown in Appendix A) measuring degree of satisfaction toward library administrators and organization, immediate supervision, and intrinsic value of the job. All three indices are important because they represent basic satisfactions which employees hope to derive as members of the library organization. Responses were categorized in terms of the respondents' sentiments toward library unionization. Pro-union librarians included union members and those who would join if a union existed in their library. Anti-union librarians included those who had not joined the union in their library and those who stated they would not join if a union existed in their library. The former represented 53 percent of the sample; the latter, 47 percent.

No significant differences were found between pro-union and anti-union librarians with respect to attitude toward immediate supervision, and attitude toward job satisfaction. As the figures in table 28 show, there was no difference between the two groups in attitude toward job satisfaction; and 89 percent of the entire sample agreed that their job was worthwhile and afforded opportunities for personal growth and development. The index of

[24] Ibid., pp. 273–74.
[25] Warren G. Bennis, ed., *American Bureaucracy* (Chicago: Aldine, 1970), p. 6.
[26] Lipset, "White Collar Workers," p. 39.

131

TABLE 28

SURVEY RESPONDENTS' ATTITUDES TOWARD THE LIBRARY
AND ITS ADMINISTRATION

(In Percentages)

Attitude	Pro-union	Anti-union	Total	Total Sample
Toward job satisfaction:				
Favorable	53	47	100	89
Unfavorable	53	47	100	11
Toward immediate supervision:				
Favorable	51	49	100	82
Unfavorable	57	43	100	18

attitude toward immediate supervision showed only a slight differentiation; and 82 percent of the entire sample held favorable opinions of the administrative aspects of their supervisor's job.

A considerably lower proportion of the total sample held favorable attitudes toward their library organization and administration, and this index proved to be statistically discriminatory of pro-union and anti-union librarians. As the following results show, about one out of every four librarians have an unfavorable attitude toward this index, and the ratio is higher among pro-union librarians.

	Pro-union	Anti-union	Total	Total Sample
Favorable	47%	53%	100%	70%
Unfavorable	66	34	100	30

Analysis of individual items which compose the index shows that those relating to library administrators were more discriminatory of union and nonunion librarians than items relating to the library organization. In addition, both groups show a higher degree of dissatisfaction with the former. The items and the percent of favorable responses of pro-union and anti-union librarians are shown in table 29.

Although the total index gives a statistically significant difference between pro-union and anti-union librarians, its significance disappears when the factor attitude toward unionism is controlled. When the index is broken down into its subcomponents—attitude toward administration and attitude toward organization—the former continues to discriminate between pro-union and anti-union librarians, even when attitude toward unionism is controlled; but the latter measure fails to be statistically significant. Hence,

TABLE 29
FAVORABLE RESPONSES TO ITEMS RELATING TO LIBRARY ORGANIZATION
(In Percentages)

	Anti-union	Pro-union
Administration items:		
The library administrators are very competent in their jobs.*	74	59
The library arminstrators have a genuine interest in the welfare of employees.*	66	46
This library operates efficiently and smoothly.	60	47
Organization items:		
There are many good positions here for those who strive to get ahead.*	56	42
The longer one is employed at this library the more he feels that he belongs.	72	68
I can feel secure about my position as long as I do good work.	90	89
Average response:		
To three administration items*	67	51
To three organization items	73	66

*Statistically significant at .01%.

it is concluded that attitude toward library administration is a significant factor in promoting union membership.

It is worthy to comment on one item in the index of attitude toward organization that proved to be statistically significant. More than half (58 percent) of the pro-union librarians, and slightly less than half (44 percent) of the anti-union librarians disagreed with the statement, "There are many good positions here for those who strive to get ahead." Dissonance over prospects of promotion is generally indicative of bureaucratic structure. Since the majority of the total sample (52 percent) disagreed with the statement, further proof is provided on the importance of bureaucratization in creating dissatisfaction among professional employees. According to Blackburn and Prandy, "Increased size and complexity of organization is often associated . . . with a reduction in the prospects of promotion to management for those in the lower levels. The diminished opportunities to share in the exercise of authority will tend to reinforce the individual's

133

rejection of its legitimacy."[27] Similarly, Lockwood found that "bureaucratization is frequently associated with a decline in the chances of upward mobility for [railway] clerks" in England.[28]

The analysis above supplies proof that unionization is a reaction to bureaucratization, although the arguments are not conclusive. Since bureaucracy is generally a function of the amount of employees administered, it can be inferred that the probability of unionization is higher in larger libraries than in smaller as a result of bureaucratic administration. It is obvious, however, that bureaucratization is not exclusive to large libraries. The personal administrative policies of a single chief librarian can introduce bureaucracy to the smallest library. The comment of one librarian illustrates this salient point: "I am a union member because I feel the small library system I worked for previously took advantage of employees. I do not want this to happen in the large system I am working for now."

Before asserting that bureaucratization is a significant factor in promoting unionization, several other factors that might explain the relationship between library size and unionization are examined. The effects of proximity to unionized employees and labor legislation are going to be analyzed here. The relationship between these factors and library size is direct. Large libraries are generally located in large cities; the latter, in turn, tend to have a greater degree of unionization and more liberal labor legislation than small cities. Thus, even though the bureaucratization of large libraries may encourage union formation, these factors may have a more direct influence in promoting union formation. Finally, the independent effects of proximity to organized employees and legislative climate, and employment concentration, will also be investigated.

Proximity to Organized Employees

Several writers on white-collar unionism have speculated that proximity to other unionized employees can increase propensity to join unions.[29] Kassalow, for example, has written that, "the spread of unionism among white-collar employees . . . has undoubtedly been due in part to the high degree of organization and the great political and social effectiveness of the manual workers' union during the past thirty years."[30] The main reason

[27] Blackburn and Prandy, "White-Collar Unionization," p. 118.

[28] David Lockwood, *The Blackcoated Worker* (London: George Allen & Unwin Ltd., 1958), p. 149.

[29] *See*, for example, C. Wright Mills, *White Collar* (New York: Oxford Univ. Pr. 1956), p. 307.

[30] Everett Kassalow, *Trade Unions and Industrial Relations* (New York: Random, 1969), p. 201.

advanced in support of this argument is that employees who are exposed to unionization are provided with a demonstration of the benefits of trade unionism.[31]

The pattern of early library unionism indicates that libraries located in cities with strong labor traditions are more likely to be unionized than those which are not. Table 1 (pp. 12–15) shows that unions formed prior to 1960 were confined to such cities. In fact, of the nineteen early unions, only two existed in localities with little trade union history. Cursory observation of the current unions further supports this hypothesis.

Analysis of the regions and states in which current library unions are concentrated shows a high correlation with the strength of overall unionization in the same regions and states. In a study of public employee unions and associations, Stieber found that the northeast region is by far the most likely to have unionization. Eighty-seven percent of the public employees in northeastern cities were represented by unions or associations in 1968. Cities in the north central and western regions reported 57 and 58 percent, respectively, of their employees represented. Southern cities with 30 percent representation are least likely to have employee organizations.[32]

A regional breakdown of the unionized libraries in table 1 shows a similar distribution. Ten libraries, or close to 40 percent of the total, are located in northeastern states; seven are located in north central states; seven in the western region; and two in the southern region.

The strength of overall unionization in individual states can be measured, in part, by the total union membership for the state as a proportion of total employment in nonagricultural establishments. It can also be measured by whether the state has enacted a right-to-work law. Under the terms of the National Labor Relations Act, a union may negotiate a union shop agreement provided the state has not enacted a so-called "right-to-work" law forbidding such agreements. Generally, such laws have failed to be enacted in highly unionized states. Table 30 shows the twelve states in which unionized libraries exist and the national ranking of each state in terms of proportion of union membership and existence of right-to-work laws. As can be seen, each state in which library unions have been formed also has a relatively high proportion of union members and no right-to-work statutes.

Another measure of the degree of union strength in individual states is provided by the extent of unionization among public school teachers. Table 30 also shows for each state with library unions: (1) the percent of instructional (professional) personnel in school systems which have writ-

[31] Bain, *White-Collar Unionism*, p. 85.
[32] *Municipal Yearbook, 1969*, p. 34.

TABLE 30
UNION STRENGTH OF STATES

States with Unionized Libraries (1971)	Ranking by Total Union Membership as Proportion of Total Non-agricultural Employment (1968)[a]	Existence of State Right-to-Work Law[a]	Percentage of Instructional Personnel in Systems with Agreements (1968–69)[b]	Percentage of Comprehensive Agreements (1967–68)[c]
California	12	No	96	0
Connecticut	23	No	87	87
Illinois	8	No	67	23
Maryland	26	No	89	10
Massachusetts	21	No	80	95
Michigan	5	No	98	100
Minnesota	15	No	83	0
New Jersey	16	No	49	2
New York	4	No	91	21
Ohio	9	No	69	2
Pennsylvania	3	No	42	6
Wisconsin	11	No	72	41
District of Columbia	—	—	100	100

[a]*Directory of National and International Labor Unions* (Washington, D.C.: Dept. of Labor, 1969).
[b]*Negotiation Research Digest* 2:B–5 (June 1969).
[c]Ibid. 2:B–2 (Mar. 1969).

ten negotiation agreements, and (2) the percent of these agreements that are comprehensive in nature. A comprehensive agreement refers to an agreement which recognizes either the American Federation of Teachers (AFT) or the National Education Association (NEA) as the teachers' representative and contains specific items relating to salaries and other personnel and employment conditions which have been negotiated by the school board and the teachers' representative. This is in contrast to a "procedural" agreement where no specific items have been negotiated or agreed upon by the parties. The existence of a comprehensive agreement represents a truer form of unionization. As can be seen in table 30, in eight out of the twelve states (including the District of Columbia), 80 percent or more of the teachers are covered by an AFT or NEA agreement. In four of the states the agreement is likely (50 percent chance) to be comprehensive in nature. By comparison, only thirteen of all states had 80 percent or more teachers covered by agreements, and only five had 50 percent or more comprehensive agreements.

Even though library unions have been formed in regions and states with high overall unionization, it is of more consequence to investigate the relationship with individual cities since the proximity effect is more immediate. Unfortunately, little comparable data are available on the extent of private or public sector unionization for individual cities. Those which are available are given in table 31. Columns 1 to 3 show unionization data for public works, fire, and police department personnel for cities where unionized libraries exist. These occupations generally represent the most highly organized municipal employees.

Column 1 gives the number of divisions of public works employees represented by unions. According to the *Municipal Yearbook*, the highest number of unionized departments in 1969 for all cities with population of 25,000 or greater was six; the modal number was one. Twelve cities had four or more unionized departments, and column 1 shows that library unions exist in four of them.

Column 2 gives the estimated percent of fire department personnel who were unionized in 1969. As can be seen, all cities with library unions for which data are available also have a high degree of unionization among firemen. The measure is practically useless, however, since over 80 percent of all cities with population of 25,000 or greater reported a high degree of unionization among firemen. Column 3 gives the degree of unionization among police personnel for 1968–69. One-third of the cities with library unions for which data are available also report union activity among policemen. This is in contrast, however, to the fact that slightly more than 50 percent of all cities with population of 50,000 or more have unionized police personnel.

137

TABLE 31
UNION STRENGTH OF CITIES

City	Public Works Unionized Employee Divisions (1969)[a]	Percentage of Unionized Fire Department Personnel (1969)[b]	Percentage of Unionized Police Department Personnel (1968–69)[c]	Number of Local Unions Affiliated with National Unions (1967–68)[d]	Existence of Negotiated Agreements for Teachers (1971)[e]	Existence of Negotiated Agreements for Nurses (1971)[f]
Baltimore	2	85	59	2	Yes (AFT)	Yes
Berkeley	2	88	0	3	—*	—
Boston	5	—	—	8	Yes (AFT)	Yes
Buffalo	—	—	0	7	—	—
Chicago	—	85	0	65	Yes (AFT)	Yes
Cleveland	—	94	97	27	Yes (AFT)	Yes
Detroit	5	94	0	9	Yes (AFT)	Yes
District of Columbia	—	—	92	6	Yes (AFT)	Yes
Enfield	1	—	—	—	—	—
Los Angeles	4	29	0	6	No	Yes
Milwaukee	3	85	—	13	Yes (NEA)	Yes
Minneapolis	—	94	0	—	Yes (AFT/NEA)	Yes
New York	5	92	0	72	Yes (AFT)	Yes
Newark	4	—	6	2	Yes (AFT)	Yes
Oakland	3	93	0	9	—	—
Oshkosh	2	99	—	2	—	—
Philadelphia	—	—	100	3	Yes (AFT)	Yes
San Francisco	—	97	0	6	No	Yes
Santa Monica	2	97	0	2	—	—
Youngstown	—	100	—	—	—	—

a 1971 Municipal Yearbook, pp. 172–78.
b 1970 Municipal Yearbook, pp. 406–37.
c 1969 Municipal Yearbook, pp. 338–69.
d 1968 Municipal Yearbook, pp. 225–38.
e Data obtained from NEA Headquarters, 1971.
f Data obtained from ANA Headquarters, 1971.
* Data not available.

Column 4 shows the number of local unions of municipal employees which were affiliated with national labor unions in 1967–68. According to the *Municipal Yearbook*, the modal number of locals for all cities with population of 50,000 or more is zero. Fourteen cities reported ten or more locals, and column 4 indicates that library unions exist in four of them.

Column 5 shows those cities where either NEA or AFT negotiated comprehensive agreements in 1971. As can be seen, comprehensive agreements exist in more than half the cities. A comparison with the total number of agreements in all cities in the United States is not possible because of lack of data.

Finally, column 6 shows those cities where state nurses' associations negotiated collective bargaining agreements in 1971. Although all cities which have library unions have American Nurses' Association (ANA) contracts as well, not all nurses in those cities are necessarily covered. Nurses are employed in many different agencies and institutions, both privately and publicly owned, within each of the cities. In some, the agreement may cover only those employed by one agency; and in others, a number of agreements may exist covering the majority of nurses in the area. Comparable data for all cities in the United States are not available.

These statistics demonstrate that library unions have emerged in cities with relatively high unionization. Although the statistics are not complete, they are sufficient to suggest that proximity to organized employees is an important factor affecting propensity to unionize.

Legislative Climate

Whether employees have the legal sanction to organize and bargain collectively may affect propensity to unionize. Historically, most public employees have lacked legislation protecting their right to unionize. The National Labor Relations Act of 1935, which insured the right of private employees to join unions, specifically excluded from its scope "employees of the United States or any State or political division thereof." Most state labor relations laws enacted about the same time were more vague as to whether they applied equally to public and private employment, but it was generally assumed that they did not. In 1946, the Florida Supreme Court sustained this assumption, declaring that a public authority had "none of the peculiar characteristics of private enterprise."[33]

Other court decisions around the same time never actually stated that public employees were prohibited from joining labor unions, but neither did they prohibit administrators from discouraging union membership. In

[33] Miami Water Works Local 654 v. City of Miami (1946) 26 So. (2d) 194.

1930, the Washington State Supreme Court upheld the right of the Seattle school board to require prospective teachers to sign "yellow-dog" contracts—declarations that they were not and would not become union members during the course of their employment.[34] Five years later the Virginia Supreme Court upheld the right of the city manager of Norfolk to issue a rule forbidding firemen to join a labor union.[35] In 1946, the United States Supreme Court refused to review a decision by the Mississippi Supreme Court upholding the discharge of policemen by the city of Jackson for joining a trade union.[36] Thus, the highest court in the land, by implication, endorsed the doctrine that as long as there is no legislation prohibiting employing authorities from limiting or preventing the organization of their employees, the former's right to do so is proper exercise of administrative discretion.

During the past ten to twenty years, the legislative climate has changed radically. One expert concluded that "it is now taken as *datum* that government employees generally, including those serving municipalities, may, even in the absence of express statutory authorization, band together for purposes of their mutual aid and protection."[37] Early court decisions have generally been reversed, and judicial guarantee has been given to the right of public employees to join labor unions. One New York court affirmed that public employees ". . . have the same right to mutual help and assistance that other citizens have, and to group themselves together for that purpose." A Connecticut court stated that ". . . in the absence of prohibitory statute or regulation, no good reason appears why public employees should not organize as a labor union."[38]

During the past ten years, many states and municipalities have enacted legislation granting their employees the right to organize and bargain collectively, although they vary widely in scope and rights conferred. Few states have granted these liberties on a basis that is par with the private sector. Most notable is the denial of public employees to strike. In addition, the right of unions to negotiate collective agreements with state and local governments is less well established than in private industry.[39] Several statutes require governmental agencies to "meet and confer" with union representatives, but do not require that they reach binding written agreement.

[34] Seattle High School Teachers Chapter 200 v. Sharpless (1930) 159 Wash. 424.

[35] Carter v. Thompson (1935) 164 Va. 312.

[36] City of Jackson v. McLeod (1946) 90 L. Ed. 1261.

[37] Everett Kassalow, "White-Collar Unionism in the United States," in *White-Collar Trade Unions*, ed. Adolf Sturmthal (Urbana: Univ. of Illinois Pr., 1966), p. 334.

[38] Ibid.

[39] Ibid., p. 335.

Experience in the private sector shows that governmental intervention protecting the right of workers to organize and bargain collectively stimulates union membership. The most important federal protective venture for the private sector was the National Labor Relations Act enacted in 1935. Immediately after its passage, and for the next two years, total union membership increased faster than at any other time in history.[40]

The same phenomenon has occurred among public employees. In 1962, President Kennedy issued Executive Order 10988, which directed federal government agencies to recognize employee organizations. This, in turn, provided the impetus for state and municipal legislation granting the right of local public employees to organize. As a result, between 1960 and 1968, public employee unionism rose by 101.4 percent.[41]

There is a positive relationship between the existence of library unions on the one hand, and favorable state and local labor legislation on the other. Table 32 summarizes labor relations policies of the twelve states

TABLE 32
STATE LABOR RELATIONS POLICY

State/Date	Right to Organize	Right to Bargain Collectively	Right to Meet and Confer	Requirement to Reach Binding Written Agreement
California, 1968	Yes	No	Yes	No
Connecticut, 1967	Yes	Yes	—	Yes
Illinois	No	No	No	No
Maryland	No	No	No	No
Massachusetts, 1965	Yes	Yes	—	Yes
Michigan, 1965	Yes	Yes	—	Yes
Minnesota, 1965	Yes	No	Yes	No
New Jersey, 1968	Yes	Yes	—	Yes
New York, 1967	Yes	Yes	—	Yes
Ohio	No	No	No	No
Pennsylvania, 1970	Yes	Yes	—	Yes
Wisconsin, 1966	Yes	Yes	—	Yes

SOURCE: *Labor Management Policies for State and Local Governments*, Advisory Commission on Inter-Governmental Relations, Washington, D.C., Sept. 1969.

[40] Irving Bernstein, "Growth of American Unions," p. 303.
[41] Abraham L. Gitlow, "Public Employee Unionism in the United States: Growth and Outlook," *Labor Law Journal* 21:766–67 (Dec. 1970).

where library unions have been formed. As can be seen, all but three states protect the right of public employees to organize; and all but five guarantee the right to bargain and to reach a binding agreement. Two of these five exceptions, California and Minnesota, stipulate that employees may "meet and confer," but do not go so far as to require public agencies to reach agreement.

Table 33 summarizes local legislation pertaining to each unionized library. Cursory observation shows that in the great majority of cases, unionization has been accompanied by favorable legislation.

The existence of favorable labor legislation partially eliminates one of the main factors that hindered early library unions. It was observed earlier

TABLE 33

LOCAL LABOR RELATIONS POLICY

City/County	Right to Organize	Right to Bargain Collectively	Right to Meet and Confer	Right to Reach Collective Bargaining Agreement*
Baltimore	Yes	—	—	—
Berkeley	Yes	No	Yes	Yes
Bloomfield, New Jersey	Yes	Yes	—	Yes
Boston	Yes	Yes	—	Yes
Brooklyn	Yes	Yes	—	Yes
Buffalo and Erie County	Yes	Yes	—	Yes
Chicago	No	No	No	No
Cleveland	No	No	No	No
Contra Costa County	No	No	Yes	No
Detroit	Yes	Yes	—	Yes
District of Columbia	Yes	—	—	—
Enfield	Yes	Yes	—	Yes
Los Angeles	Yes	No	Yes	No
Los Angeles County	Yes	Yes	—	Yes
Milwaukee	Yes	Yes	—	Yes
Minneapolis	Yes	No	Yes	No
Morris County, New Jersey	Yes	Yes	—	Yes
New York	Yes	Yes	—	Yes
Newark	Yes	Yes	—	Yes
Oakland	Yes	No	Yes	No
Oshkosh	Yes	Yes	—	Yes
Philadelphia	Yes	Yes	—	Yes
Queens Borough	Yes	Yes	—	Yes
San Francisco	Yes	No	Yes	Yes
Santa Monica	Yes	Yes	—	Yes
Youngstown and Mahoning County	No	No	No	No

*Or Memorandum of Understanding

that approximately half of the unions which dissolved between 1917 and 1945 did so as a result of strong opposition by library administrators. Today, administrators in some states would face court charges of "unfair labor practices" for similar opposition. One administrator of a recently unionized library commented, "I am not happy with it [unionization] but according to the law I have no choice."

Several studies imply that today, most library administrators have a more favorable view of unionization. In a 1967 survey of seventy administrators, 68 percent stated they were neutral toward unionization of library employees; 3 percent stated they would encourage unionization; 20 percent said they would discourage it; and 9 percent made no comment.[42] In a survey of Pennsylvania libraries, Vignone found that library directors and librarians did not differ significantly in reaction toward a model of collective bargaining procedures for public library employees. Library trustees, however, were significantly less amenable to the procedures.[43] It is noteworthy to mention that the opinions reflected in these surveys are generally based on the assumption that unionization will not actually occur. A 1969 survey asked the following question of 100 public library administrators, "Do you anticipate unionization anytime in the near future?" Seventy-five percent responded with "no"; 9 percent, "yes"; 9 percent were not certain; and 7 percent gave no reply.[44]

Net Effect of Environmental Factors

The preceding sections established that the three environmental factors studied are potentially significant in promoting library unionism. But the interrelations between the factors has prevented the verification of any one as being singularly significant. That is, the concentration of unions in large libraries may be due to the effects of bureaucratization; to the fact that the larger cities in which the libraries are located tend to be more extensively unionized, thus enabling the concept of proximity to organized employees to take effect; or to the fact that favorable labor legislation is more likely to exist in larger cities.

To determine the independent effect of each factor, the analysis must proceed in a manner which enables each factor to be controlled. The small number of library unions and the relative scarcity of data do not allow a complete analysis of this type. Nevertheless, by using the data which are available, a rough attempt has been made to perform a controlled form of

[42] "Collective Bargaining: Some Questions Asked," p. 975.

[43] Vignone, *Collective Bargaining Procedure*, pp. 116–18.

[44] Bundy and Wasserman, *The Public Library Administrator,* Preliminary Analysis, p. 33.

TABLE 34
Controlling for Employment Concentration: States

State	National Ranking by Union Membership (1968)[a]	Proximity to Organized Employees		
		Right-to-Work Law (1968)[a]	Percentage of Instructional Personnel in Systems with Agreements (1968–69)[b]	Percentage of Comprehensive Agreements (1967–68)[c]
Union:				
Connecticut	23	No	87	87
Illinois	8	No	65	22
Maryland	26	No	89	10
Massachusetts	21	No	80	95
Michigan	5	No	98	100
Minnesota	15	No	83	0
New Jersey	16	No	(49)	(2)
New York	4	No	91	21
Pennsylvania	3	No	(42)	(6)
Wisconsin	11	No	72	41
District of Columbia	—	—	100	100
Nonunion:				
Colorado	24	No	82	4
Florida	44	Yes	43	0
Hawaii	19	No	0	0
Indiana	6	No	39	4
Kentucky	18	No	37	0
Missouri	7	No	47	0
Oregon	13	No	90	(0)
Texas	46	Yes	30	0
Washington	2	No	95	1

study. For this purpose, proximity to organized employees and legislative climate are treated as a combined factor. Information is completely inadequate to permit examination of their independent effects upon unionization.

HOLDING EMPLOYMENT CONCENTRATION CONSTANT. The effect of employment concentration has been controlled by comparing large union and nonunion libraries with respect to the other two factors. The country's fifty largest libraries in terms of number of professional positions were taken from the 1968 *Library Statistics*. County libraries were eliminated from the list since data on the other factors are not available for counties. In addition, libraries which would be subject to similar influences were excluded from consideration (i.e., Brooklyn, Queens Borough, and New York libraries would be similarly influenced by the same legislative climate). The result is a list of twenty-six libraries, exactly half of which currently have union activity. Tables 34 and 35 compare these libraries

TABLE 34 (Continued)
CONTROLLING FOR EMPLOYMENT CONCENTRATION: STATES

	Legislative Climate: 1969			
State	Right to Organize	Right to Bargain Collectively	Right to Meet and Confer	Requirement to Reach Binding Written Agreement
Union:				
Connecticut	Yes	Yes	—	Yes
Illinois	No	No	No	No
Maryland	No	No	No	No
Massachusetts	Yes	Yes	—	Yes
Michigan	Yes	Yes	—	Yes
Minnesota	Yes	No	Yes	No
New Jersey	Yes	Yes	—	Yes
New York	Yes	Yes	—	Yes
Pennsylvania	Yes	Yes	—	Yes
Wisconsin	Yes	Yes	—	Yes
District of Columbia	—	—	—	—
Nonunion:				
Colorado	No	No	No	No
Florida	Yes	No	No	No
Hawaii	Yes	No	No	No
Indiana	Yes	No	Yes	No
Kentucky	Yes	No	Yes	No
Missouri	Yes	No	Yes	No
Oregon	Yes	Yes	—	No
Texas	Yes	No	No	No
Washington	Yes	Yes	—	Yes

NOTES: Data in parentheses represent unionization data for individual states that are not strictly comparable because labor legislation was enacted during the intervening years. All data regarding Legislative Climate, 1969, are from *Labor Management Policies for State and Local Governments*, Advisory Commission on Inter-Governmental Relations (Washington, D.C., 1969).

[a]*Directory of National and International Labor Unions* (Washington, D.C.: Dept. of Labor, 1969).
[b]*Negotiation Research Digest* 2:B–5 (June 1969).
[c]Ibid. 2:B–2 (Mar. 1969).

with respect to state and city data, respectively, on degree of unionization and legislative climate. The tables were created by expanding tables 30, 31, and 32 to include data for each nonunion library.

A few explanatory notes are in order. In the case of local legislation covering union and nonunion libraries, specific data are not available for all of the latter. So a new measure is used in table 35. The *Municipal Yearbook* reports for most cities whether there exists formal collective

TABLE 35
Controlling for Employment Concentration: Cities

City	Public Works Unionized Employee Divisions (1969)	Proximity to Organized Employees				
		Percentage of Unionized Fire Department Personnel (1969)	Percentage of Unionized Police Department Personnel (1968–69)	Number of Local Unions Affiliated with National Unions (1967–68)	Existence of Negotiated Agreements for Teachers (1971)	Existence of Negotiated Agreements for Nurses (1971)
Union:						
Baltimore	2	85	59	2	Yes (AFT)	Yes
Boston	—	—	—	8	Yes (AFT)	Yes
Chicago	—	85	0	65	Yes (AFT)	Yes
Cleveland	5	94	97	27	Yes (AFT)	Yes
Detroit	—	94	0	9	Yes (AFT)	Yes
District of Columbia	—	29	92	6	Yes (AFT)	Yes
Los Angeles	4	85	0	6	No	Yes
Milwaukee	3	94	—	13	Yes (NEA)	Yes
Minneapolis	—	—	0	0	Yes (AFT/NEA)	Yes
Newark	4	—	(6)	(2)	Yes (AFT)	Yes
New York	5	92	0	72	Yes (AFT)	Yes
Philadelphia	—	—	100	3	Yes (AFT)	Yes
San Francisco	—	(97)	(0)	(6)	No	Yes
Nonunion:						
Akron	—	91	98	2	Yes (NEA)	No
Cincinnati	3	96	95	6	Yes (NEA)	Yes
Dallas	—	70	78	—	No	Yes
Denver	1	61	0	11	Yes (NEA)	No
Honolulu	1	86	28	2	No	Yes
Indianapolis	—	97	—	1	Yes (NEA)	No
Long Beach	3	90	0	2	No	Yes
Louisville	2	—	100	3	—	Yes
Miami	2	85	100	3	No	No
Portland	—	98	80	12	Yes (NEA)	Yes
San Diego	2	—	0	2	Yes (NEA)	Yes
Seattle	3	99	0	25	Yes (NEA)	Yes
St. Louis	5	90	0	17	—	—

Legislative Climate

City	Collective Bargaining Policy with Unions of City Employees (1967–68)[a]	Collective Bargaining Policy with Public Works Departments (1969)[b]	Labor Contract with Public Works Departments (1969)[b]	Labor Contract with IAFF (1969)[c]	Contract with Library Union
Union:					
Baltimore	No	Yes	Yes	—	(—)
Boston	Yes	—	—	—	(Yes)
Chicago	No	—	—	No	(No)
Cleveland	Yes	—	—	No	(No)
Detroit	Yes	Yes	Yes	Yes	(Yes)
District of Columbia	Yes	Yes	No	—	(—)
Los Angeles	Yes	Yes	No	No	(No)
Milwaukee	Yes	Yes	Yes	Yes	(Yes)
Minneapolis	—	—	—	No	(No)
Newark	(No)	Yes	No	—	(Yes)
New York	Yes	Yes	Yes	Yes	(Yes)
Philadelphia	Yes	—	—	—	(Yes)
San Francisco	(No)	—	—	(No)	(No)
Nonunion:					
Akron	Yes	—	—	No	—
Cincinnati	Yes	Yes	No	No	—
Dallas	—	—	No	No	—
Denver	No	No	No	No	—
Honolulu	No	Yes	No	No	—
Indianapolis	No	—	—	No	—
Long Beach	No	No	No	Yes	—
Louisville	No	Yes	Yes	No	—
Miami	No	No	No	Yes	—
Portland	No	—	—	—	—
San Diego	No	Yes	No	Yes	—
Seattle	No	Yes	Yes	Yes	—
St. Louis	No	No	No	No	—

NOTE: Data in parentheses represent unionization data for individual cities that are not strictly comparable because labor legislation was enacted during the intervening years.

SOURCE: For first part of table, see table 31.

[a] *1968 Municipal Yearbook*, pp. 225–38.
[b] *1971 Municipal Yearbook*, pp. 172–78.
[c] *1970 Municipal Yearbook*, pp. 406–37.

bargaining and a negotiated contract with public works department unions, with the International Association of Fire Fighters (IAFF), and whether there is a formal policy of collective bargaining with unions of city employees. A comparison of these data for unionized libraries in table 35 with data contained in table 33 shows the measures are generally accurate in predicting how local legislation would apply to organizing and bargaining rights of nonunionized libraries. In addition, all the data contained in tables 34 and 35, and all the proceeding tables of this section, are from 1967–68 to 1971 sources. In some cases, unionization data for individual cities or states are not strictly comparable because labor legislation was enacted during the intervening years. Where this is known to be the case, the data are enclosed in parentheses. In all instances, the more recent data should predominate. Finally, in table 34, states have been disregarded in cases where they would occur in both the union and nonunion sections.

The first part of table 34 shows that among states, little difference exists between the degree of unionization in the union and nonunion sectors. The data indicate that library unions could be just as likely to emerge in several nonunion states as in the union states. The only significant variation is in the percent of comprehensive agreements for teachers, which differs markedly between the two sections. But this is more of a reflection of legislative climate than extent of unionization, since the existence of a comprehensive agreement is dependent upon permitting legislation.

The second part shows that although the right to organize is prevalent in both sections, there is some difference in the right to bargain, and a significant difference in the right to reach a binding agreement. All but two of the union states grant the right to bargain or to meet and confer, compared with four exceptions among the nonunion states. However, most nonunion states only permit parties to meet and confer, and only one specifies that a contract be reached.

The first part of table 35 reveals little variation in the degree of unionization of public works department, police, fire, teacher, and nursing personnel. The only outstanding difference in the first part is the predominance of AFT in the union, and of NEA in the nonunion sections. The second part again reveals a slight variation in legislative climate. Both sections generally permit the right to organize, but labor contracts are more common in the union section, indicating a more liberal legislative climate.

Hence, the tables demonstrate that when library size is roughly controlled, there does exist a difference between union and nonunion sectors. The variation is more significant with respect to measures of legislative climate than with degree of unionization.

HOLDING DEGREE OF UNIONIZATION AND LEGISLATIVE CLIMATE CONSTANT. To control for the factor proximity to organized employees, a measure of extent of unionization is used. The measure for state comparisons is total union membership as a proportion of nonagricultural employment. Column 1 of table 36 gives the twenty states with the highest proportion of union membership, and column 2 the number of library unions that exist in each state. Significantly, all but four of the current unionized libraries exist in states with a relatively high degree of unionization.

Column 3 of table 36 shows the sixteen states which, in one expert's opinion, have the most comprehensive legislative enactments in the area of public employee bargaining rights.[45] Five of the thirteen states in which library unions exist (including the District of Columbia) do not have relatively comprehensive legislation. When degree of unionization and legislation are considered together, they can "explain" only twelve of the twenty-six unionized libraries (see boxes).

An index of union strength in individual cities was developed by using the number of unionized public work departments and the number of locals of city employees affiliated with national labor unions. Part 1 of table 37 shows all cities which have either three or more unionized public work departments or five or more locals of city employees. For the former measure, the mode of all cities in the United States is one; for the latter, the mode is zero. The limits of three and five, respectively, were chosen so as not to bias the measure to include only large cities. As can be seen from Part 1, nine of the current twenty-one unionized libraries included in the table exist in cities which according to the index represent the most extensively unionized in the country. Data were not available for three of the nine exceptions, but these are generally known to be strongly unionized (Philadelphia; Minneapolis; and Youngstown, Ohio). Five unionized libraries were not included in the table because of lack of data (Brooklyn, Queens, Los Angeles County, Morris County, and Contra Costa County). Three of these libraries—Brooklyn, Queens, and Los Angeles County— are known to be located in strongly unionized areas. Thus, it can be said that only eight of the twenty-six unionized libraries are in localities where unionization is not particularly strong.

Measures of local legislative climate used previously are shown in Part 2 of table 37. As the table indicates, in most cities where there is a library union, there is also a contract with IAFF or unions of public works employees, or a formal policy of collective bargaining with city employees. This indicates a relationship between library formation and favorable legislative climate. The reverse relationship does not always hold, how-

---

[45] Seidman, "State Legislation," pp. 13–14.

TABLE 36
CONTROLLING FOR DEGREE OF UNIONIZATION AND
LEGISLATIVE CLIMATE: STATES

Rank by Union Membership (1968)	Number of Library Unions	Comprehensive Legislative Enactment (1971)
West Virginia (1)	0	No
Washington (2)	0	Yes
Pennsylvania (3)	1	Yes
New York (4)	4	Yes
Michigan (5)	1	Yes
Indiana (6)	0	No
Missouri (7)	0	No
Illinois (8)	1	No
Ohio (9)	2	No
Alaska (10)	0	No
Wisconsin (11)	2	Yes
California (12)	7	No
Oregon (13)	0	Yes
Montana (14)	0	No
Minnesota (15)	1	Yes
New Jersey (16)	3	Yes
Nevada (17)	0	No
Kentucky (18)	0	No
Hawaii (19)	0	Yes
Delaware (20)	0	Yes
Others:		Others:
Connecticut	1	Connecticut
Massachusetts	1	Massachusetts
Maryland/District of Columbia	2	Maine
		Rhode Island
		South Dakota
		Vermont
	26	

ever. There are several instances where a favorable climate seems to exist, but where no library unions have been formed.

When degree of unionization and legislative climate are considered together, the lack of this inverse relationship becomes more prominent.

150

That is, in several cities where measures indicate unionization is strong and legislation is favorable, library unions do not exist.[46] Significantly, the total and professional staff sizes of libraries in these cities are relatively small, with only two exceptions. Hence, it is concluded that proximity to organized employees and legislative climate only partially explain library unionization, and that library size (employment concentration) has an independent influence on union formation.

Conclusion

The three environmental factors that have been examined here appear to have relevance in explaining library unionization. On the basis of the analyses presented, it is concluded that: (1) unions have emerged predominantly in large libraries as a result of the bureaucratization that is inherent in large organizations; (2) library unions are likely to emerge in areas where the degree of general unionization is high; and (3) library unions are likely to emerge in areas where legislative climate is conducive to public employee collective action. The latter two factors are seemingly interrelated: a high degree of unionization tends to foster favorable labor legislation; and favorable legislation, in turn, tends to encourage additional unionization. Data were not sufficient to investigate the direction or strength of these relationships. The controlled form of analyses conducted here suggests that library size (employment concentration), and proximity to organized employees and labor legislation, have independent influences on library union formation.

[46] These libraries are: Seattle, Washington; Cincinnati, Ohio; Dayton, Ohio; Bridgeport, Connecticut; Tacoma, Washington; Great Falls, Montana; Schenectady, New York; Anchorage, Alaska; Granite City, Illinois; Kenosha, Wisconsin; Lawrence, Massachusetts; Manitowoc, Wisconsin.

TABLE 37
CONTROLLING FOR DEGREE OF UNIONIZATION AND LEGISLATIVE CLIMATE: CITIES

	PART 1				PART 2		
City	Library Staff: Total/Professional (1968)	Unionized Public Works Departments (1969)	Number of Local Public Unions (1967–68)	Library Union (1971)	Collective Bargaining Policy with Public Unions (1967–68)	Public-Works Department: Collective Bargaining/Union Contract (1969)	IAFF Contract (1969)
Detroit, Mich.	521/209	5	9	Yes	Yes	Yes/Yes	Yes
Houston, Tex.	—	3	—	No	—	No/No	No
Los Angeles, Cal.	967/300	4	6	Yes	Yes	Yes/No	No
New York, N.Y.	2220/698	5	72	Yes	Yes	Yes/Yes	Yes
Buffalo, N.Y.	840/329	5	7	Yes	Yes	Yes/Yes	Yes
Boston, Mass.	354/86	—	8	Yes	Yes	—	Yes
Cleveland, Ohio	715/150	—	27	Yes	Yes	—	No
Atlanta, Ga.	—	1	6	No	No	No/No	No
Chicago, Ill.	1199/100	—	65	Yes	No	—	No
Denver, Colo.	—	1	11	No	No	No/No	Yes
Kansas City, Mo.	—	1	5	No	No	No/No	No
Milwaukee, Wis.	421/86	3	13	Yes	Yes	Yes/Yes	Yes
Phoenix, Ariz.	—	4	4	No	No	No/No	No
Pittsburgh, Pa.	—	3	12	No	No	No/No	Yes
St. Louis, Mo.	—	5	17	No	No	No/No	No
San Francisco, Cal.	282/110	—	(6)	Yes	(No)	—	(No)
Seattle, Wash.	342/125	3	25	No	No	Yes/Yes	Yes
District of Columbia	490/101	—	6	Yes	Yes	—	No
Cincinnati, Ohio	436/197	3	6	No	No	Yes/No	No
Dayton, Ohio	206/46	2	6	No	No	Yes/Yes	Yes
Long Beach, Cal.	—	3	2	No	No	No/No	No

Newark, N.J.	262/60	(4)	(2)	Yes	(No)	(Yes/No)	(No)
Oakland, Cal.	220/—	(3)	(9)	Yes	(No)	(No/No)	(No)
Portland, Ore.	—	—	12	No	No	—	Yes
St. Paul, Minn.	133/25	—	19	No	No	—	No
San Jose, Cal.	—	3	4	No	No	No/No	No
Des Moines, Ia.	—	4	9	No	No	No/No	No
Fresno, Cal.	—	6	10	No	No	No/No	No
Pasadena, Cal.	—	3	4	No	No	No/No	No
Bridgeport, Conn.	—	2	6	No	No	Yes/Yes	Yes
Chattanooga, Tenn.	—	—	5	No	Yes	—	Yes
Flint, Mich.	129/46	—	8	No	No	No/No	Yes
Peoria, Ill.	—	3	6	No	No	—	No
Syracuse, N.Y.	—	—	6	No	Yes	—	Yes
Tacoma, Wash.	96/26	—	22	No	No	—	Yes
East St. Louis, Ill.	—	—	6	No	No	—	—
Euclid, Ohio	—	—	6	No	No	No/Yes	No
Dubuque, Iowa	—	3	4	No	No	No/Yes	No
Great Falls, Mont.	32/4	3	1	No	Yes	Yes/Yes	Yes
Oak Park, Ill.	—	3	4	No	No	—	—
Richmond, Cal.	—	4	4	No	No	No/No	No
Schenectady, N.Y.	88/23	4	—	No	—	Yes/Yes	Yes
Anchorage, Alaska	11/2	3	—	No	—	Yes/Yes	Yes
Florence, Ala.	—	3	0	No	No	No/No	—
Granite City, Ill.	8/3	4	5	No	No	Yes/Yes	Yes
Hamilton, Ohio	52/3	2	5	No	No	Yes/Yes	No
Joliet, Ill.	—	—	8	No	Yes	—	No
Kenosha, Wis.	41/11	1	6	No	No	Yes/Yes	Yes
Lawrence, Mass.	19/0	1	10	No	No	Yes/Yes	Yes
Newton, Mass.	—	2	5	No	No	Yes/Yes	No
Springfield, Ill.	—	—	6	No	No	—	—
Daytona Beach, Fla.	—	—	5	No	No	—	No
Highland Park, Mich.	—	—	7	No	No	—	No
Manitowoc, Wis.	18/3	2	5	No	Yes	Yes/Yes	Yes

153

TABLE 37 (Continued)
CONTROLLING FOR DEGREE OF UNIONIZATION AND LEGISLATIVE CLIMATE: CITIES

City	PART 1				PART 2		
	Library Staff: Total/Pro-fessional (1968)	Unionized Public Works Departments (1969)	Number of Local Public Unions (1967–68)	Library Union (1971)	Collective Bargaining Policy with Public Unions (1967–68)	Public-Works Departmen: Collective Bargaining/ Union Contract (1969)	IAFF Contract (1969)
OTHER CITIES WITH LIBRARY UNIONS							
Santa Monica, Cal.	67/22	2	2	Yes	No	Yes/Yes	Yes
Philadelphia, Pa.	752/193	—	—	Yes	—	—	—
Youngstown, Ohio	146/27	—	—	Yes	—	—	Yes
Minneapolis, Minn.	283/79	—	—	Yes	No	—	No
Berkeley, Cal.	68/22	(2)	(3)	Yes	(No)	—	No
Oshkosh, Wis.	35/5	2	(2)	Yes	—	Yes/Yes	Yes
Bloomfield, N.J.	42/9	—	—	Yes	(No)	—	—
Enfield, Conn.	—	(1)	—	Yes	—	Yes/Yes	—
Baltimore, Md.	640/172	2	(2)	Yes	(No)	Yes/Yes	—

Chapter 7

A Theory of Library Unionism

In order to present a theory of the library union movement, it is necessary to establish the type of questions such a theory should answer. Dunlop, after reviewing several theories of labor organizations, posed several questions: (1) what accounts for the emergence of labor organizations; (2) what explains their pattern of growth; (3) what are their ultimate goals; and (4) why do individual workers join labor organizations.[1] Since the focus of this study is on aggregate union growth, Dunlop's fourth question is inapplicable. An additional point to be made here is that a theory be capable of forecasting the permanence of the union movement; that is, the theory should identify independent variables whose nature determine the future growth or decline of unionization. This is closely related to Dunlop's first question, but it is explicitly mentioned as a criterion of labor theory since the library union movement has only recently reached momentum.

The suggested criteria that a theory of the library union movement should satisfy are that it: account for the emergence of library unions, define their ultimate goals, explain their pattern of growth, and forecast their permanence. The theory presented here is developed in light of existing theories discussed in the first chapter and the empirical evidence presented in other previous chapters.

Observations

Thus far, the pattern of library unionism has been established and the effects of certain factors in shaping this pattern have been examined herein. These analyses provide observations which serve as tenets upon

[1] Dunlop, "The Development of Labor Organizations," pp. 164–65.

which the theory is centered. The observations can be summarized as follows:

1. Library unions have existed since the late 1910s. They have generally been a phenomenon of large libraries.

2. Their formation has been a reaction to low earnings and undesirable methods of library administration. Programs of early unions emphasized improvements in salaries and working conditions; current unions are giving attention to both earnings and "professional" matters.

3. Several factors demonstrated significance in affecting union formation. Favorable legislation, proximity to organized employees, and bureaucratization will encourage unionization. On the other hand, substitute organizations (staff associations and public employee associations), unfavorable attitude toward unionism, and belief in the incompatibility of union membership and professional standards will discourage unionization.

4. Certain occupational characteristics of the profession, such as the large proportion of females, the advanced median age, and higher social origins, are not significant in deterring or promoting library unionization.

Emergence of Library Unions: A Proposed Theory

It is hypothesized that an important condition leading to the emergence of library unions is that there exists a diminished degree of contact and communication between administrators and librarians. That is, unionization is a reaction to the diminution of daily interactions between the two, created either through the hierarchical structures of bureaucratization or through administrative policy. The motivation toward unionization occurs from an awareness of an incongruence between desired and realized job status. As professionals, librarians have expectations of what their job should entail with respect to function and remuneration. Dissatisfaction arises when the present job is not in accord with expectations. When conditions are such that the dissatisfaction cannot be rectified through personal contact or individual bargaining with management, group action must be relied upon in order to place the staffs' interests to management. The function of the union is to enhance the professional status of the job.

Other writers on library unionization have commented on the importance of the same condition in fostering union formation. Eldred Smith, who wrote one of the first authoritative discourses on the current library union movement, noted the "chasm that has developed between the administrative and nonadministrative librarians." He described the nature of this cleavage at one library:

> Library policy [at University of California, Berkeley] is made by the university librarian, in consultation with a few top admin-

istrators. Once these policies are decided upon, they are discussed, if at all, only with the members of the librarians' Advisory Conference, which is composed of the University librarian, the associate and assistant librarians, the heads of the various library departments and branch libraries, some miscellaneous (and nonprofessional) administrators.

Nonadministrative librarians are not encouraged to concern themselves with policy. Their opinions are not sought in any organized way. . . . If a nonadministrative librarian has any suggestions to make, he is expected to pass them up through the hierarchical structure, beginning with his supervisor.[2]

Another writer, Alice Bryan, concluded in a 1949 study of public libraries, "The growth of library staff organizations and library unions has unquestionably been fostered by the failure of communication between and management and staff."[3]

The division between administrators and staff was also mentioned in the periods of early unionization. For instance, in 1919 a leader of the Library Employees Union of New York made the following comment on the cause of union action: "We have worked under boards of trustees for all these years. They are away from direct contact with us. . . ."[4] In the same year, a *Library Journal* editorial on library unionism stated, "What is needed is a more thoro mutual understanding between Boards of Trustees and administrative officers, on the one hand, and the body of workers on the other."[5] In 1949, a brochure of the Detroit Public Library Employees Union stated that growth in library size had gradually weakened the personal ties between employer and employees, creating the need for an organization to bridge the distance between administration and the staff.

The motivation toward unionization was proposed as a result of an awareness of an incongruence between desired and realized job status, and the function of the union to rectify the incongruence by enhancing the professional status of the job. Activities of library unions suggest two areas where incongruences have occurred: (1) economic remuneration; and (2) participation in library administration.

The constitutions and bylaws of current library unions support this proposition. The Los Angeles Public Library Guild states in its guide

[2] Eldred Smith, "Librarians and Unions: The Berkeley Experience," *Library Journal* 93:719 (Feb. 15, 1968).

[3] Bryan, *The Public Librarian*, p. 264.

[4] "Asbury Park Conference," p. 379.

[5] "Editorial," *Library Journal* 44:350 (June 1919).

lines, "As professional colleagues with the administration, we feel that our ideas are of value and that each of us from our vantage point in the library system has a contribution to make toward policy formulation."[6] Objectives of the San Francisco Public Library Guild are: ". . . to promote the profession of Librarianship by improving salaries and working conditions, by promoting the active participation of members in the formulation of Library policies, by providing a forum from which members can speak to the community about the profession's needs, services and objectives."[7] The purposes of the Librarians' Association of the Buffalo and Erie County Public Library are:

> (a) to further individual and collective professional development; (b) to advance the professional competence of librarians and librarian trainees . . . through studies, research bibliographies, lectures and other suitable means of promoting professional growth; and (c) to achieve improvement in the economic and professional status of its members through implementation of professional negotiations. . . .[8]

The emphasis of early unions was on economic matters. Since the unions emerged during periods when the question of higher salaries was of interest to all workers, it is difficult to justify that the unions' motive was to elevate professional status. Documentation does show that unions frequently drew salary comparisons with other professional workers, particularly teachers, and a few unions stressed the necessity of achieving salaries commensurate with the librarians' training.[9] In addition, Berelson remarked in 1939 that another phase of economic matters with which unionization was concerned ". . . involves the wide spread in library salaries and its implications."[10] The concern was over the wide percent difference between salaries of chief librarian and other administrative positions and that of the library staff. Berelson cites a study showing salary movements between 1934 and 1937. The conclusion was,

> . . . the gains [in 1937] . . . have been largely in the higher salary brackets as compared with 1934. . . . In the lower levels the situation is distinctly less favorable. . . . The average salary of general assistants was $1,395 in 1934, and that average was not raised by a single

---

[6] Librarians' Guild Guide Lines, mimeographed, undated.

[7] Bylaws of the Librarians' Guild of the San Francisco City and County Employees Union, Local 400, mimeographed, undated.

[8] Constitution and bylaws of the Librarians Association of the Buffalo and Erie County Public Library, as amended Feb. 18, 1970, mimeographed, undated.

[9] See, for example, Lucile Speer, "The Professional Worker in Organized Labor," PNLA Quarterly 8:100–1 (Apr. 1944).

[10] Berelson, "Library Unionization," p. 506.

dollar in 1937. The salaries in 1937 of librarians in administrative or executive positions, however, had increased over those of 1934. . . . The efforts of the profession to raise salaries should certainly be centered for some time to come upon the lower brackets.[11]

Previous chapters show that early unions also evidenced some concern over library administration. Towards this end, union programs dealt mainly with seeking improvements in personnel policies. As early as 1935, however, there was proof that sentiments were developing in the direction of "professionalizing" staff positions. This was illustrated by one librarian who was enumerating the contributions staff associations might make to the profession.

> In years past there was frequently a wide diversity between the quality of training of the chief librarian and that of individual members of his staff, but this difference in quality of training is rapidly being eliminated. While it is still an accepted dictum that every library must have an individual who is responsible for the policies and procedures of the institution and who must of necessity have authority commensurate with such responsibility, it seems just as true that as the level of the professional equipment of librarians rises, more cognizance must be granted the right of individual librarians in the ranks to have a voice in the policies of libraries.[12]

Fifteen years later, the first union was organized which explicitly stated as a purpose "affording the employee a greater opportunity to participate in the policies and decisions affecting him."[13]

It was stated in the proposed theory that the function of the library union is to enhance the professional status of the librarians' job. This is accomplished through collective bargaining with administrators or other forms of concerted action such as political lobbying or legislative campaigns. In pursuing its function, it is important to clarify whether the library union is an expression of a conflict of interest with administrators. The clarification is important because as such, the library union takes on the elements of a class ideology; and its members, as professionals, by joining the union must, to some extent, give up a part of their status ideology in favor of a class ideology.[14] It is proposed that librarians' efforts

[11] Ibid., p. 507.

[12] Herman H. Henkle, "The Staff Association as a Unit in Professional Organization," *Library Journal* 60:459–60 (June 1, 1935).

[13] The Detroit Public Library Employees Local 1259, AFSCME, AFL, organized in 1949.

[14] Kenneth Prandy, *Professional Employees* (London: Faber and Faber, Ltd., 1965), pp. 42–43.

to achieve higher professional status do not involve a rejection of administrators' authority, but rather a belief that the staff has a right to share in the exercise of authority. This implies that library unions have emerged from a status ideology rather than from a class ideology where there is a rejection of administrators' authority and a belief that their power must be challenged.

The inclination toward a status ideology is demonstrated to a degree by librarians' rejection of the trade union–class ideology image. Fourteen of the twenty-six current library unions considered in this study have avoided the designation "union" in preference to such titles as "guild" or "association." There has also been a low level of militancy, which connotes a rejection of a concept of conflict.

More importantly, the activities of library unions are closely related to a status ideology. Only several early unions displayed tendencies toward class consciousness. Most notable is the New York union organized in 1917, which disclaimed that librarians are professionals, and declared that ". . . librarians are industrial workers in as high a degree as members of any of our allied trades."[15]

The programs of the majority of early unions to improve salaries and working conditions do not reflect an employer-employee conflict. In most cases, improvements were sought through legislative campaigns conducted in cooperation with administrators. For instance, in 1940 an officer of the Chicago Public Library Employees Union commented on the union's program, which included proper salaries and working conditions and adaptation of modern, democratic personnel policies: "The importance and chief strength of any program lies, of course, in the active support that can be rallied around it. To that end the union has launched an intensive organizational and educational campaign involving the library staff, the administration, and the public."[16] In 1919, the head librarian of the District of Columbia Public Library praised the efforts of the newly organized union. "The avowed purpose of the organizers was to secure a better future for the library and to safeguard it from further disintegration thru constant resignations rather than primarily a hope for personal advantage. Emphatically this is not an anti-administration movement."[17]

The approach taken by current unions to attain greater participation in administrative decisions also is in the form of helping to run the library. For instance, the situation described above by Eldred Smith was met by the union in the following manner: "In its efforts to change this stultifying pattern, the Library Chapter has made two proposals: the institution of

---

[15] "Report of the Library Employees' Union No. 15590," p. 512.
[16] "Letters to Editor," p. 419.
[17] Powerman, "Unionism," p. 365.

professional staff meetings and the inclusion of nonadministrative librarians in the librarian's Advisory Committee."[18]

Even in collective negotiations current unions have enunciated a pattern of participating in library administration rather than challenging its authority. Salary negotiations have departed from standard union practice of establishing automatic salary increases with little leeway for merit consideration; and few agreements give any weight to seniority, most specifying that merit is to take precedence as the basis for rewards.

This general pattern of participation rather than conflict is substantiated by a recent survey indicating librarians' and administrators' opinions of changes in library procedures or methods of decision-making as a result of collective bargaining. One administrator replied, "Staff on all levels might be more closely involved with all kinds of library decisions." Another administrator stated, "Inevitably the staff will have much more voice in budgeting and programming decisions. Priorities in use of available resources will be arrived at through joint consideration." A union leader stated, "Ideally, this process should give the professional staff a stronger voice in policy decisions."[19]

Thus far, it has been proposed that an important condition leading to the emergence of library unions is a diminished degree of contact and communication between administrators and librarians; and that the motivation toward unionization results from an awareness of an incongruence between desired and realized job status. Since the incongruence cannot be rectified through personal contact or bargaining with administrators, it becomes the function of the union to represent the staffs' interests in order to enhance the professional status of the job. This function of the union is based upon a status ideology since there is no evidence that librarians' intentions are to challenge or supplant administrators' authority.

Earlier reference was made to four theorists of the labor movement whose insights aided in the analytical framework of this study. Each of these theorists claimed universality in the application of their particular concepts. But when each theory is analyzed with respect to those criteria a labor theory should satisfy, and in context of the analyses and empirical evidence on the library union movement, three of the four appear to be incomplete or inadequate as a theory of library unionism. A brief statement giving the shortcomings of these theorists in this instance is in order.[20]

Robert Hoxie viewed the union as constituting a group interpretation of the existing social situation, with its function being a remedial program aimed at establishing and maintaining certain conditions of living. The

18 Smith, "Librarians and Unions," p. 719.

19 "Collective Bargaining: Questions and Answers," pp. 1386–87.

20 The reader is referred to the discussion of these theorists in chapter 1.

function of the union is determined by the problems of the specific situation, the attitudes of its members, and the economic conditions of the period. Hoxie's theory is significant in explaining variant forms of unionism since form is dependent upon the particular environmental and personal factors. However, Hoxie's theory does not provide satisfactory answers to each of the four questions posed at the outset of this chapter, and, in fact, Hoxie's socio-psychological interpretation of the emergence of unions denies a "theory of the labor movement." Hence, Hoxie's theory does not provide a satisfactory explanation of the emergence of library unionism, although it may be suited to explaining the particular form and character which library unions have taken.

Sidney and Beatrice Webb gave an economic interpretation of unionism, with the essential cause being the divorce of the worker from the ownership of the means of production. The function of the union is to provide for the democratic participation of workers in the conditions of sale of their services. The Webbs' contribution has been credited more as a statement of the "economic consequences of a labor organization, virtually a theory of wages or collective bargaining," than as a theory of trade unionism.[21] Like Hoxie, the Webbs provide no definitive answers to the four questions posed earlier. It might be argued that the Webbs viewed the economic revolution that separates workers and capitalists as the initiating cause of trade unions, but they contend that the "divorce" does not in itself supply "a complete explanation of the origin of trade unions."

Frank Tannenbaum viewed the origins of unions arising from technological change. As enterprises grew larger, contact between the worker and his employer became less frequent. Unions arise as defense organizations to protect the worker from the dehumanizing effects of the machine process. This argument is similar to that in the proposed theory, with the effects of bureaucratization substituting for (or accompanying) the effect of technological change. However, Tannenbaum goes on to state that through the unions, workers attempt to limit the employer's decision-making function. He envisioned the unions' ultimate triumph over capitalistic opposition, and displacing it by "industrial democracy." It was argued above that library unionism stems from a status ideology. Since Tannenbaum's theory implies a class struggle—a challenge to employer control and an inherent conflict between employer and workers until the unions' triumph—the theory does not accurately conform to the observations of library unionism.

Selig Perlman's theory is centered, in part, on the role of opportunity consciousness. When workers are conscious of a scarcity of job oppor-

---

[21] Dunlop, "Development of Labor Organizations," p. 167.

tunity, the union becomes the instrument by which they assert their collective ownership over the whole amount of opportunity, and parcel it out fairly among their members. The union achieves this through collective bargaining; it seeks to establish "rights" to the jobs by incorporating into the trade agreement regulations applying to, among others, overtime, priority and seniority in employment, apprenticeship, and the introduction of machinery. The union, through collective bargaining, does not attempt to displace or abolish the employer, but attempts to gain rights and considerations for its members equal to those of the employer.

Opportunity consciousness is the crux of Perlman's theory. Without scarcity of job opportunity there would appear to be little need for unions. Perlman states that scarcity consciousness is a product of two main causes. The first stems from a psychic self-appraisal where the worker acknowledges

> . . . his lack of native capacity for availing himself of economic opportunities as they lie amidst the complex and ever shifting situations of modern business. He knows himself neither for a born taker of risks nor for the possessor of a sufficiently agile mind ever to feel at home in the midst of the uncertain game of competitive business.[22]

The second source comes from a survey of accessible opportunity. As a result of "natural" causes (such as a shortage of land) or the "institutional order of things," the worker learns from experience that not only is entrepreneur opportunity limited, but that "the number of jobs available is almost always fewer than the number of job seekers."[23]

Does Perlman's theory of scarcity consciousness relate to librarians' experience with unionism? It was observed that librarians have more or less always enjoyed plentiful job opportunities in the sense that only once during the 1900s has there existed a scarcity of jobs. It was also observed that library unionism has generally been a phenomenon of large bureaucratically structured libraries. Evidence cited earlier showed that bureaucratic structures are often associated with a reduction in the prospects of promotion into the administrative hierarchy. (A surprising 52 percent of the total southern California sample survey for this study disagreed with the statement, "There are many good positions here [in the library system] for those who strive to get ahead.") Perlman's concept of scarcity consciousness conceivably could encompass this form of limited horizontal mobility. Those librarians who believe opportunity is plentiful and that

[22] Charles A. Gulick and Melvin K. Bers, "Insight and Illusion in Perlman's Theory of the Labor Movement," *Industrial and Labor Relations Review* 6:518 (July 1953).
[23] Ibid., p. 519.

the chances are good of moving into the upper echelons of the administrative bureaucracy would not submit to group control. The majority of librarians—those who foresee little chance of mobility into the upper echelons and are conscious of the scarcity of opportunity—may turn to group control. The purpose of group control is to strive toward status equivalent to the administrators not through advancement, but by expansion of the responsibility and authority of present positions.

How does this interpretation of Perlman's theory relate to the proposed theory of library unionism? It was proposed that the condition leading toward the emergence of library unions is a diminished degree of contact and communication between administrators and librarians, created by the hierarchical structures of bureaucratization or administrative policy. It was also proposed that the motivation toward unionization results from an awareness of an incongruence between desired and realized job status. The incongruence cannot be rectified through personal contact or individual bargaining with administrators due to the diminished degree of contact between administrators and librarians. Therefore, collective action is relied upon to represent the staffs' interests to administrators in order to enhance the job to its desired status. The insights of Perlman's concepts enable a refinement of the proposed theory.

In the proposed theory, the condition leading toward unionization is the inopportunity of a close relationship between staff and administrators. In the interpretation of Perlman's theory, the condition is consciousness of scarcity of promotional opportunities. The research and survey findings on bureaucratization presented earlier suggest that the condition in the proposed theory is actually a symptom of limited promotional opportunity, and that the latter condition, in turn, generally stems from the effects of a bureaucratically administered organization. The motivating power toward collective action in both the proposed theory and Perlman's theory is a desire to achieve greater professional and job status. The basic ideology underlying the two theories is the same. The proposed theory postulated that the function of the union is not to challenge administrators' authority, but to share in decision-making and otherwise obtain equivalent status as that of the administrators (with equivalent status defined in terms of both material and nonmaterial rewards). Similarly, Perlman viewed the function of the union not as a vehicle to displace the employer, but as a means to gain rights and considerations equal to those of the employer.

A possible discrepancy between the two theories is Perlman's belief that unions "ration" opportunities among their constituencies and control their members in relation to the conditions upon which members as individuals are permitted to occupy a portion of the opportunity. These functions imply union security provisions and preference of seniority over merit, programs generally not implemented by unions of professional employees. For instance, it was seen that library unions have given little weight to seniority, and have stressed the voluntary nature of membership. However, Perlman attributes these functions only to "mature" trade unionism, which is dependent upon the "psychology" of the laboring man. The psychology, in turn, centers around the concept of opportunity consciousness.

The proposed theory and Perlman's theory can be partially reconciled if opportunity consciousness is considered to be a matter of degree. With a highly pessimistic outlook toward opportunity, the worker psychology will dictate a highly protective attitude toward available opportunities. Since professionals have not been highly protective of opportunities, as deduced from the activities of their representative organizations, it can be inferred that their degree of opportunity consciousness is not overly pessimistic, and that they have not yet reached a "trade union mentality."

Alternatively, Perlman states that the psychology of the laboring man will lead to mature trade unionism when given certain preconditions, namely, the opportunity to exist legally. Professionals' exclusion of union security and seniority rights is deduced from the practices of their unions. But it has been shown here that most state statutes forbid bargaining over traditional union security provisions, and many protect the merit systems of civil service. If given legal sanction, it can only be a matter of speculation whether professionals would respond with a more protective psychology.

Regardless, implicit in Perlman's theory is the prediction that the development of mature trade unionism, through either increasing consciousness of limited opportunity or permitting legislation, will lead to a parcelling of opportunities only among union members. Whether the present emphasis of professional unionism on the voluntary nature of membership and the de-emphasis on seniority rights mark a new dimension in the labor movement, and hence a discrepancy with Perlman's theory, cannot as yet really be determined.

This will be an important question for future research once environmental conditions (namely, labor legislation) are equal for private and public employee unionization. Perlman's concepts of mature trade unionism and the psychology of the laboring man have been attacked as being deduced from less than adequate observations. Perlman's notion of these concepts is derived from practices of labor unions: "Labor's own 'home grown' ideology is disclosed only through a study of the 'working rules' of labor's own 'institutions.' "[24] Gulick and Bers charge Perlman with circular

[24] Ibid., p. 520.

reasoning in this respect. They claim that Perlman was greatly impressed with American labor's preoccupation with control over jobs and wage rates to the exclusion of other types of activity, such as formation of a labor party. They continue that Perlman's psychology of the laboring man is

> inferred from the observed fact of almost exclusive preoccupation with control of job opportunities and the renunciation of other types of activity. On the other hand, the "psychology" is in turn defined as that which is typically preoccupied with "job control" to the exclusion of other types of activity.[25]

Ultimate Goals of Unions

It follows from the preceding section that the ultimate goal of library unions is to "professionalize" librarians' positions, or more exactly, to achieve professional equality with administrators, as defined below. Professionalization is admittedly an inexact term. Prandy notes the numerous attempts to define the terms "profession" and "professionalism," and adds,

> Carr-Saunders and Wilson, the authors of the fullest account of the professions in Britain, did not feel themselves able even to attempt the task, accepting the O.E.D. definition of "a vocation in which a professed knowledge of some department of learning or science is used in its application to the affairs of others or in the practice of an art founded upon it."[26]

The constitutions and programs of library unions signify that "achievement of professional equality with administrators" refers to achieving earnings and utilization of skills and knowledge which are commensurate with librarians' professional training. Since few unions have adopted a class ideology, it appears that professional equality does not encompass achievement of the power and social prestige that may accompany administrative positions.

Pattern of Growth

The pattern of library unionism is affected by several key factors. If the interpretation given to Perlman's theory is acceptable, union emergence

---

[25] Ibid., pp. 520–21.
[26] Prandy, *Professional Employees*, p. 175.

is ultimately determined by the degree of scarcity consciousness, or extent of perceived opportunity. Within this framework, four major influences will shape the pattern of collective action.

1. Growth in library size and staff will tend to generate conditions that provoke collective action. The relationships between library size, bureaucratization, and union formation have been discussed and it is sufficient to say that in the long run, as public libraries increase in size, the prospects of unionization are enhanced.

2. A factor interrelated with library size (bureaucratization) is the aggregate degree of professional training.[27] It was stated in the proposed theory that the motivation toward unionization results from an awareness of an incongruence between desired and realized job status. That is, as professionals, librarians have expectations of what their job should entail with respect to function and remuneration. These professionally orientated expectations are primarily formulated during the years of formal professional training.[28] Several researchers of professionalization have noted the process of "professional socialization" where an individual during the period of professional training, develops a commitment to his professional career and internalizes a professional image which becomes an integral component of his self-concept. Hughes, for example, theorized that "professional education involves the replacement of stereotyped images by more subtle, complex . . . perceptions of the professional role."[29]

As a result of the process of professional socialization, the individual carries to the job a set of expectations regarding the professional status of the job. Material presented earlier showed that conflict often arises when the professional, with his professional expectations, is placed in the context of a bureaucratic organization. Evidence of this conflict is apparent in the survey of southern California librarians. It was found that younger librarians are more likely than older librarians to have earned a master's degree; and, at the same time, less likely to possess favorable attitudes toward job satisfaction and toward the library organization and admin-

---

[27] This refers to the general level of professional training among the nation's librarians, and normally would be measured by the proportion of librarians receiving graduate degrees in library science. The rise in the education level of librarians over the past twenty years was discussed in chapter 5. As of 1969, 74 percent of the librarians in large public libraries reported receiving graduate degrees.

[28] Although professional expectations normally are initially derived during the years of professional training, it has been recognized by some writers that professional orientation continues to develop after graduation from a professional school. *See*, for example, Dan C. Lortie, "Professional Socialization," in *Professionalization*, eds. Howard M. Vollmer and D. L. Mills (New Jersey: Prentice-Hall, 1966), pp. 98–101.

[29] Ibid., p. 101.

istration. Among librarians under 30 years of age, 89 percent held master's degrees; and among those between 30 and 44, 87 percent held master's degrees; but of those librarians 45 years or older, only 65 percent reported having master's degrees. The distribution in attitudes is as follows:

	Under 30	30 to 44	45 and Over
Favorable attitude toward organization and administration	79%	91%	92%
Favorable attitude toward library job satisfaction	58	56	79

A rise in the aggregate degree of professional training alone is not likely to influence the pattern of library unionism. Rather, a rise in the aggregate degree of professional training when accompanied by a bureaucratic organization is likely to lead toward increased motivation for unionization, as librarians attempt to rectify the incongruence between desired (expected) and realized (actual) job status.

3. The utility of substitute organizations will partially determine whether unions emerge. It was concluded earlier that unionization can be thwarted by effective professional and public employee associations. A prime case is the nursing profession, which has received economic and professional representation from local affiliates of ANA. In fact, most professionals have achieved representation through their professional associations. From this pattern comes the dialogue of a new dimension in the labor movement, "a merger of elements of the professional society with those of the labor union."[30]

Public librarians, with no national professional association to turn to (since ALA has excluded itself), appear to have three main alternatives if they seek representation: unions, local staff associations, and public employee associations.[31] The one chosen depends upon an assessment of its utility. The utility of a representative organization can be determined by four factors:

a. Degree of autonomy from administrators. Since the purpose of a representative organization is to present the staff's views to management, it can be assumed that employees will want their organization to be independent from administrators. Unions have the clearest advantage in this respect.

b. Degree of power the organization has to make administrators acknowledge its existence and seriousness of purpose. Once again

[30] Bernard Goldstein, "Some Aspects of the Nature of Unionism Among Salaried Professionals in Industry," *American Sociological Review* 20:205 (Apr. 1955).

[31] A fourth alternative is the state library association, but at this time none has assumed a protective role.

unions are normally the best alternative in this regard, because of the increased power which goes along with labor affiliation. The classic example is the Butte, Montana, union formed in 1934. Library administrators voted to close the library because of inadequate funds. The library staff disagreed with the decision, but was cognizant of its limited power to affect the administrator's choice. So the staff formed a union, affiliated with AFL, and through labor support succeeded in its campaign.

c. Acceptability of the organization. Obviously, an organization formed to represent the staff must be acceptable in form to the majority of librarians. Here, the staff and public employee associations have an advantage over unions, due to the unfavorable connotation unionism denotes to some librarians. This is evidenced by the survey of southern California librarians. Practically all librarians surveyed desired some form of representation, but among those who rejected the library union as this vehicle, the majority gave unacceptability of labor unions as the major reason. Aforementioned studies showed that connotation of unionism is often influenced by proximity to unionized employees. Hence, library unions have been concentrated in areas where overall unionization is common; conversely, few library unions have emerged in nonunion localities. Attitude toward the compatibility of union membership and professional standards also influences the expediency of unionization. The southern California survey showed that the majority of anti-union librarians regard union membership as inconsistent with their professional standards. In the long run, as unionism becomes more accepted and respected as an institution, thus creating less attitudinal resistance, unionization is likely to become a more acceptable alternative to many librarians.

d. The ability of the organization to meet librarians' needs. The staff will select an organization which has the capacity to implement their needs. Currently, the most essential requirement is that the organization be able to represent librarians' "professional" concerns. Public employee associations are at a disadvantage in this regard, particularly when librarians are included in bargaining units representing a variety of public employees. Similarly, many librarians doubt the unions' ability to work toward professional goals.

4. The pattern of library unionism is also affected by labor legislation and proximity to organized employees. The strong relationship between labor legislation supporting public employee rights to organize and library union formation was demonstrated earlier, as was the relationship between proximity to unionization of other employees and library union formation. As protective legislation becomes more widespread and unionization be-

comes a more accepted institution among all employees, the conditions for union formation among librarians become more favorable.

The pattern of library unionism shows that the incidence of unionization among public librarians is relatively low. This is largely influenced by two factors. One important factor is that unions have not been readily available to librarians. This is coupled with the reality that librarians are not actively recruited for unionization. Hence, most library staffs are in the situation of deciding whether or not to organize a union, which is a more arduous decision than debating whether or not to join an available organization. Mills notes that the same phenomenon accounts for the low degree of unionization among white-collar workers in general. "An immensely greater effort over a longer period of time has been given to wage-worker unionism. For most white-collar employees to join or not to join a union has never been a live question, for no union has been available, or, if it has, was not energetically urging affiliation."[32] The lower degree of organization among librarians as compared with such other professions as teaching and nursing is similarly explained by the absence of a national union or representing organization to which librarians can easily become attached.

The lack of a readily available representative organization can reduce propensity to unionize in at least three ways. First, dissatisfaction may be tolerated to a certain extent when there is no accessible vehicle to serve as an outlet. Second, the utility of substitute organizations, particularly staff associations, becomes higher because of their immediacy. Third, if unions were readily available, their active recruitment could cultivate awareness of the necessity of organization.

A second factor explaining the low incidence of unionization among librarians is found in the speculation that librarians are not extensively unionized because there has been no desire for collective action. For instance, one union leader stated that librarians are not a prime target for unionization because they "seem happy and satisfied with pay and working conditions in general."

Although this factor may be obvious, it has considerable merit. The motivation toward unionization was hypothesized to be consciousness of the incongruence between desired and realized status. This motivation, in turn, was shown to be more prone to occur in large-scale organizations because of the greater probability of blockage in interactions between administrators and staff and limited prospects of promotions. Given these conditions, library unionization is likely to be sparse simply because there are not many large-scale libraries. The 1968 *Library Statistics* shows that

32 C. Wright Mills, *White Collar* (New York: Oxford Univ. Pr., 1956), pp. 305–6.

only eighty-three libraries in the country have a total staff of over one hundred; only thirty-three have a professional staff of fifty or more.[33] Hence, employment concentration, which was demonstrated to be a significant factor in promoting particular instances of library unionization, tends to operate against the extensive unionization of the profession.

A related consequence of low employment concentration is that the average library staff size is not conducive to great bargaining power. Undoubtedly, the presumption that organization would have little effect prevents some library staffs from initiating collective action. But this is basically a function of the unavailability of representative organizations. The Butte, Montana, union distinctly illustrates that a small staff can affect a major administrative decision through labor affiliation.

In addition, the claim often advanced that librarians inherently have a minimum degree of bargaining power due to the nonessential nature of library service is not necessarily warranted. Although the instances have been few, militant action by librarians has more often than not been effective. Demonstrations by the Brooklyn and Queens Borough library unions were instrumental in advancing negotiations with library administrators. A strike by the Berkeley union apparently convinced city authorities of the union's seriousness, and a salary agreement was soon reached. A threatened strike by the Chicago union resulted in a last minute appeasement session with the mayor and library administrators, and a resultant agreement giving the union the right to represent its members in processing grievances and submitting suggestions to the library board. Library employees cannot cause severe economic damage, but labor disputes in public agencies can create political repercussions and political embarrassment which can sometimes be as effective as economic damage.

Earlier analyses showed that personal characteristics which characterize librarianship—namely, predominance of females, advanced median age, and higher social backgrounds—are not highly important in influencing aggregate unionization.

Permanence of Library Union Movement

The history of library unionization shows that most unions existed for only a short period of time. The average existence of unions formed prior to 1943 was between four and five years. Their temporal nature is partially explained by some factors discussed in preceding chapters. For instance, many early unions disbanded because of strong opposition by library administrators. This obstacle is removed to a large extent as pro-

---

[33] Boaz, *Statistics of Public Libraries*, pp. 47–64.

tective legislation becomes more widespread and organization among public employees becomes more common. In addition, inadequate and ineffective leadership contributed to the demise of at least several of the early unions.

Using the advantage of retrospect, one variable emerges as highly contributory to the short existence of most unions. It involves the myopic purposes of the majority of unions. As stated previously, the mission of most early unions was improvement in salaries. This objective was relatively easily satisfied through a successful legislative campaign to increase library appropriations, or by better general economic conditions which automatically brought higher library appropriations, and salary raises. Once salary increases were achieved, regardless of the means, interest in the unions generally subsided. The same pattern can occur when the purposes are not purely economic. For example, the primary goal of the Washington, D.C., union organized in 1918, was to secure passage of a reclassification act. The union disbanded the same year as the Reclassification Act was passed. As stated previously and according to a union member, after the act went into effect, ". . . various members of the library staff kept individual [union] memberships . . . out of gratitude and loyalty for what had been accomplished. Little by little, however, there seem [to be] no problems that concerned the library and the members dropped out one by one."[34]

Thus, a distinguishing characteristic of most early unions was the immediacy of their purposes. This bears little relationship to the degree of excellence of the early unions, but rather is more indicative of the short-run concerns of their membership. In contrast, the majority of current unions have combined economic considerations with longer-range professional purposes. The latter have been shown to principally involve increased participation in administrative processes.

For several reasons, the adoption of professional objectives implies a longer duration of unionization. First, administrators are unlikely to give immediate agreement to specific programs proposed by the union to achieve these objectives, largely because administrators will be understandably guarded in protecting their management prerogatives. Second, once agreement is reached, many programs will instill the union's permanence. For instance, agreement on periodic meetings between administrators and staff representatives implies the continuous existence of a representative organization. Third, a union's assumption of professional objectives may lessen librarians' resistance to unionization. If a library union demonstrates that professional issues, such as censorship, are as essential an ingredient of its program as salary considerations, more librarians would be likely to accept union representation.

[34] Berelson, "Library Unionization," p. 495.

Whether the assumption of professional objectives will lead to more permanency in the library union movement than existed in early periods cannot, of course, yet be determined since these objectives have emerged only recently. Theoretically, the current union movement should be relatively stable, provided there is seriousness of purpose in attaining professional objectives.

Conclusion

The purpose here was to present a theory of the library union movement. The theory was developed on the basis of the empirical evidence and analyses conducted in previous chapters and insights provided by existing theories of labor organization.

It was hypothesized that union formation is a reaction to the diminution of daily interactions between the library staff and their administrators. The diminution of interactions is created either through the hierarchical structures of bureaucratization or through administrative policy. Either phenomenon creates a situation where policy formulation and decision-making processes are allocated to administrators, and librarians are relegated to a position of subordination. The motivation toward unionization occurs from an awareness of an incongruence between desired and realized job status. As professionals, librarians have expectations of what their job should entail with respect to function (which includes participation in library administration) and remuneration. Dissatisfaction arises when the present job is not in accord with expectations. When conditions are such that the dissatisfaction cannot be rectified through personal contact or individual bargaining with management, group action must be relied upon in order to place the staff's interests to management. The function of group action, or unionization, is to enhance the professional status of the job so it is in accord with the group's desired status as professionals.

This hypothesized theory was then "refined" through insights provided by Selig Perlman's theory of the labor movement. Perlman's theory centered on the role of opportunity consciousness. When workers are conscious of a scarcity of job opportunity, they will unionize in order to assert their collective "ownership" over the whole amount of opportunity. While it was noted that library unions have not as yet attempted to obtain ownership over available opportunities (through such union programs as seniority, etc.), it was recognized that diminution of interactions between librarians and administrators (through bureaucratic structure or administrative policy) not only removes librarians from the policy formulation and decision-making processes of the library, but also tends to decrease the prospects of promotion into the administrative hierarchy where they can participate in these functions. Thus, when it becomes apparent to librarians that the opportunity to share in administrative functions no longer exists, and when it becomes apparent that the opportunity to later share in these functions through promotion is limited, scarcity of opportunity is realized. With such an outlook, the rational reaction is to adapt to the situation by achieving desired professional status within the scope of present positions by expanding the responsibility and authority of the jobs.

Thus, the goal of unionization is to enhance the "professional" status of the job in order to achieve status equivalent with expectations. Expectations are measured by the amount of professional training and status of administrators. To this end, library unionization is more of an expression of a status than a class ideology since there is no apparent rejection of administrative authority or attempt to displace the administrative hierarchy.

Within this framework, the growth of the library union movement will be influenced by several key factors: (1) growth in library size will tend to generate conditions that provoke unionization; (2) a rise in the aggregate degree of professional training, which influences the professional expectations of the job within the environment of a bureaucratic organization, is likely to intensify the motivation toward unionization; (3) the utility which librarians place on substitute organizations, such as local staff associations, will determine whether unions are selected as a vehicle of representation; (4) supportive labor legislation and proximity to organized employees will promote unionization.

The relatively low degree of aggregate unionization in the library profession is explained largely by the fact that unions have not been readily available to librarians, and by the low degree of employment concentration in most libraries. Personal characteristics which typify the profession do not appear to significantly inhibit unionization.

The permanence of library unions is essentially a function of their purposes. Early unions were characterized by rather immediate purposes, and hence most existed for only a limited time. Most current unions have assumed long-range professional goals as well as short term objectives. Given the seriousness to strive toward the former, current library unionism should be a relatively stable phenomenon.

Basically, the reasons for the emergence of library unions are not too dissimilar from the growth of unionism in general. Both result from Perlman's concept of scarcity consciousness. Thus far, however, library and other professional unions differ in some respects from the form and practices of manual worker unions. It is too early to judge whether this is a manifestation of a new direction in the labor movement, or a result of differing environmental circumstances, such as labor legislation.

Chapter 8

Conclusion

The first task undertaken in this study was a review of early and current library unions. This educed a pattern of library unionism which can be summarized as follows:

1. The aggregate degree of unionization among public librarians is relatively low: an estimated 7 to 10 percent of the country's public librarians were unionized in 1968–69. The degree of unionization is increasing, however. There are more library unions today than existed in total prior to 1960.
2. Both early and current unions emerged predominately in large public libraries; and both have been concentrated in specific geographical regions (eastern and midwestern states, and California).
3. Both economic and noneconomic, i.e., professional, issues have been pursued by the unions. The former were of central importance to early unions, while attention to professional concerns has become more prominent among current unions.
4. Strong administration opposition was instrumental to the demise of many early unions. On the other hand, favorable labor legislation seems to be instrumental in fostering the formation of many current unions.
5. Most library unions have affiliated with national labor organizations, primarily at the instigation of the librarians. There has never existed a systematic effort, either by national unions or by librarians, to organize the profession.

The next procedure in this study was to analyze factors that conceivably could affect the pattern of library unionism. The conclusions can be summarized as follows:

1. Professional and employee associations have not played a major role

in hindering unionization. The American Library Association, the dominant professional association, has been relatively inattentive to economic problems of the profession during the past ten to twenty years. In addition, there is mounting criticism that ALA's organizational structure has made it incapable of adequately representing librarians. (Before 1950, ALA's educational and economic programs were more receptive to needs of librarians. While ALA's programs may not have necessarily hindered unionization, the association did not encourage unionism through neglect of librarians' concerns.) Furthermore, ALA has recently precluded itself from becoming an agent for collective bargaining, an action which could induce more librarians to turn to unions. Several state library associations have deliberated the notion of representing librarians in bargaining situations, but as yet no action has been taken. Local staff associations exist in many large libraries, but studies of their activities show that most are not used extensively as bargaining agents. Public employee associations offer librarians the best alternative to unionization since many are becoming "near unions" as they negotiate for improved salaries and working conditions. Today, however, librarians are paying as much attention to professional concerns as economic improvement, and the ability of public employee associations to accommodate the former is questionable, particularly when librarians are grouped with other public employees.

2. Occupational characteristics were not found to be significant in explaining propensity toward unionization. Pro-union librarians tend to be younger, male, earning a lower salary, better educated, and from lower social origins; but this profile does not significantly differentiate them from anti-union librarians. On the other hand, two attitudinal characteristics demonstrate high significance in impeding union membership. Librarians who perceive membership as being inconsistent with their professional standards, and those who adversely view unionism in general, are highly unlikely to become union members.

3. Economic position of librarians has had a differential effect upon the pattern of library unionism. Most early unions emerged as a reaction to low salaries and high inflationary prices. In contrast, while economic issues are topics of concern to most current unions, they do not emerge as highly significant in promoting current union formation. In addition, there is no evidence to suggest that concerns of unemployment or other matters of employment security have been important in fostering union formation. The only possible exception

is the 1930s depression, when high unemployment may have accompanied low wages in encouraging union formation.

4. Three environmental factors were found to be important in influencing unionization. One is employment concentration. The bureaucratization inherent in large libraries tends to create a structural barrier between administrators and librarians which inhibits their degree of personal contact and communication. A second factor is legislative climate. There is a high positive relationship between the existence of legislation granting public employees the right to organize and bargain collectively, and the formation of library unions. Third, areas with strong labor traditions are more conducive to library unionization than areas with little trade union activity.

The final part of this study presented a theoretical interpretation of the pattern of library unionism. Selig Perlman's concept of opportunity consciousness was interpreted to include opportunity for promotion, and it was hypothesized that unions emerge where there is a pessimistic outlook toward vertical mobility. Additionally, it was hypothesized that the motivation toward unionization stems from an awareness of an incongruence between desired and realized professional status. The goal of unionization is to professionalize librarians' positions in order to achieve status equivalent with their expectations, which are measured by their professional training and status of administrators.

The findings of this study can be usefully summarized in the following three equation descriptive model:

(1) $U = f(O, C)$
(2) $O = g(B, T)$
(3) $C = h(L, P, A)$
Where: U = Library unionization
   O = Degree of opportunity consciousness
   C = Exogenous factors that promote or hinder unionization
   B = Degree of bureaucratization
   T = Degree of aggregate professional training
   L = Legislative climate
   P = Proximity to organized employees
   A = Availability of unions

The first equation states that library unionization is a function of the degree of opportunity consciousness and the nature of certain exogenous factors that promote or hinder unionization. Consciousness of the scarcity of opportunity must exist before there is a desire to improve present status through unionization. While scarcity consciousness is a necessary condition for unionization, it is not by itself always sufficient. Environmental conditions must be conducive to union formation. Furthermore, when environmental conditions are favorable for unionization, the degree of scarcity and status consciousness is often raised. For instance, the demonstration effects of proximity to unionized employees, or union recruiting, can increase the awareness that comparably situated employees are in a much better position. This can generate an assessment of available opportunity and present status, which can lead to increased propensity to unionize.

The second equation specifies factors that influence opportunity consciousness. An explanatory comment is in order. In this equation, bureaucratization is used synonymously with high degree of employment concentration. The latter is inherent in large libraries, which in turn tend to be bureaucratically administered. But bureaucratization is not an exclusive property of large libraries since it can be effected through administrative policy in small libraries. Because bureaucratization is the most fundamental of these relationships, it is used in the equation instead of employment concentration. Another equation could be added, showing that degree of bureaucratization is a function of employment concentration or administrative policy:

$$(4) \quad B = i(E, AP)$$
Where: E = Employment concentration
AP = Administrative policy

The second equation states that degree of opportunity consciousness is influenced, in part, by bureaucratization. Prior to the development of bureaucratization, administrators and librarians tend to share in policymaking and the exercise of authority. Institutionalization of bureaucracy creates a structural division between administrators and librarians which is based upon specialization of functions. This specialization generally allocates functions involving policymaking and exercise of authority to administrators, and relegates librarians to a position of subordination. When it becomes apparent that the opportunity to share in administrative functions no longer exists, or when it becomes apparent that the opportunity to later share in these functions through promotion is limited, scarcity of opportunity is realized. The same process tends to diminish the librarians' realized professional status.

At the same time, bureaucratization inhibits the degree of contact and communication between administrators and librarians. As a result, when librarians experience grievances or dissatisfactions (over economic and professional matters) they have little opportunity to confront administra-

tors on an individual basis. When enough librarians share similar grievances or dissatisfactions, collective action must be relied upon to effect
changes.

The second equation additionally specifies that degree of opportunity
consciousness is influenced by the aggregate degree of professional training. This factor is interrelated with bureaucratization since in order for an
increase in the aggregate degree of professional training to affect unionization, it must exist within the context of bureaucratization. However, degree
of professional training is included in the model as a factor separate from
bureaucratization because while the *effects* of an increase in professional
training are dependent upon the existence of bureaucratization, the entire
dimensions of the factor are not explained or necessarily influenced by
bureaucratization. In addition, bureaucratization describes an integral endogenous environment in which unionization is likely to occur, but by
itself it does not explain the motivation toward unionization. Professional
training, on the other hand, provides an explanation for the motivation
toward unionization.

As discussed in the preceding chapter, professional training initiates the
process of professional socialization, where the individual develops a commitment to his profession and internalizes a professional image. As a
result of professional socialization, the individual carries to the job a set
of expectations concerning the professional nature of the job. Because of
this professional cognizance, there will always be a natural consciousness
and assessment of professional status (including future opportunity). The
motivation toward unionization occurs when there exists an incongruence
between the desired (expected) and realized (actual) professional status
of the job. If this incongruence occurs in an endogenous environment
where it cannot be rectified on an individual basis with administrators, and
if it becomes apparent that there is limited opportunity to later rectify the
situation through promotion, scarcity of opportunity is realized and unionization is likely to occur.

As the aggregate degree of professional training increases, the aggregate
level of professional cognizance increases, which leads to a more intense
natural consciousness and assessment of professional status and opportunities. If this occurs in a bureaucratic environment (as described above),
the prospects of unionization are enhanced. If there is a low degree of
aggregate professional training, professional cognizance is lower, the natural consciousness and assessment of professional status is less intense,
and the motivation toward unionization is less, whether or not the endogenous environment is bureaucratic.

Hence, degree of opportunity consciousness is influenced by the aggregate degree of professional training, since the level of the latter determines

the level of the professional consciousness and assessment of job status. Degree of opportunity consciousness is also influenced by bureaucratization since the latter determines the extent to which there exists (either presently or in the future) the opportunity to fulfill professional expectations.

The third equation identifies exogenous factors that promote or hinder unionization. Labor legislation guaranteeing the right of public employees to organize and bargain collectively promotes union formation. On the other hand, the absence of favorable legislation does not always prevent unionization. This is exemplified by the existence of library unions during the 1910s and 1930s. But legislative climate indirectly hindered early unionization since judicial interpretation of existing legislation permitted public employers to discourage union membership through a variety of means.

The third equation also states that proximity to organized employees influences unionization. When there is an immediacy of unionization among allied employees, union membership can be fostered by the demonstration of the benefits of labor unions. This, however, is the most speculative of the factors included in the model. Data were not sufficient to allow a thorough analysis of the effects of proximity to unionized employees. In addition, it is entirely possible for this factor to discourage union membership since proximity to unionism can demonstrate the disadvantages of unions as well as the advantages. Furthermore, it is not certain that legislative climate and proximity to organized employees are completely independent factors. Data were inadequate to test the degree of interdependence. The factor is included in the model on the basis of two findings: early and current unions, with few exceptions, have emerged in geographical regions with strong labor union traditions; and the limited analysis conducted earlier signifies that most current unions have emerged in cities with relatively high degrees of public employee unionization.

Finally, the third equation also specifies that unionization will be influenced by the availability of unions. When union membership is readily available, the prospect of unionization is increased. Conversely, as has been the case of librarians, when employees must deliberate not on whether to join but on whether to form a union, the act of unionizing becomes more formidable, and as a result is less likely to occur. Availability of unions also affects the extent of union recruitment. When unions are readily available, employees will be recruited for membership, which provides further inducement toward unionization.

Availability of unions can influence union membership in yet another way. Many professional employees are in a position not normally shared by manual workers: they have a choice of organizations to represent them;

namely, unions, professional associations, and public employee associations. Provided all are available, the one chosen depends upon an assessment of its utility. Utility can be determined by at least four major criteria: degree of autonomy from employers; degree of power the organization has to make employers acknowledge its existence and seriousness of purpose; acceptability of the organization to the employees; and the ability of the organization to meet the employees' needs. If unions are not available, and substitute organizations meet these criteria, labor unionization will be thwarted.

The availability of unions bears some relationship to the legislative climate and proximity to organized employees. When the latter two factors are favorable for unionization, it is more likely that unions will be readily available. Nevertheless, this factor is treated independently in the model because while the above relationship probably holds for many employees, particularly manual workers, it will not always be the case for a numerically small profession such as librarianship.

The equations of the model contain, either explicitly or implicitly, all factors found in this study to be significant in influencing unionization, except for two. Attitude toward unionism and perception of the compatibility of union membership and professional standards were determined to be significant impediments of union membership. To a large extent these factors are important in explaining individual decisions to unionize. But they can also be of consequence in explaining aggregate unionization. To this extent, these factors are related to legislative climate and proximity to organized employees. Several reasons support this association. First, and most importantly, neither factor was found to be significantly correlated with such personal characteristics as age, sex, education, and social origin. By implication it can be inferred that the attitudes reflected by these factors are cultivated by environmental variables. Second, as several writers have noted, it is not unreasonable to expect that the respectability of unions is enhanced by favorable legislation and contact with union members in allied occupations. Arguments to this effect were presented in earlier chapters.

The descriptive model is claimed to be adequate in explaining the library union movement. It states that library unionization is essentially a function of the degree of opportunity consciousness and certain exogenous factors that promote or hinder unionization. The former is influenced by the degree of bureaucracy (determined by employment concentration or administrative policy) and the degree of aggregate professional training; the exogenous factors include legislative climate, proximity to organized employees, and availability of unions. Opportunity consciousness is a necessary prerequisite for union formation, but is not always a sufficient condition unless one or more of the exogenous factors are favorable for unionization.

The model meets the stated objective of this study: it provides an explanation of the patterns of library unionism. Unions have been organized in large libraries and in specific geographical regions as a result of, respectively, bureaucratization and proximity to organized employees. Librarians have sought labor unions because of the disutility of substitute organizations. The incidence of library unionization is greater now than at any other time in history because of higher employment concentration, increased professional training of librarians, and enactment of favorable labor legislation. The low aggregate degree of organization among librarians is accountable by the low level of employment concentration that characterizes the profession and the unavailability of representative organizations. Finally, the trend of increasing unionization among librarians should continue as librarians grow larger, favorable labor legislation becomes more pervasive, and the level of aggregate professional training among librarians continues to rise (within the context of bureaucratization).

The model does not necessarily give an exhaustive explanation of the pattern of library unionism. All that is claimed on its behalf is that the included factors have a systematic and repetitive affect on aggregate library unionization. If the equations of the model were to be estimated, each would contain a standard error to compensate for errors in measurements of the factors included in the model and to account for the influence of omitted factors that have an unsystematic and random influence on library unionization. Nor is the model necessarily suitable in explaining the pattern of aggregate U.S. union membership or patterns of unionism in other occupations, although it should have a basic resemblance to models constructed for these patterns. The model presented here was developed to provide an explanation of aggregate unionization for a particular pattern of unionism.

Appendixes

Appendix A: Questionnaire Distributed to Professionals

Shown in this appendix is a copy of the questionnaire distributed to 715 professionals of six southern California public libraries. For analytical purposes, responses were recoded. The recoded values of each question are given in parentheses. In addition, response categories of individual questions were often grouped. These groupings are evident from the recoded values.

Name of Library _____

PLEASE DO NOT SIGN YOUR NAME

PART I   Check the appropriate response.

1. Sex: Male   (1)
        Female   (0)

2. Age: Under 30   (1)
        30 – 44   (2)
        Over 45   (3)

3. Salary: Under $7,000   (1)
           7,000– 9,000   (1)
           9,000–11,000   (2)
           11,000–14,000 (3)
           14,000–18,000 (4)
           Over 18,000   (4)

4. Education: (Check appropriate blank(s))
   High School (0)   Doctoral:
   Bachelors Degree: PhD (0)
     BA   (0)   DLS (0)
     Lib. Major (0) Other (0)
   Masters:
     MA   (1)
     MALS (1)

5. Marital Status: Single   (1)
                   Married   (0)
                   Widowed   (1)
                   Divorced or
                   Separated (1)

6. Is your spouse employed?
   Yes   (1)
   No   (0)
   Not
   Applicable _____

183

7. How long have you been employed at your present library system?

Less than one year   (1)
   1 – 2 years   (2)
   3 – 5 years   (3)
   6 – 10 years   (4)
 11 – 15 years   (5)
 Over 16 years   (6)

8. How long have you been employed as a librarian?

Less than one year   (1)
   1 – 2 years   (2)
   3 – 5 years   (3)
   6 – 10 years   (4)
 11 – 15 years   (5)
 Over 16 years   (6)

9. At how many library systems have you worked since becoming a librarian?

 1 (0)
 2 (0)
 3 (1)
 4 (1)
 5 (1)
Over 6 (1)

10. Father's Occupation:

Professional   (1)
Businessman or Proprietor   (1)
White-Collar Worker   (1)
Skilled Laborer   (0)
Unskilled Laborer   (0)

PART II   Read each sentence and indicate by circling the appropriate letters whether you Strongly Agree, Agree, Disagree, or Strongly Disagree. A few questions deal with library administrators. These questions pertain to the head librarian and his assistants (i.e., those at the administrative top of the library system). Some questions pertain to your supervisor. They refer to the person to whom you directly report.

	STRONGLY AGREE (SA) (0)	AGREE (A) (0)	DISAGREE (D) (1)	STRONGLY DISAGREE (SD) (1)
11. The library administrators are very competent in their jobs.	SA	A	D	SD
12. I have little opportunity to use my abilities in this organization.	SA	A	D	SD
13. The library's (city's) employee benefit program is adequate.	SA	A	D	SD

	STRONGLY AGREE (SA)	AGREE (A)	DISAGREE (D)	STRONGLY DISAGREE (SD)
	(0)	(0)	(1)	(1)
14. My work gives me a feeling of pride in having done the job well.	SA	A	D	SD
15. I very much like the type of work that I am doing.	SA	A	D	SD
16. The longer one is employed at this library the more he feels that he belongs.	SA	A	D	SD
17. There are many good positions here for those who strive to get ahead.	SA	A	D	SD
18. My supervisor really tries to get our ideas about things.	SA	A	D	SD
19. My job gives me a chance to do the things that I do best.	SA	A	D	SD
20. I am very much underpaid for the work that I do.	SA	A	D	SD
21. This library operates efficiently and smoothly.	SA	A	D	SD
22. The library administrators have a genuine interest in the welfare of employees.	SA	A	D	SD
23. My work is my most rewarding experience.	SA	A	D	SD
24. My supervisor gives us credit and praise for work well done.	SA	A	D	SD
25. My salary is enough to live on comfortably.	SA	A	D	SD
26. My supervisor knows very little about his job.	SA	A	D	SD
27. I really do not feel a sense of pride or accomplishment as a result of the type of work that I do.	SA	A	D	SD

	STRONGLY AGREE (SA)	AGREE (A)	DISAGREE (D)	STRONGLY DISAGREE (SD)
28. I can feel secure about my position as long as I do good work.	(0) SA	(0) A	(1) D	(1) SD
29. It is good for persons in an occupation such as yours to have at least one organization which looks out for the job and professional interests of the members of the occupation.	(1) SA	(1) A	(0) D	(0) SD
30. Unions must bear the major responsibility for the inflation during the past 10 years.	(1) SA	(1) A	(0) D	(0) SD
31. In the long run, unions will do more for librarians than will library administrators.	(1) SA	(1) A	(0) D	(0) SD
32. As compared with management and government, the labor movement represents the best interests of most people.	(1) SA	(1) A	(0) D	(0) SD
33. It is generally known that most unions are corrupt.	(1) SA	(1) A	(0) D	(0) SD
34. The grievance machinery is one of the most important benefits of the collective bargaining contract.	(1) SA	(1) A	(0) D	(0) SD
35. No union can afford to publicly renounce the use of the strike as a collective bargaining weapon.	(1) SA	(1) A	(0) D	(0) SD
36. It is impossible for a librarian to belong to a union, and at the same time to maintain the standards of his profession.	(0) SA	(0) A	(1) D	(1) SD

	STRONGLY AGREE (SA)	AGREE (A)	DISAGREE (D)	STRONGLY DISAGREE (SD)
	(0)	(0)	(1)	(1)
37. The American Library Association should assume a more direct role in improving salaries and other conditions of employment for librarians.	(1) SA	(1) A	(0) D	(0) SD

PART III Check the appropriate response.

38. When did you definitely decide to become a librarian?
    During high school or before   (0)
    As an undergraduate   (0)
    During graduate school   (1)
    After completion of college   (1)

39. If you could do things over, would you choose librarianship again?
    Yes (0)   No (1)   Don't Know (1)

40. Which of the following best describes how you feel about making a job change to another occupation in the near future?
    I have no desire to change occupations. I am satisfied being a librarian. (0)
    I am not actively seeking a change, but I would be prepared to change occupations if the right opportunity came along. (1)
    I am actively interested in changing to another occupation. (1)

41. Are you a member of the American Library Association?
    Yes (1)   No (0)

42. Are you a member of a local professional library association?
    Yes (1)   No (0)   None Exists

43. Are you a member of a union organized within your library or a union of other city or municipal employees?
    Yes (1)   (Proceed to Question 45)
    No (0)   (Proceed to Question 45)
    None Exists

44. If there currently is not a union which you may join, would you be likely to join if one were organized?
    Yes (1)   No (0)

45. If a library union does exist, or if one were to exist, do you think that "professional" and "non-professional" librarians should be included in the same bargaining unit?

Yes <u>(1)</u>   No <u>(2)</u>   Don't Know <u>(3)</u>

Thank you for your cooperation. On the back of this page, please feel free to indicate why, or why not you are a union member; or, if no union exists, why, or why not you would like to become a union member.

Appendix B: Factors of Employee Satisfaction

FACTOR	ITEM NUMBERS ON QUESTIONNAIRE
Organization and Management: Deals with the employee's relationship with management and the organization which management represents to him. It reflects sentiments of identification with the organization and of security for the present and future.	11, 16, 17, 21, 22, 28
Immediate Supervision: Deals with the employee's attitude toward his immediate supervision—both the human relations aspect and the purely administrative aspects of the supervisor's job.	18, 24, 26
Material Rewards: Deals with the material rewards the employee receives from his work both in terms of pay and in terms of employee benefits.	13, 20, 25
Job Satisfaction: Represents the intrinsic satisfactions associated with actually doing the job and with the belief that the job is worthwhile and affords opportunities for personal growth and development.	12, 14, 15, 19, 23, 27

Appendix C: Statistical Tests Used in Study

Shown in this appendix are the statistical tests and formulas used in interpretation of the questionnaire data. All the computations were carried out by the UCLA Western Data Processing Center, using its Statistical Package for the Social Sciences (SPSS). Tests of statistical significance were judged at the .01 level of probability.

Pearson Correlation: Used to obtain a beginning summary statistic describing the strength of association between any two factors measured by the questionnaire.

$$r = \frac{\Sigma_{i=1}^{N} X_i Y_i - (\Sigma_{i=1}^{N} X_i)(\Sigma_{i=1}^{N} Y_i) / N}{[[\Sigma_{i=1}^{N} X_i^2 - (\Sigma_{i=1}^{N} X_i)^2 / N][\Sigma_{i=1}^{N} Y_i^2 - (\Sigma_{i=1}^{N} Y_i)^2 / N]]^{1/2}}$$

Chi-Square: Used to test the independence (or lack of statistical association) between two factors. Its greatest use was to determine the independence between union membership or desirability of union membership and other factors (such as age, sex, etc.)

$$x^2 = \Sigma_i \frac{(f_o^i - f_e^i)^2}{f_e^i},$$

where f_o^i equals the observed frequency, and f_e^i equals the expected frequency.

Partial Correlation: Used to test the association between a dependent factor and a given independent factor while eliminating the effect of other independent factors. For example, it enables testing the association between union membership and age, while "controlling" for salary, education, etc.

$$r_{ij.k} = \frac{r_{ij} - (r_{ik})(r_{jk})}{\sqrt{1 - r_{ik}^2} \sqrt{1 - r_{jk}^2}},$$

where k is the control factor and i and j are the independent and dependent factors.

Scalogram Analysis (Guttman Scaling): Used to analyze the underlying operating characteristics of questionnaire items given in table 9 in order to determine if their interrelationships meet several special properties which define a Guttman Scale. A Guttman Scale is: (1) unidimensional—the component items must all measure movement toward or away from the same single underlying object; (2) cumulative—operationally, a cumulative scale implies that the component items can be ordered by degree of difficulty and that respondents who reply positively to a difficult item will always respond positively to less difficult items and vice versa. Statistical criteria used in this study in evaluating the scalability of items in table 9 were that the coefficient of reproducibility be above .9 and that the coefficient of scalability be above .6. (For a complete explanation of scalogram analysis, see Allen L. Edwards, *Techniques of Attitude Scale Construction* [New York: Appleton-Century-Crofts, Inc., 1957], pp. 172–200.)

Bibliography

Books

American Library Annual, 1958. New York: Bowker, 1958.

Bain, George Sayers. *The Growth of White-Collar Unionism.* Oxford: Clarendon Press, 1970.

Bennis, Warren G., ed. *American Bureaucracy.* Chicago: Aldine, 1970.

Blau, Peter M., and Richard Scott. *Formal Organizations.* San Francisco: Chandler, 1962.

Bok, Derek, and John T. Dunlop. *Labor and the American Community.* New York: Simon and Schuster, 1970.

Bostwick, Arthur E. *The American Public Library.* New York: Appleton, 1929.

Bowker Annual of Library and Book Trade Information. New York: Bowker.

Bryan, Alice. *The Public Librarian.* New York: Columbia Univ. Pr., 1952.

Carr-Saunders, A. M. *Professions: Their Organization and Place in Society.* Oxford: Clarendon Pr., 1928.

Certification of Public Librarians in the United States. Chicago: American Library Assn., 1965.

Clopine, John. *History of Library Unions in the United States.* Washington, D.C.: Catholic Univ. Pr., 1951.

Fogel, Walter, and Archie Kleingartner, eds. *Contemporary Labor Issues.* Belmont, Calif.: Wadsworth Publishing Co., 1966.

Goldstein, Melvin S. *Collective Bargaining in the Field of Librarianship.* New York: Pratt Institute, 1968.

Hoxie, Robert F. *Trade Unionism in the United States.* New York: Appleton, 1936.

Kassalow, Everett. *Trade Unions and Industrial Relations.* New York: Random, 1969.

Leigh, Robert D. *The Public Library in the United States.* New York: Columbia Univ. Pr., 1960.

Lieberman, Myron, and Michael H. Moskow. *Collective Negotiations for Teachers.* Chicago: Rand McNally, 1966.

Lockwood, David. *The Blackcoated Worker.* London: George Allen & Unwin Ltd., 1958.

191

McDiarmid, E. W., and John McDiarmid. *The Administration of the Public Library.* Urbana, Ill.: Univ. of Illinois Pr., 1943.

Mills, C. Wright. *White Collar.* New York: Oxford Univ. Pr., 1956.

Municipal Yearbook (annual). Illinois: The International City Managers' Association.

Munthe, Wilhelm. *American Librarianship from a European Angle.* Hamden, Conn.: Shoe String Pr., 1964.

National Industrial Conference Board. *White-Collar Unionization.* New York: National Industrial Conference Board, No. 220, 1968.

Perlman, Selig. *A Theory of the Labor Movement.* New York: Augustus M. Kelley, 1968.

Prandy, Kenneth. *Professional Employees.* London: Faber and Faber, Ltd., 1965.

Salaries of Library Personnel, 1952. Chicago: American Library Assn., 1953.

Spicer, Erik J. *Trade Unions in Libraries: The Experience in the U.S.* Ann Arbor: Univ. of Michigan Pr., 1959.

Spyers-Duran, Peter. *Public Libraries: A Comparative Survey of Basic Fringe Benefits.* Rochester, N.Y.: Libraries Unlimited, Inc., 1967.

A Survey of Libraries in the United States. Volume 1. Chicago: American Library Assn., 1926.

Tannenbaum, Frank. *A Philosophy of Labor.* New York: Knopf, 1952.

Vignone, Joseph A. *Collective Bargaining Procedures for Public Library Employees.* Metuchen, N.J.: Scarecrow, 1971.

Webb, Sidney and Beatrice. *The History of Trade Unionism.* New York: Longmans, 1920.

Articles

"Activities Committee, Library Unions." *ALA Bulletin* 33:796 (1939).

"ALA Salary Standards for 1946." *ALA Bulletin* 45:102 (1951).

"ALA Salary Survey: Personal Members." *American Libraries* 2:409–17 (1971).

"Asbury Park Conference: Catalog Section—Trustees Section." *ALA Bulletin* 13:375–86 (1919).

Baehr, Melany E., and Richard Renck. "The Definition and Measurement of Employee Morale." *Administrative Science Quarterly* 3:157–84 (Sept. 1958).

Bauman, Alvin. "Measuring Employee Compensation in U.S. Industry." *Monthly Labor Review* 93:17 (Oct. 1970).

Berelson, Bernard. "Library Unionization." *Library Quarterly* 9:477–510 (1939).

Bernstein, Irving. "The Growth of American Unions." *American Economic Review* 44:301–18 (1954).

Blackburn, R. M., and Kenneth Prandy. "White-Collar Unionization: A Conceptual Framework." *The British Journal of Sociology* 16:111–22 (1965).

"Board on Personnel Administration." *ALA Bulletin* 40:369 (1946).

Boaz, Martha. "Labor Unions and Libraries." *California Librarian* 33:104–8 (1971).

Bowerman, G. F. "Unionism and the Library Profession." *Library Journal* 44:365 (1919).

"Collective Bargaining: Some Questions Asked." *ALA Bulletin* 62:973–76 (Sept. 1968).

"Collective Bargaining: Questions and Answers." *ALA Bulletin* 62:1385–90 (Dec. 1968).

"Committee Reports, Annuities and Pensions." *ALA Bulletin* 30:363 (1936).

"Committee Reports; Salaries, Staff, and Service." *ALA Bulletin* 31:601 (1937).

Compton, Charles H. "Our Obligation to Maintain Standards." *ALA Bulletin* 26:91 (1932).

————. "Salary and Employment Conditions." *ALA Bulletin* 27:12 (1933).

"Death of the Manpower Shortage." *Library Journal* 95:3735–44 (Nov. 1, 1970).

"Democratization of the Association." *American Libraries* 1:366–78 (1970).

Ellsworth, Ralph E. "Critique of Library Associations in America." *Library Quarterly* 31:382–400 (1961).

Ferguson, Milton James. "The Library Crosses the Bridge." *ALA Bulletin* 32:421–26. (1938).

Ferguson, Trach H. "Collective Bargaining in Universities and Colleges." *Labor Law Journal* 19:778–804 (1968).

Garbarino, Joseph W. "Precarious Professors: New Patterns of Representation." *Industrial Relations* 10:1–20 (1971).

"General and Salary Statistics—Public Libraries." *ALA Bulletin* 34:271, 285 (Apr. 1940).

Gitlow, Abraham L. "Public Employee Unionism in the United States: Growth and Outlook." *Labor Law Journal* 21:766–78 (1970).

Goldstein, Bernard. "Some Aspects of the Nature of Unionism Among Salaried Professionals in Industry." *American Sociological Review* 20:199–205 (1955).

————. "Unions and the Professional Employee." *Journal of Business* 27:276–84 (1954).

Goldstein, Bernard, and Bernard P. Indik. "Unionism as a Social Choice: The Engineers' Case." *Monthly Labor Review* 86:365–69 (Apr. 1963).

Golodner, Jack. "The Librarian and the Union." *Wilson Library Bulletin* 42:387–90 (1967).

Goode, William J. "The Librarian: From Occupation to Profession?" *Library Quarterly* 31:306–20 (1961).

Gulick, Charles A., and Melvin K. Bers. "Insight and Illusion in Perlman's Theory of the Labor Movement." *Industrial and Labor Relations Review* 6:518 (July 1953).

Henkle, Herman H. "The Staff Association as a Unit in Professional Organization." *Library Journal* 60:459–60 (1935).

Herzog, Donald R. "Fringe Benefits: The Federal Government v. Private Industry." *Labor Law Journal* 22:89–99 (1971).

Hopkins, Joseph A. "Unions in Libraries." *Library Journal* 63:3403–7 (1969).

Howard, Paul. "Associations and United States Legislation." *Library Trends* 3:279 (1955).

Jain, T. C. "Role and Functions of Library Associations." *Herald of Library Science* 2:21–22 (1963).

BIBLIOGRAPHY

Kellam, W. P. "What ALA Means to the Library Profession." *Library Journal* 85:1055–57 (1960).
Kleingartner, Archie. "Nurses, Collective Bargaining and Labor Legislation." *Labor Law Journal* 18:236–45 (1967).
———. "Professionalism and Engineering Unionism." *Industrial Relations* 8:224–35 (1969).
———. "The Unionization of White-Collar Workers." Institute of Industrial Relations, University of California, Los Angeles, Reprint No. 182, 1968.
Kornhauser, Ruth. "Some Social Determinants and Consequences of Union Membership." *Labor History* 2:30–61 (Winter 1961).
Lancour, Harold. "The Librarian's Search for Status." *Library Quarterly* 31:369–81 (1961).
Lewis, Robert. "A New Dimension in Library Administration—Negotiating a Union Contract." *ALA Bulletin* 63:455–64 (1969).
McDonough, Roger H. "An Inaugural Address." *ALA Bulletin* 62:873 (1968).
Miller, George A. "Professionals in Bureaucracy: Alienation Among Industrial Scientists and Engineers." *American Sociological Review* 32:759 (Oct. 1967).
"Minimum Library Salary Standards for 1948." *ALA Bulletin* 42:104–6 (1948).
Mitchell, Sydney B. "Ways and Means of Limiting Library School Output." *ALA Bulletin* 26:424 (1932).
Mleynek, Darryl. "Professional Unions." *California Librarian* 31:110 (Apr. 1970).
Mosher, W. E. "Implications of an Enlightened Personnel Policy." *Library Journal* 62:849 (1937).
Nyren, Karl E. "Librarians and Labor Unions." *Library Journal* 92:2115–21 (1967).
"Opinions on Collective Bargaining." *ALA Bulletin* 63:803–9 (June 1969).
Orman, Oscar C. "550 Librarians Speak." *Wilson Library Bulletin* 14:573 (Apr. 1940).
"Papers and Proceedings, Detroit Conference, 1922—Annual Reports, Salaries." *ALA Bulletin* 16:215–17 (1922).
Parker, Ralph H. "Ports of Entry to Librarianship." *Library Quarterly* 31:344–55 (1961).
"Proceedings, ALA Conference, June 23–27, 1919." *ALA Bulletin* 13:359 (1919).
"Proceedings of the Fifty-sixth Conference, Unemployment." *ALA Bulletin* 28:718 (1934).
"Report of the Library Employees' Union No. 15590 Greater New York, 1917 to 1919." *Library Journal* 44:512 (1919).
Ryan, Mary Jane. "Career Development of Librarians." *Catholic Library World* 40:167 (Nov. 1968).
"Salaries and Unemployment." *ALA Bulletin* 27:94–95 (1933).
"Salaries and Working Conditions of Library Employees, 1949." *ALA Bulletin* 43:297–98 (1949).
Schein, Bernard. "Certification of Public Librarians in the United States." *ALA Bulletin* 50:659–61 (1956).
Schiller, Anita R. "A Survey of Salary Surveys." *ALA Bulletin* 58:279–86 (1964).
———. "The Disadvantaged Majority." *American Libraries* 1:345–49 (1970).

Seidman, Joel. "State Legislation on Collective Bargaining by Public Employees." *Labor Law Journal* 22:13–22 (1971).

Sheridan, Robert. "A Membership Dilemma." *American Libraries* 1:52–55 (1970).

Sherman, Clarence E. "The Unionization of the Profession as One Librarian Sees It." *Special Libraries* 30:38–41 (1939).

Shister, Joseph. "The Logic of Union Growth." *Journal of Political Economy* 61:413–33 (Oct. 1953).

Smith, Eldred. "Librarians and Unions: The Berkeley Experience." *Library Journal* 93:717–20 (1968).

Smith, Stewart W. "In Union—Is There Strength?" *Wilson Library Bulletin* 11:310–11 (1937).

Speer, Lucile. "The Professional Worker in Organized Labor." *PNLA Quarterly* 8:100–1 (1944).

"Trends in Library Manpower." *Wilson Library Bulletin* 43:269–78 (1968).

"Trends in Library Salaries." *ALA Bulletin* 22:805 (1928).

Wight, Edward A. "Standards and Stature in Librarianship." *ALA Bulletin* 55:871–5 (1961).

Willacy, Hazel M. "Changes in Factory Workweek as an Economic Indicator." *Monthly Labor Review* 93:28 (Oct. 1970).

Zeigler, Helen T. "The Staff Association Picture, 1936." *Library Journal* 61:944 (1936).

Articles in Collections

Dunlop, John T. "The Development of Labor Organization: A Theoretical Framework." In *Readings in Labor Economics and Labor Relations*, edited by R. L. Rowan and H. R. Northrup. Homewood, Ill.: Richard D. Irwin, 1968.

Kassalow, Everett. "White-Collar Unionism in the United States." In *White-Collar Trade Unions*, edited by Adolf Sturmthal. Urbana: Univ. of Illinois Pr., 1966.

Lortie, Dan C. "Professional Socialization." In *Professionalization*, edited by Howard M. Vollmer and D. L. Mills. Englewood Cliffs, N.J.: Prentice-Hall, 1966.

Northrup, Herbert. "Collective Bargaining by Professional Societies." In *Insights into Labor Issues*, edited by Richard A. Lester and Joseph Shister. New York: Macmillan, 1948.

Scott, W. Richard. "Professionals in Bureaucracies—Areas of Conflict." In *Professionalization*, edited by Howard M. Vollmer and D. L. Mills. Englewood Cliffs, N.J.: Prentice-Hall, 1966.

Van Deusen, Neil C. "Professional Education for Librarianship: Summary." In *Education for Librarianship*, edited by Bernard Berelson. Chicago: American Library Assn., 1949.

Government Publications

Advisory Commission on Intergovernmental Relations, *Labor-Management Policies for State and Local Government*, A Commission Report. Washington, D.C.: ACIR, September, 1969.

Boaz, Ruth. *Statistics of Public Libraries Serving Areas with at Least 25,000 Inhabitants, 1968*. Washington, D.C.: Office of Education, 1970.

Bolino, August C. *Supply and Demand Analysis of Manpower Trends in the Library and Information Field.* Washington, D.C.: Office of Education, July, 1969.

Bundy, Mary Lee, and Paul Wasserman. *The Public Library Administrator and His Situation.* Washington, D.C.: Office of Education. Final Report, June, 1970.

Census of Governments: *1967, Compendium of Public Employment.* Washington, D.C.: Bureau of the Census, 1967.

College Women Seven Years after Graduation. Washington, D.C.: U.S. Dept. of Labor, 1960.

Directory of National and International Labor Unions. Washington, D.C.: Bureau of Labor Statistics, 1970.

Drennan, Henry T., and Richard L. Darling. *Library Manpower: Occupational Characteristics of Public and School Librarians.* Washington, D.C.: Office of Education, 1966.

————, and Doris C. Holladay. *Statistics of Public Library Systems Serving Populations of 35,000 to 49,999: Fiscal Year 1960.* Washington, D.C.: Office of Education, May, 1962.

Historical Statistics of the U. S. Washington, D.C.: Dept. of Commerce, 1960.

Labor Management Policies for State and Local Governments, Advisory Commission on Inter-Governmental Relations, Washington, D.C., Sept., 1969.

Manpower Report of the President. Washington, D.C.: Dept. of Labor, 1970.

Municipal Public Employee Associations. Washington, D.C.: Bureau of Labor Statistics, Bulletin No. 1702, 1971.

Occupational Outlook Handbook. Washington, D.C.: Bureau of Labor Statistics, 1969.

Schick, Frank L., *et al. Statistics of Library Systems Serving Populations of 50,000 to 99,999: Fiscal Year 1960.* Washington, D.C.: Office of Education, November, 1961.

Interviews

Armstrong, Carol. President, Librarians' Guild, Santa Monica Chapter, Local 1634, Council 36, AFSCME.

Barrett, Douglas. Educational Representative, California Area, AFSCME.

Carter, Lyda. President, Chicago Public Library Employees Union, Local 1215, AFSCME.

Collison, Robert. Professor and Assistant Dean, School of Library Service, University of California, Los Angeles.

Dillon, T. President, San Francisco Public Library, Librarians' Guild, Local 400, SEIU.

Georgi, Charlotte. Librarian, Graduate School of Management, University of California, Los Angeles.

Hammet, Barry. San Diego Municipal Employees Association.

Henselman, Frances. City Librarian, City of Long Beach, California.

Kaye, Edwin H. Humanities Bibliographer, Research Library, University of California, Los Angeles.

Lippert, Thomas. President, Los Angeles Public Library, Librarians' Guild, Local 1634, Council 36, AFSCME.

Mafrica, Anthony. Departmental Personnel Officer, Los Angeles Public Library.
Manchak, Barbara. Personnel Assistant, LAD, American Library Association.
Pederson, Wally. Business Representative, Librarians Employee Representation Unit, LACEA, SEIU.
Rowe, Harry M. Jr. County Librarian, County of Orange, California.
Scogren, Mrs. L. President, Berkeley Public Library Employees Union, Local 2077, AFSCME.
Shelton, Jim. Director of Employee Relations, County of Orange, California.
Smith, Winton. Chief Analyst, Orange County Employees Association.
Thorne, Marco. City Librarian, City of San Diego, California.
Vosper, Robert. University Librarian, University of California, Los Angeles.

Miscellaneous

ALA Organizational Information. Chicago: American Library Assn., 1970–71.
American Association of University Professors. AAUP Chapter Conference Letter, No. 4, May 23, 1972.
Barbash, Jack. *Union Philosophy and the Professional.* Pamphlet, American Federation of Teachers, AFL-CIO, n.d.
Certification of Public Librarians in the United States. Chicago: American Library Assn., 1965.
Classification and Pay Plans for Municipal Public Libraries. Chicago: American Library Assn., 1938.
Egly, Edward C. *Fringe Benefits for Classified Employees.* Association of School Business Officials of the U.S. and Canada, Bulletin No. 19, 1959.
Executive Committee, National Governors' Conference. *Report of Task Force on State and Local Government Labor Relations.* Illinois: Public Personnel Association, 1967. Also, *Supplement,* 1968.
Kassalow, Everett. "Occupational Frontiers of Trade Unionism in the United States." *Proceedings of the Industrial Relations Research Association,* 1960, 13th Annual Meeting, pp. 183–215.
Lipset, Seymour Martin. "White Collar Workers and Professionals—Their Attitudes and Behavior Towards Unions." In *Research Developments in Personnel Management.* Mimeographed. Institute of Industrial Relations, Univ. of California, Los Angeles, 1962.
Miller, S. M. "Discussion of 'The Occupational Frontiers of Union Growth.' " *Proceedings of the Industrial Relations Research Association.* Thirteenth Annual Meeting, Dec., 1960.
Personnel Organization and Procedure: A Manual Suggested For Use in Public Libraries. Chicago: American Library Assn., 1968.
Position Statement. "The American Library Association and Library Collective Bargaining." Adopted by the Library Administration Division Board of Directors, January 21, 1970.
Schlachter, Gail Ann. "Professional Librarians' Attitude Toward Professional and Employee Associations as Revealed by Academic Librarians in Seven Midwestern States." Ph.D. dissertation, Univ. of Minnesota, 1970.
Williamson, Charles C. *Training for Library Service.* A report prepared for the Carnegie Corporation of New York. Boston: Merrymount Pr., 1923.

197

Index